THE WEALTH OF NATURE

ENVIRONMENTAL HISTORY
AND THE
ECOLOGICAL IMAGINATION

Donald Worster

OXFORD UNIVERSITY PRESS

New York   Oxford

D0018274

Oxford University Press

Oxford   New York
Athens   Auckland   Bangkok   Bombay
Calcutta   Cape Town   Dar es Salaam   Delhi
Florence   Hong Kong   Istanbul   Karachi
Kuala Lumpur   Madras   Madrid   Melbourne
Mexico City   Nairobi   Paris   Singapore
Taipei   Tokyo   Toronto

and associated companies in
Berlin   Ibadan

Copyright © 1993 by Donald Worster

First published in 1993 by Oxford University Press, Inc.,
200 Madison Avenue, New York, New York 10016

First issued as an Oxford University Press paperback, 1994

Oxford is a registered trademark of Oxford University Press

All rights reserved. No part of this publication may be reproduced,
stored in a retrieval system, or transmitted, in any form or by any means,
electronic, mechanical, photocopying, recording, or otherwise,
without the prior permission of Oxford University Press.

Library of Congress Cataloging-in-Publication Data
Worster, Donald, 1941–
The wealth of nature: environmental history and the
ecological imagination / Donald Worster.
p.   cm.   Book of essays which previously appeared in
various journals or books or given as lectures.
Includes bibliographical references (p.   ) and index.
ISBN 0-19-507624-9
ISBN 0-19-509264-3 (Pbk.)
1. Human ecology—United States—History.
2. Landscape assessment—United States—History.
I. Title.   GF503.W68   1993
304.2'8'0973 — dc20   92-15360

987654321

Printed in the United States of America
on acid-free paper.

For Jeanne and Norvin Hein

Preface

◆

NEARLY three decades ago, while engaged in the postgraduate study of American history, I began reading a book of nature writing by Joseph Wood Krutch, *The Twelve Seasons,* and immediately saw what was missing from my seminars. There was no nature in their history—no sense of the presence and influence of the land on past human experience, no soil, no countryside, no smell of fungus, no sound of spring peepers trilling from the marsh at dusk. Historians seemed to have forgotten completely that, until very recently, almost all people lived as intimately with other species and with the wind and weather as they did with their own kind. To ignore that long intimacy was to distort history. Writing history is, to be sure, always an act of distortion, imposing on the past the experience and outlook of the present. We heard much in my seminars about the need for objectivity, about letting the past speak for itself; but the most "objective" scholars seemed unaware of how deep their own distortions ran. They had forgotten, or perhaps had never known, the natural things that mattered greatly to people of another era.

"Man's development," wrote Krutch, "takes him farther and farther away from associations with his fellows, seems to condemn him more and more to live with what is dead rather than with what is alive."[1] Although a well-known drama critic and professor at Columbia University, a man with strong urban attachments, Krutch began in his middle years to discover the land. In 1930 he read Thoreau's *Walden,* then moved to rural Connecticut, then in 1952, baffling many of his city associates, moved off to the Sonoran desert, where he could be among white-winged doves and lizards the rest of his life. Living myself in the state of Connecticut, I was not yet ready to go that far (though the Southwest and Great Plains had been my early home), but first wanted to see whether academic history could become more alive than dead. This book of essays is one outcome of that search; they represent my own intellectual turning to the land.

The first group of essays deals with the new academic field of environmental history, which can be defined as the interdisciplinary study of the relations of culture, technology, and nature through time. The essays pursue the connections that the new history has made with such natural sciences as ecology and with such fields as anthropology and geography. I know that some of my colleagues in the new history will find a few of my positions different from their own; after all, conflicting politics and values must separate even this small group of scholars into rival positions on the role or meaning of nature in human life. We disagree over whether the natural world constitutes any kind of order or pattern that we can know and, if it does, over whether that order can be apprehended by means of science or not. We debate what is "natural" and what is not, what is "cultural" in the landscape and what is not, whether Indians in the precontact period "managed" the whole environment or only some small part of it, how much was wilderness and how much was the white pioneer's mythology or fetish. We have divergent opinions over the extent to which nature influences human affairs, some taking up a position of limited environmental determinism, others insisting that culture determines all. Readers of these essays will not find such debates covered in depth here. Instead, they will find the views of one man only, who is less interested in correcting others' errors than in saying how history looks to him.

Other themes in these essays include agriculture, its present as well as its past; agriculture considered ecologically more than economically. Certainly for me, the history of the land includes the history of people dwelling on the land, though I do not mean to limit them to rural people. Everyone, after all, in the city as much as in the country, must live from the land; there is no place else to go. Other essays are on such subjects as water, especially water development in the arid western states, the rise of the public lands movement and of environmentalism in the United States, the history of ecology, and the cultural roots of the modern environmental crisis. Diverse though the subjects may be, they are held together by a belief that history ought to be more than knowledge chasing its own tail. Environmental history ought to have a few *ideas* to offer the public, and those ideas ought to have a little conviction in them as well as reason and evidence. The historian should let people know what he cares about and encourage them to care about it too. He should not hide all day in the archives or write only for a graduate seminar, but now and then try to take part in the great public issues that animate our times: the fate of rural communities, for example, the aspirations of developing countries, the future of the earth.

Some of these essays appeared earlier in academic journals or books, often scattered in places where readers might have trouble finding them or even knowing of their existence. A few were given as public lectures, which will explain their informality of style, and have never before been in print. Inevitably, since they were written over a span of several years and for various audiences, they overlap here and there in content, though I have tried to eliminate any egregious repetition of data or argument. More seriously, they may seem to readers to be filled with contradictory ideas that the author has not quite reconciled. I realize, for instance, that at times I express a strong sense of, and respect for, the order of nature while at other times admitting that order is a troubled idea, one that even scientists, our traditional guides in the matter, seem to be losing a grip on. In this postmodernist, poststructuralist age, when all that has seemed solid melts into the air, this is a familiar dilemma; however, it will not be resolved by yielding to complete historical relativism. Historians, impressed by the variability of human ideas over time, are wont to take that way out, leading the public off into the deserts of relativism and leaving them stranded there with no map, no waterhole, no sense of direction, no way out. Environmental history is no exception; it too can seem about as bewildering to readers as any other history, confusing their ideas about what nature refers to. The temptations are great, but I believe historians ought to struggle against that tendency. Although I am critical of some aspects of science, I am nonetheless sure that because it is a changing, imperfect, culturally bound guide does not mean that science should be no guide at all. If these essays do not present fully coherent answers to all the ultimate questions, if they leave some matters more tentative or muddled than readers like, at least I hope they offer good, thoughtful reasons for acknowledging a set of forces and lives beyond the merely human, the merely cultural, and for learning to respect them.

My philosophical position as an environmental historian might be described as "antimaterialistic materialism." I want to draw attention back to the material reality of the natural world as it impinges on human society, now shaping, now being shaped, by that society. My dissatisfaction with non-environmental history is that it commonly ignores that material reality, an ignorance that extends far beyond the cloisters of history into contemporary popular attitudes. Our politics, economics, highway engineering, music, newspapers, all could use a little more materialism of the right kind: a greater awareness of the materiality of the planet, its limits, diversity, and dynamics. On the other hand, I do not believe that materialism, defined in either ethical or ontological terms, is a fully adequate way to understand the past, let alone organize our desires. I do not mean to argue in these pages that humans can live by bread alone. Or that ecological, let alone economic, creatures are all that we are. Or that nature has ever exercised total power over our existence. Or that human ideals are trivial, ineffectual, epiphenomenal, always wrong, always arrogant, or always destructive. The cultural history of nature is as significant as the ecological history of culture. That may be the core message of environmental history, and if it seems too paradoxical, then that is where fate has caught us: in paradoxes that we can never fully escape. Perhaps the core paradox of the modern era has been that, while over the past three hundred years we have gained a valuable new appreciation of the material world around us, we have also taken a narrowly materialistic attitude toward it. Environmental history, therefore, might be seen as part of a broader search to discover a less reductive, less ecologically and spiritually nihilistic, less grasping kind of materialism.

A few heartfelt acknowledgements remain to be. I want to express thanks to all the journals and audiences who first received these thoughts and helped shape them into something better; to my students and colleagues in environmental history, who have taught me much about both the large and small questions; to the members of my family, who happily share with me a piece of land that is more than ours alone; to the two people named in the dedication, who many years ago provided a home and friendship in the Connecticut woods. Also, I want to thank my agent, Gerry McCauley, and the staff at Oxford University Press, in particular, Sheldon Meyer and Leona Capeless. And finally, thanks to Joe, who many years ago helped turn me in the right direction.

Rock Creek, Kansas   D. W.
October 1992

Contents

◆

1. The Nature We Have Lost   3

2. Paths Across the Levee   16

3. History as Natural History   30

4. Transformations of the Earth   45

5. Arranging a Marriage: Ecology and Agriculture   64

6. A Sense of Soil   71

7. Good Farming and the Public Good   84

8. Private, Public, Personal: Americans and the Land   95

9. The Kingdom, the Power, and the Water   112

10. Thinking Like a River   123

11. An End to Ecstasy   135

12. The Shaky Ground of Sustainable Development   142

13. The Ecology of Order and Chaos   156

14. Restoring a Natural Order   171

15. John Muir and the Roots of American Environmentalism   184

16. The Wealth of Nature   203

    Notes   221

    Index   245

THE WEALTH OF NATURE

1

The Nature
We Have Lost

◆

NOSTALGIA runs all through this society—fortunately, for it may be our only hope of salvation. My own version, which I probably share with a few million others, takes me back to walk in pristine natural places on this continent. I dream of traveling with our second native-born naturalist, William Bartram (his father John was the first), a slightly daft Pennsylvania Quaker who botanized from the Carolinas down into Florida in the early 1770s. I would travel with him, "seduced by . . . sublime enchanting scenes of primitive nature," through aromatic groves of magnolia, sweet gum, cabbage palmetto, loblolly pine, live oak, the roaring of alligators in our ears.[1] I would gaze with Thomas Jefferson through his elegant white-framed windows at Monticello toward the Blue Ridge Mountains, speculating about the prodigious country stretching west. Best of all, I imagine entering that west with Lewis and Clark in 1804–5, standing beside them on Spirit Mound in present-day South Dakota, beholding, as Clark put it in his execrable spelling, "a most butifull landscape; Numerous herds of buffalow were Seen feeding in various directions; the Plain to North N. W. & N.E. extends without interuption as far as Can be seen."[2] And I think what it must have been like for them warping and poling up the muddy Missouri River, penetrating farther into the vast open country of the unplowed, unfenced prairies when wolves still howled in the night; of heading into "the great unknown," panting over the unpainted, unmined, unskiied Rocky Mountains and rafting down the uncharted, undammed Columbia to the gray-green drizzly shore of the Pacific Ocean.

How much has been lost in our short years as a nation, how much have we to be nostalgic about. In the beginning of white discovery North America must have been a glorious place, brimming with exquisite wild beauty, offering to agriculturists some of the earth's richest soils, incredible stands of trees, booty on booty of mineral wealth. Think for a moment of the infinitude of animals that once teemed but are now diminished or gone.

In the most comprehensive, detailed analysis yet offered, Frank Gilbert Roe estimated that forty million bison roamed the continent as late as 1830.[3] One of the first Europeans to see them, the Spanish explorer Francisco Vasquez de Coronado, wrote almost three hundred years before that date: "I found so many cattle . . . that it would be impossible to estimate their number. For in traveling over the plains, there was not a single day, until my return, that I lost sight of them."[4] So impressed by this animal were later Americans that they put its picture on one of their most common coins; now there are far more of those nickel images saved by coin collectors than bison that survive.

Ernest Thompson Seton estimated forty million white-tailed deer before there were farms and guns. Someone else has said there may have been five billion prairie dogs, as many as the present total human population of the world. And as many as three to five billion passenger pigeons, migrating in dark, torn clouds that blotted out the sun, breaking trees when they came down to roost; now they too have vanished into carbon and gas.[5]

Navigators encountered off Newfoundland schools of fish so dense they blocked their passage, holding them prisoner, and waterfowl so thick they could feast forever on wild duck eggs. In 1985, however, as one index of change, the U.S. Fish and Wildlife Service counted only 62 million among all the major duck species, down more than half from a few decades earlier. If that seems like plenty of ducks, remember that we have about as many tennis rackets in our closets and far more beer cans in our refrigerators. In this year there are over a thousand species on the endangered list, and many more are threatened.

What we have left in abundance, rivaling ourselves in magnitude, are the bugs. We have not really dented their numbers; 10,000 of them per acre can still be found in some American habitats, along with billions of mites, whole Manhattans, whole miniature Chinas, crawling underfoot.

Besides losing so many of the larger animals, we have lost entire ecological communities, complete landscapes, and with them have lost a considerable range of human feelings—the delight and the joy, the humility that may come from standing in the presence of what we have called the wilderness. In most parts of the country such feelings are gone forever.

Environmental historians debate whether the wilderness ever really existed or whether it was merely a figment of the astonished, naive European imagination. Several have argued that the white man invaded a long inhabited, and much managed, country, the home of Indians for tens of thousands of years. North America, they say, was not a "virgin" land but a "widowed" one, as millions of aborigines died from contact with European diseases. But neither adjective will quite do, for the continent was far too big and diverse to be so simply gendered and personalized. It was neither a widow nor a virgin, neither bride nor groom, nothing like any person we have known. But we may accurately say it was, over most of its extent, an untrammeled land by the standards of either early modern western Europe or today's America. Immense stretches of it seldom knew a human foot, let alone a fence or building. The most plausible current estimate of the native human population living north of Mexico in the era of Christopher Columbus runs about five million—extreme figures go as high as eighteen million.[6] Either figure is tiny, compared with all those bison or prairie dogs or compared with most nations today. They had all to themselves a territory of 7.4 million square miles, the combined extent of the United States and Canada, or more than a square mile apiece. In some places, of course, like Florida, the coastal fringe of the Pacific Northwest, the lower Mississippi valley, they lived in much denser populations than that—but then over some part of the landscape virtually no one must have lived: zero humans per square mile. And however numerous or scarce they were or however distributed, they were a Stone Age people, living by hunting and gathering or, where they were agricultural, cultivating their scattered, shifting fields with bones and digging sticks; by far their most potent technology was fire, which they used liberally but undoubtedly controlled even less effectively than we control our nuclear reactors and pesticides. To describe their relationship with the whole continent as "management" would be a considerable exaggeration. Without bogging down in pedantic wrangles over definitions, we can say that before contact the native peoples were dwelling on a largely undomesticated continent, wild or nearly wild over much of its extent. In contrast, the newcomers, the white and black and Asian immigrants, have, in the space of two or three centuries, steadily cleared and paved, mowed and malled their way through that territory, until today less than 2 percent of the lower 48 states is in a condition of wilderness, roadless and uninhabited.

What was it that destroyed so much of America's wild natural beauty and the Indian's habitat? What turned so much of the continent into the agricultural-urban-industrial-commercial excrescence we see sprawling everywhere today—into Greater Cleveland, the Las Vegas Strip, Harlan County, Kentucky, the Great Plains wheat belt? Merely saying it was the coming of "new immigrants" does not explain very much. What was it about those immigrants that produced such promethean effects? This is a question that environmental historians have sought to answer, though they have not arrived at any consensus. One set of explanations they offer emphasizes tangible, material forces, including such things as demography, technology, and energy. These, many say, have been the revolutionary forces, and we, like the land on which we live, have been inextricably held in their grip. Let us give those forces their due and briefly recall how they have operated to transform the ecological conditions of the continent.

First, consider the explosive growth in North America's human population following in the wake of the European discoveries. Certainly, and it is obvious to everyone, this has been a massive reason for the dramatic environmental changes that have occurred. The recording of immigration to the United States began only in 1819, two centuries after Jamestown was founded and eleven years after the end of the African slave trade. From that beginning of official documentation until 1970, over 45 million persons legally entered our doorways from abroad. The high annual point was 1907, when 1,285,349 of them were registered. Since 1970 the gate has been opened wide again, and Congress has just recently, in the immigration law of 1990, opened it even wider, allowing in 770,000 per year. Many more, of course, crawl under the fence and enter illegally from Mexico or Canada. Only about 30 percent of the nation's demographic growth now comes from legal immigration, most of the rest from natural increase, but immigration alone adds every decade more than the aboriginal Indian numbers I mentioned above. And now in the late twentieth century we have dwelling in this country over 250 million citizens—an astounding quarter of a billion. That gives us an average density of about seventy persons per square mile, compared with a global average (leaving out the land mass of Antarctica) of one hundred per square mile—and remember that there may have been less one person per average square mile in Indian North America. The places where most Americans live are now among the most densely settled on earth. The state of Virginia, for example, has 144 residents per square mile, compared with Iraq's 83. The state of Pennsylvania is more densely peopled than France, with 264 per square mile. Ohio is more thickly settled than Thailand or China. Oklahoma has a greater human density than Finland, Sweden, or Norway. Florida exceeds the density of Spain, Massachusetts exceeds that of India and the United Kingdom, and New Jersey has a hundred more people per square mile than the Netherlands.[7]

Those numbers, massive though they are, account for only a small part of Americans' total ecological impact. Historians go on to stress a second material factor, the growth of technology and industrialism and what they have done to the biophysical environment. The rise of mass production processes and of mass consumption, starting with the manufacture of cotton textiles in Massachusetts during the 1790s, has completely revolutionized people's relation to the land. Industrialism has filled our wardrobes, larders, and bookcases, filled our households, offices, and barns, with a quantity of goods that come to us almost effortlessly, and come from every part of the country and beyond, from places we have never seen or have little interest in. Since 1914, when Henry Ford set up his assembly lines at the new, advanced River Rouge plant near Detroit, it has been the automobile that has most dramatically symbolized the industrial economy; now, some 100,000 automobiles roll off the world's assembly lines each day, and there are well over a hundred million passenger cars on our nation's streets and highways, as well as millions of trucks and vans. Throughout America and the rest of the industrial world, the automobile has become the most common and the most potent technological force for environmental modification and destruction we have, voraciously consuming wood, aluminum, steel, rubber, plastic, farmland, city space, wetlands, quiet.[8]

And the proliferation of the automobile suggests a third material factor, the rise of the fossil fuels, which have likewise profoundly altered the ecological conditions of the continent. By discovering and tapping those ancient buried stores of energy, coal, oil, and natural gas, we have unleashed incredible changes on the face of the earth here and abroad. In the mid-nineteenth century the average northern household required for fuel sixteen to eighteen cords of wood a year.[9] Today, Americans produce commercially over 58,000 petajoules of energy per year—the equivalent of 9.5 billion barrels of oil—or 38 barrels apiece.[10] A family of four would thus use 152 barrels annually or their equivalent—those are barrels, not gallons. Imagine that today we got our energy supply delivered once a year and had to store it in the backyard, as we once did our fuelwood. Think of all the tidy suburbs of the nation with black barrels of oil plunked down on the neatly mown bluegrass lawns. Never mind for the moment that much of our energy supply is lost in the form of heat, doing us no good whatsoever, or that so much of it is wasted that often the real purpose of fossil fuel consumption seems to be to vent excess CO_2 into the atmosphere. Despite the waste, the continent has been radically transformed during the fossil fuel era. Put those barrels to work on remaking the landscape, as they are every day, every year, and there is no mountain or river that can defy them, if the human will is there, no species that can run away. If you doubt that power, try building an interstate highway with an elk's shoulder blade tied to a stick.

So we have to acknowledge those powerful material forces and their history in order to explain the radical transformation of North America since the days of Bartram, Jefferson, Lewis and Clark. But most environmental historians urge caution and even skepticism about letting such materialist explanations become the whole story. Demography, technology, and energy seem impressive forces, all right, but they are also inadequate as explanations, often concealing as they do the real forces of change that lie more hidden and subtle than a coal seam. Historians say it is in the area of the immigrant white man's culture, his and her ideas or ways of seeing, that we can locate the profoundest causes of environmental change. Even the runaway force of American population growth, if scrutinized carefully, is a reflection of cultural attitudes. We have those mounting numbers to deal with not simply because of reproductive biology but because of our common perceptions of what the country's environment will sustain, what it's good for. Why does the United States continue to admit more immigrants than all the other nations of the world? Why does New Jersey vote to admit more people even though it's more crowded than Japan? Because the great American fertility goddess, the Statue of Liberty, keeps whispering in our ears that there's always room for more, that somewhere out in North Dakota there's plenty of space left, that this is and must be the opportunity society. It's a cultural thing.

So let us turn to some deeper cultural sources to explain the destruction of nature that has gone grinding along, so inexorably, so fatally, in North America. The most adequate explanation for that destruction (or should we call it "settling the place," as we once thought we were doing?) lies in American attitudes toward nature and our place in it. Those attitudes, I believe, took indelible form in the eighteenth century, the very period when the nation itself emerged and began seeking an identity, forming national ambitions, and planning for the future. We keep harking back to that period because it was then that we ceased to be Europeans and set in motion those distinctive, identifying ideas and institutions that would bring us down to the present. To be sure, those ideas had roots going far back into an archaic past, all the way back to the Greeks and Romans and the ancient Israelites. But it was not until the eighteenth century that the ideas came together into a recognizably modern form, becoming an intellectual mold that has fashioned our national thinking ever since. Those ideas would have cataclysmic ecological consequences; they would drive us relentlessly to create the man-made landscape we inhabit today and in the process nearly wipe out that wilder America. They would also leave us, for many intricate reasons, feeling guilty about what we have done and would encourage that peculiar search for national atonement we have called environmentalism. All in all a fertile, potent set of ideas. And they came boiling out of quaint little villages like Colonial Williamsburg and Puritan Boston, from taverns redolent with the musty odor of ale, from solemn assembly rooms where politicians orated, from domestic hearthsides where they were spun out with the thread on a spinning wheel.

The key American environmental idea, and at once the most destructive and most creative, the most complacent and most radical, is the one that ironically has about it an aura of wonderful innocence. America, we have believed, is literally the Garden of Eden restored. It is the paradise once lost but now happily regained. In Judeo-Christian mythology the first humans, Adam and Eve, discovering evil after yielding to the Devil's temptation, had to be kicked out of the Garden on their nearly naked bums. But *mirabile dictu,* Americans of the eighteenth century found a way to sneak back into the garden. A band of their ancestors had made their way to the New World and there rediscovered it, with the gate standing wide open, undefended. What a blessed people. They brought along with them some Africans in chains to help enjoy the place, and by and by they let in a few others from Asia, but mainly it was a fortunate band of white Europeans that destiny allowed to re-enter and repossess the long-lost paradise. No other people in the world has ever believed, as Americans have, that they are actually living in Eden: not the Italians or the Swiss, though they probably thank their stars for who they are; not the Brazilians or the Mexicans, though they have been living like us among the riches of the New World; not even the Australians or the Canadians, who like us have conquered a lot of valuable real estate; and of course not any of those people who have lived outside the Judeo-Christian tradition, the Koreans or Tibetans, for example. All of them undoubtedly have loved their land and loved it deeply; they have praised its beauty, identified its sacred places, but they have had no grand, mythic illusions about it.

Many times they have even felt compelled to apologize to the world for the poverty of their soil or the paucity of their resources. Not so with the Americans; we understood early on that the planet's last best place had been kept sequestered for us. That mythic belief in Eden restored lies at the very core of our peculiar national identity. It is the primary source of our self-confidence and our legendary, indefatigable optimism. It has made us the Teflon-coated people, completely impervious to the stark, damming evidence of our own folly. And it has encouraged a rather condescending, pitying attitude toward the rest of the world, who are so sadly condemned to live in such manifestly inferior settings.

There are a couple of themes densely embedded in America's Edenic image of itself, and I want to pull them apart for analysis. The first is the belief that nature, as found in North America, is a complete, eternal, and morally perfect order. To be sure, nature displays the same general handicraft in every corner of the planet, but only here is the perfection of her workmanship supposed to be so clearly realized. At some ancient point in time, eighteenth-century Americans believed, the natural world was created by a supreme intelligence, someone I can't help picturing as a kind of divine Albert Einstein figure, incredibly smart and wonderfully kind, whose frizzy halo of hair has been pressed down under a powdered wig. When he got done creating, he shuffled off and sat in the corner, leaving nature to roll marvelously round and round forever, finished and invulnerable and beautiful beyond flaw. Obviously, much of that notion can be traced back to Moses (or to whomever she was who wrote the book of Genesis) but the salient point for Americans was that we are privileged to witness that divine creation as perfectly intact as it was at the beginning of time, and what's more, we can actually walk through it.

So tell us, fortunate American citizen, exactly what the properties of your Eden are. Without hesitation, the answers come surely and easily, the familiar stuff of many eighteenth-century writings. We may imagine, for instance, the authoritative voice of Thomas Jefferson answering the question. To begin with, he would reply, nature is eminently rational, laid out by Great Reason itself and accessible to our lower faculties. It is completely transparent to scientific, inquiring minds, though its creation required more rationality than a whole college of professors could furnish. Furthermore, nature is permanent; it is designed to endure forever as the exact same order of objects interacting with one another in the same old way, surmounting all the vicissitudes of time. Individual plants and animals may come and go, but the order of the whole can not be altered by any force, including humans acting with all their power. "Such is the economy of nature," wrote Jefferson in *Notes on the State of Virgina,* "that no instance can be produced, of her having permitted any one race of animals to become extinct; of her having formed any link in her great work so weak as to be broken."[11] He was writing to refute rumors that a great-clawed sloth had once walked the North American continent but was now gone. The Indians, Jefferson pointed out, told of such an animal still prowling the northern latitudes, far from human eyes, but their testimony was superfluous; for him abstract reason alone was enough to establish the creature's survival. How could America be the perfect garden if sloths went about dying in it? Show me a supposedly fossil bone and I'll find the living animal to match it, even if I have to paddle my canoe to darkest Arkansas. Another characteristic of nature is that she is frugal and efficient; nothing is ever wasted or useless in her workings. Then, and perhaps most important, nature is amazingly abundant. Every tiny niche is filled with life, and each little life contributes to the welfare of the whole. Here is Thomas Paine's enthralled account of that cornucopia:

> If we take a survey of our own world . . . our portion in the immense system of creation, we find every part of it, the earth, the waters, and the air that surround it, filled, and as it were crowded with life, down from the largest animals that we know of to the smallest insects the naked eye can behold, and from thence to others still smaller, and totally invisible without the assistance of the microscope. Every tree, every plant, every leaf, serves not only as an habitation, but as a world to some numerous race, till animal existence becomes so exceedingly refined, that the effluvia of a blade of grass would be food for thousands.[12]

In the face of such plentitude, the human being can only consume in a spirit of gratitude whatever he or she can. Nature demands our respect, but how do we show it? By the degree of our enthusiasm, the intensity of our enjoyment, the size of our appetite. We are not required to pinch and save, to conserve or protect, because some one much more intelligent has done all that for us. Nature will look out for itself. Our only work is to be active in making good and full use of the abundance spread before us. Could anything be more Edenic than that?

The power of the eighteenth-century myth of an American Eden reverberates down through our history to these very times. We are still a people in love with our prolific Garden. We continue to explore it, as Jefferson's generation did, traveling with pride and satisfaction from valley to mountain to plain, fencing in what we can, owning and possessing as much as we can, mining and exploiting it with great glee, now and then settling down to enjoy the view. We demand maximum freedom to drive our new

Buicks (advertised under the Edenic sign of the American eagle) to and through the garden, bumper to bumper with our Nissan Pathfinders, our Ford Broncos, our Vagabond motorhomes. We have scattered Edenic images all across the country's map, from Garden City, Long Island, and the Garden State of New Jersey to Garden City, Kansas, and the Garden of the Gods, Colorado. In our national gazeteer you can find an Eden, Michigan, an Eden, Mississippi, an Eden, New York, an Eden, Wyoming, as well as an Eden Valley and Eden Prairie in Minnesota. Many of them may be marred these days by a K-Mart, a Wendy's, an overflowing land-fill, or by air pollution from a nearby smelter; never mind, the names on the map often sounded more glamorous than the reality looked.

Americans, even in these days of rising concern, still tend to look on nature through an eighteenth-century rose-colored window—Palladian is understood. I speak not only of the creationists, who still consider Moses the best biologist ever and vehemently reject the overwhelming testimony of scientists about evolution, but also of economists, politicians, manu-facturers, and happy summer campers, for all of whom nature is forever infinitely generous, forgiving, and abundant. We cannot do any real dam-age to her, we still say to ourselves; she is now, as ever, a mother who never says no to her children. Eden survives for us, if only in the endlessness of our material expectations.

Ironically, many environmentalists today, though disagreeing with so much of the thinking I have just described, also hold fast to some eigh-teenth-century notions of nature. They look to the last remaining wilder-ness for proof of a benevolent moral order existing outside human culture, a standard by which the fall of humankind may be measured. Such is the essential creed, I believe, of groups like the Wilderness Society and the Sierra Club, though for them that natural Eden is no longer protected or secured by divine intelligence, nor is it infinitely abundant, able to satisfy all our demands. Eden has been much spoiled in their eyes, and reversing the tables, it is now up to us to redeem what is left of it.

As these environmentalist revisions indicate, the whole idea of an invulnerable Eden waiting through the ages on the North American con-tinent has been slowly breaking down for a long time now. Even before Thomas Jefferson died in 1826, scientists had firmly established that many species had truly gone extinct, leaving large holes in the natural order. The publication in 1859 of Charles Darwin's *On the Origin of Species* only added to the sneaking awareness that we cannot actually go back to some primeval Eden, if it ever existed in quite the way Jefferson's age believed. Today, most well-informed Americans readily grant that we live in the midst of a nature that has never been exactly perfect, not for the last hundred million or hundred billion years, a nature that has always been evolving and changing, though we may agree that it has shown an impressive trial-and-error adaptativeness, far more than our recently contrived economy or laws. The nature we now see looks far more fragile and vulnerable than it once did, less efficient in many ways, and far less bountiful in light of the demands we make on it. We are moving at long last, even on this uniquely favored continent, toward an awareness of universal resource scarcity and limits.

How much enthusiasm can we work up for this less than perfect nature revealed by the modern era? Is reverence really possible any longer? Is nature in this post-Edenic era still worthy of great respect, or should we put more faith in our own human intelligence, in our technological inventiveness? Must our hopes now rest not on the land but on our ingenuity, and if so, is our ingenuity really up to the challenge? Conversely, can we now ignore the need to accept responsibility for the environmental damage we do? Such ethical questions did not puzzle our ancestors, who were serious moral thinkers but seldom thought they had any moral obligations to the earth. They plunge us back into the dark, tangled, disordered web of history we have made.

Thus the image handed down to us from the eighteenth century of America as a restored Eden is in a most confused state these days—not completely discredited but less credible than before. That image is sharply contradicted by modern experience and more and more seems downright complacent and naive. One thing is clear to the historian: out of our resulting intellectual confusion we are growing toward a more realistic sense of what the natural world will allow us to do.

But there is a second theme in our national myth of Eden that holds on quite tenaciously still, driving us unwittingly to do further havoc to ourselves and the earth: the notion that human nature in America is a mirror image of that perfect garden of nature and is itself benevolent and good. Supposedly, we live in a society that, though admittedly not yet perfect, is moving in that direction. We are humanity's last best hope. We can trust in ourselves if not in the rest of nature.

To believe, as we have long done, that America will provide the world with a model society, is a bold, ambitious, and arrogant faith. It has implied that we are a people who can bring off an unprecedented moral revolution in human character, one that all the previous history of the species failed to do. That revolution, Americans announced as early as the eighteenth century, was already beginning to happen; under the benevolent influence of New World nature, the old vices and evils of humanity were fast disappearing. Take greed, for example. Every major religious teacher of the Old World had denounced greed as one of the cardinal sins. Jesus, for instance, had declared that it was harder for a rich man to enter the Kingdom of Heaven than for a camel to squeeze through the eye of a needle. Apparently in America, however, our camels were smaller and our needles larger. In this fortunate place we maintained that human greed could actually metamorphose into a virtue. The more we freed greed from laws and regulations, the more we would prosper; and the more we prospered, the more we would become enlightened, happy, and decent. This is, of course, the fundamental moral argument we associate with the rise of capitalism and the market economy, the dominant economic philosophy and institution of the modern world. Capitalism, in order to become so dominant, had to convince people, against all the weight of tradition, that greed was really a virtue. That transvaluation may have owed much of its theoretical argument to an Edinburghian economist named Adam Smith, but it found the greatest receptivity, its most zealous believers, among Americans. In other countries the promoters of capitalism had to fight harder against such traditional opponents as the Christian Church, older social elites, and some intellectuals and artists, who tended to be suspicious and critical. But then that hostile opposition was not living in Eden and found it hard to believe in the actuality of moral revolution; the greedy, they insisted, still needed, as always, to be watched and restrained. In contrast, Americans tended to dismiss all such suspicion of human nature as outmoded and unnecessary. Everybody might become innocent in this providential environment—at least all the well-dressed white guys. And so it is today. Our rich men are as well esteemed as ever and have not only entered into but are in control of our secular heaven, from Wall Street to Malibu Canyon. No matter how they got their money, we still tend to admire and praise them, and to forgive their sins easily. Even the rogue serving ten years in the slammer for bilking widows of their life savings, or for stealing from public housing funds, or for conning his television audience into sending in donations can do no wrong in some eyes. He loudly proclaims his innocence and virtue—"I was only trying to do my job, I am not a crook"—and millions of Americans believe him.

This notion that America is the land where vice is transformed into virtue, where everybody is as innocent as a child, has admittedly begun to wobble a bit, but it is still strong in our thinking, particularly in our economic thinking, which is about all that our thinking amounts to much of the time.[13] Every announcement of higher economic growth is greeted as proof of our improving virtue and idealism, rather than of our insatiable, ruinous greed. Despite plenty of evidence that selfishness is as ugly and rampant here, and the lust for power as corrupt, as in other nations, despite many examples of the fact that Eden has not cleansed or restored us to innocence, we resist the logical conclusion that we need more law, regulation, and good government in the national political economy as in the private domestic one. We resist that conclusion when we elect men to high office whose only qualification is their fervent, unquestioning belief that we are still the unblemished moral light of the world—if only the government would get out of the way.

Will this charming set of self-images ever seem as naive as Jefferson's theory that animal species can never become extinct? Will we ever decide that the hunger for unlimited wealth and power is as dangerous in the New World as in the Old? Will all of us ever come to see and regret the impact that unrepressed human appetite has on the natural environment? Regaining paradise is an ancient, wonderful dream, and the Edenic dream and the Edenic nature that inspired it are the most wonderful things about America. They explain why we are a nation of idealists. They explain the fact that we are an avid group of nature lovers, as our snapshots, our coffee table books, and our calendar art all demonstrate, and that the United States has been, in many respects, a world leader in environmental protection. On the other hand, we have also been a nation of consummate nature destroyers, perhaps the most destructive ever; and again it has been the dream of living innocently in a bountiful Eden that is heavily responsible. Innocence, no matter how contrived or willful, can, after all, produce tragedy. So it has done in America. We have created out of our Edenic musings a peculiar sort of tragedy. Confident of having regained paradise, complacent and blissful in its midst, we have lost much of what we have most loved.

2

Paths Across the Levee

◆

IN 1821 a man came exploring across the prairies and plains of the North American continent. His name was Jacob Fowler, and with his companions he would be the first Euro-American to ascend the whole length of the Arkansas River from what is now Fort Smith, Arkansas, to the Rocky Mountains. After eight days of poling against the current, "we stoped," he writes in his untutored spelling, "at the mouth of a bold sreem of Watter" emptying into the Arkansas, a tributary about seventy feet wide.[1] They followed that stream north through the sand hills that cover part of present-day Reno and Rice counties in the state of Kansas. Only a few cottonwood trees grew along its banks, affording scant shelter from the big sky, but the bluestem grass was so high one could not see the river ahead as it meandered across the prairie. Beyond the rich moist bottomlands the vegetation became buffalo grass, and the bison grazed there in black, drifting multitudes; the local Indians called the stream after the female bison, a name that became "Cow Creek" in the white man's tongue. There were pronghorn antelopes in those days, so light and agile, counterpointing the shaggy herds. Fowler and his crew might also have seen deer, elk, coyotes, and dense flocks of ducks and geese. Then, their curiosity satisfied and their senses pleased, they pushed on west.

Fowler had no idea that almost three centuries earlier another Euro-

pean, Don Francisco Vásquez de Coronado, had come here from the opposite direction, crossing this very same Cow Creek on his quest for the
fabled city of Quivira. Coronado found in the vicinity only the Wichita
Indians living in domed huts thatched with grass, but he did remark that

> the country itself is the best I have ever seen for producing all the products
> of Spain, for besides the land itself being very fat and black, and being very
> well watered by the rivulets and springs and rivers, I found prunes like those
> of Spain and nuts and very good sweet grapes and mulberries.[2]

Not until this present century would archaeologists locate the Indian village sites that Coronado came upon and dig up a few pieces of chain mail
his men dropped in the prairie grass, thus confirming that the great con-
quistador ended his penetration of the country not too far from the head-
waters of Cow Creek. He was disappointed by the lack of gold but amazed,
after trekking so long across the southwestern deserts, by the unexpected
bounty of nature in these parts.

Jacob Fowler then only rediscovered what Coronado, not to mention
many Indian tribes, had already discovered. Others *after* Fowler came to
explore and marvel too, including merchants traveling west on the Santa
Fe Trail, which crossed the creek; buffalo hunters, including Buffalo Bill
Cody, who worked on a ranch along the creek (stealing his famous moni-
ker from its proprietor); cowboys driving longhorns from Texas grazing
lands to the Kansas railheads and homesteaders bringing plows from the
east. In 1871 a railroad town began to build on the creek; its founder, Clin-
ton C. Hutchinson, was a former Baptist minister, Indian agent, newspaper editor—and always a conniving opportunist—from the town of
Lawrence. He promised prospective settlers "more miles . . . of clear, constant running streams than any county in eastern Kansas, and more
water running in these streams." If that seemed implausible in a climate
distinctly drier than the eastern part of the state, it was true that now and
then Cow Creek filled its banks to the brim and slopped out onto the prairies. To the bewilderment of early settlers, within a few years of its beginning the town was flooded by the creek and Main Street suddenly became
a fishing pond. Still the settlers came, including four hundred Mennonite
families from Russia, who commenced to grow winter wheat on the prairie, floods and grasshopper plagues notwithstanding. A second flood ram-
paged in 1886 and another in 1903, then still others, decade after decade;
yet on either bank the wood-frame houses continued to proliferate, along
with banks and grain elevators and red-brick churches.[3] Then in October
1941, a full 120 years after Jacob Fowler's expedition, the creek rose spectacularly and turned the whole city into a Venetian swamp, while people

paddled their boats from store to store or watched the swirling waters from their rooftops. This time, angry and determined never again to suffer such an outrage, they called in the Army Corps of Engineers, which undertook to spend millions of federal dollars to make the town safe from the erratic creek. The Corps constructed a series of levees up to fourteen feet high and diversion ditches two hundred feet wide. Now at long last these good Kansas folk, having vanquished the Indians and the bison and the sandhill cranes and the antelope, had managed to vanquish Cow Creek. Abruptly, it disappeared from their lives. Safe behind their immense ramparts of dirt, living like medieval burghers in walled cities, they could devote their full attention to watching television, waxing automobile tail fins, fending off the insidious threat of godless communism, and dancing to the Tennessee waltz.

I grew up within a few hundred feet of Cow Creek, but we could not see it from our windows; we could only see the levee. Had it not been for a grandfather who remembered that once upon a time catfish could be caught in the creek and who led me over the levee to discover the other side, I might have grown up with little sense of that lost world of water. Hardly anyone else but the two of us ever climbed the levee, intruded on the silence, and went fishing. The poet Gerard Manley Hopkins asks, "What would the world be, once bereft of wet and of wildness?" It was not a question that occurred to the townspeople of Kansas in the 1950s. They were not aware of being bereft of anything, unless it was a backyard swimming pool. But in the process of vanquishing Cow Creek, and then in the process of forgetting its former splendor of wet and of wildness, they lost more than the presence of a volatile, complicated, sometimes destructive nature in their lives; they lost much of their history as well. The Indians, the buffalo hunts, the searches of Coronado and Jacob Fowler, and so much else tended to vanish with the creek from local memory.

I tell this provincial little story to illustrate several points: first, we have in my home state of Kansas, as we do in every part of the globe, a story to tell not only of human history but also of the history of nature—a history of environmental transformation; second, what was transformed was a nature that was at once lovely and beguiling, inscrutable and threatening; and third, our history can never be truly complete unless we realize how much of it really centered on a process of interaction with the forces of nature. Even today, and even in the neighborhood of the old lost Cow, that fact remains true. The creek may no longer flood the valley, but the water cycle remains as critical as ever. Today, a troubled question locally is how a scarce supply of water should be divided among the remnant waterfowl that live in and migrate through the area and ever-thirsty irrigating farmers. And how the excrement from livestock concentrated on feedlots is polluting the streams and might be controlled. And how inorganic fertilizer applied to fields is raising the nitrate levels of groundwater to dangerous levels. We can no more get out of a relationship with nature than we can get out of history.

Historians, however, have not always remembered that truth. As in my Kansas story, many historians have built levees around their work and tried to live safely behind them. To be sure, there have been exceptions: In the nineteenth century Francis Parkman, in his narratives on the French and Indian wars, got the reputation of being "the historian of the North American forest," and Frederick Jackson Turner, the founder of frontier history, pointed to the influence of the land and wilderness on American institutions, while in the mid-twentieth century the Kansas historian James Malin talked presciently about uniting "ecology and history." And today one can still find an American history textbook or two where nature puts in a brief appearance, though usually in the dullest section in the book, where students may find a black-and-white map of the major physiographic provinces—Piedmont, Central Lowlands, Basin and Range—and that's about all. Hardly any textbook reminds readers, for example, of the thick green pineries that once stretched from Maine to Minnesota, where Americans cut the lumber to build millions of balloon-frame houses in Boston, Detroit, Chicago, St. Louis, and Kansas City. The books have commonly failed to convey even a hint of the lively, vital interaction with the land—with all its organisms and microorganisms, with such natural resources as soil and water—that has gone on through time. Thus, the standard account of American history has become a lot like the deodorized, fluorescent-lit, saran-wrapped supermarkets of the nation, where one can push a cart up and down the aisles every week and never be stimulated to wonder where the milk or bread comes from on which our politics, our heroes and villains, our social order, even (or perhaps most particularly) our economic life, have fed.

We might be tempted to blame this academic indifference, as we blame so many of our ills, on the urbanization of modern life, which has put so much distance between people and the land. But another important source, I believe, lies in the way we organize our academic life. Nature and history have become separate areas of specialization. Historians have not been *expected* to deal with nature or even with the imaginations of roving outdoor painters, the politics of environmentalism, or the changing models of natural science. Somewhere, it seems, a great lawgiver has enscribed on a tablet of stone that water cycles, deforestation, animal populations, soil nutrient gains and losses are reserved for Science, while History must confine itself to tariffs, diplomatic negotiation, union-management conflict, race and gender. Science is supposed to deal with Nature; the scientists even have a journal proclaiming that fact in its title. History, on the other hand, must deal with People, Society, and Culture.

Nobody is quite sure which great lawgiver decreed this state of affairs. One leading suspect is René Descartes, who in the mid-seventeenth century announced that the world was divided into two opposing forces, mind versus matter. Others have pointed to the much older argument between Democritus and Lucretius, on the one hand, and Plato on the other, over the primacy of mind or matter. And some would argue we must go back even before the rise of Western civilization to some broad human tendency to divide the world into binary oppositions.[4] Whatever the origins of the split, we suffer today from a too rigid set of categories that set us apart from one another in the academy. Nature is set apart from culture. The material order is set apart from, and over, the spiritual. The realm of objective data is strictly demarcated from the realm of subjectivity, feeling, and value. This division has worked to balkanize our various university departments and professions, our intellectual loyalties, and even our scholarly languages. I cannot adequately express the enormous damage that this balkanization has done not only to our intellectual and moral life but also to the natural world of western Kansas and to planet Earth.

However, I can cheerfully announce that we are beginning to blaze a small pathway across the levee. The name of the pathway is environmental history, and its essential purpose is to put nature back into historical studies, or, defined more elaborately, to explore the ways in which the biophysical world has influenced the course of human history and the ways in which people have thought about and tried to transform their surroundings.[5]

Once historians assume this purpose, then all the natural sciences suddenly become an essential ally to call on, a tool to use, an intellectual circle to penetrate and understand. The new environmental historians are busy reading books and papers written by scientists in ecology, physical geography, soil chemistry, climatology, plant genetics, parasitology, reproductive biology, and groundwater hydrology. In one recent work by a historian (a historian no less!) I found references to the following scientific journals: *Annual Review of Ecology and Systematics, Science, BioScience, Canadian Journal of Fisheries and Aquatic Science,* and the *Proceedings of the California Academy of Science.*[6] Apparently, to do environmental history really well, one must have some familiarity with, if not advanced training in, more scientific fields than many scientists would venture to acquire. That requirement is a bit frightening to the historian who once thought he or she had a rather simple art to master, except for those foreign language exams, but now discovers he or she needs to know how to read, among other things, the historical record of atmospheric methane concentration based on measurements of air trapped in an ice core from Antarctica.[7]

So what has all this trail-making across the levee so far produced? A picture of the human past that is radically unlike anything you will find in the standard undergraduate history textbooks. A past that is wider in scope than any of our conventional nation and state territories, taking in whole continents, even the earth itself. A past that is far older than the American constitution, or the Magna Carta, or even the Pyramids, as old as the species itself. And yet is as new as the automobile or aerosol sprays or the greenhouse effect.

I have said that natural scientists have begun to play a vital role in redefining the historian's field. That is so most basically because it has been scientists, by and large, who have discovered that we are in a state of crisis with our environment, a crisis that is getting more serious with each new decade. The discovery began with the publication in 1962 of Rachel Carson's *Silent Spring,* followed by the warnings of scientists like Paul Ehrlich, Barry Commoner, Edward O. Wilson, Dennis and Donella Meadows, Daniel Jantzen, and others (to name only some of the more prominent Americans). Their collective impact, and that of the media following in their wake, was to awaken a new set of perspectives in a number of disciplines, from economics and philosophy to history, verifying once more the observation that scholars tend to examine their subjects with the concerns of the present uppermost in mind. As Lewis Mumford once insisted, the new turn of events means that "all thinking worthy of the name must now be ecological, in the sense of appreciating and utilizing organic complexity, and in adapting every kind of change to the requirements not of man alone, or of any single generation, but of all his organic partners and every part of his habitat."[8]

Some of the significant ways that scientists have helped environmental historians see the past with new eyes have had to do with the history of climate change and its impact. Only in the last few years have we assembled reasonably complete data on historic temperatures and rainfall for many parts of the world, so that we now know, for example, that, between 1550 and 1700, temperatures in western Europe were unusually cold and the climate was very unstable, bringing on a crisis of subsistence, the long-term social and economic effects of which we still do not fully understand.[9] Historians have begun to look at new data on China also and to ask what may have been the relationship of rainfall and drought cycles to the rise and expansion of the Central Asian steppe peoples.[10] Other recent evidence suggests the hand of climate in the shifting fortunes of the Mayan civilization of Central America. And going back much farther in time, we have new reason to think that agriculture, which involves turning wild annual grasses into domesticated cereals, may have begun in the southern Levant 12,000 years ago under the simultaneous pressure of drought, high temperatures, overpopulation, and overexploitation of natural resources.[11] The study of climate depends on scientific models, but it is no longer exclusively a scientist's concern.

Scientists and engineers can also take credit for reminding historians of the importance of energy in our lives and of the profound social consequences that may follow when energy supplies began to run low. The first great energy crisis in history was not the one caused by the 1973 oil embargo by the OPEC cartel but rather the much earlier one caused by the depletion of forests, and it occurred not once but many times and in many places. There was an energy crisis forming in England by the sixteenth century, and it forced the English to turn to dirty, smelly coal to keep from freezing through the winter; any sensible Englishman would much rather have had a nice oak log on the grate instead of a shovelful of coal, but most had little choice in a landscape severely overcut and turned into sheep pasture.[12] The Chinese likewise depleted their forest reserves and went through a long, painful energy squeeze long before OPEC, a squeeze lasting from 1400 to 1800 A.D., during which they were forced to burn straw and build with bamboo.[13] The consequences of the transition from wood to the fossil fuels—first to coal, then to oil—have been more far-reaching than we once realized; they include changes in technology, the social mode of production, political institutions, and, of course, air quality and human health. On the positive side, the mining of coal helped realize an affluence that was quite unprecedented in human experience. By the early nineteenth century, writes R. P. Sieferle, "the whole area of England should have been planted with wood for energy purposes, had there been no coal." Instead, after opening up their coal mines, the English could devote the rest of their lands and human energies to laying out country estates, growing more food crops, supporting a larger population, and putting up rows and rows of workingmen's cottages.[14]

Those cottages for the poor, on the other hand, indicate that with the new affluence came a new kind of environmental degradation, one especially borne by the rising numbers of poor people. This degradation we now call pollution, but it has been around since the advent of modern fossil fuel energy use and mining processes. Nowhere has pollution's impact been more deadly than in Europe of the last century. For example, in the

German city of Freiberg ("city of freedom") industrial emissions became so bad by the 1840s that "not a blade of greening grass" could be found in the area, and "the rooftops were covered with sediment from the poisonous smoke." Even relatively non-industrial cities like York, England, suffered from the smokestack soot that came streaming in the open windows, ruining furniture and clothing, driving the wealthy to sell their houses at cut-rate prices and to move toward the clean air of the country.[15] The work of scientists—chemists and others—on contemporary air and water pollution is helping historians to understand the social and ecological effects of that past pollution, though finally it may be only historians who can tell us whether the air has gotten better or worse since the beginning of the industrial era.

The impact of technology on the natural environment, we can see, goes back much farther than Rachel Carson's target of chlorinated hydrocarbons and other pesticides, even farther back than the industrial cities of Victorian England. Technology has been around as long as humans, and it has been the means of altering nature during that entire span of evolution. Go back far enough in fact, and it gets more and more difficult to determine just where technology began and where it left off in the landscape. For example, thanks to the work of a group of fire ecologists who have been studying the role of fire in ecosystems, we now understand that many of our so-called pristine landscapes, like the tallgrass prairie, were in fact the product of fires burning across the land from time immemorial. The unresolved, and probably unresolvable, question raised by that discovery is how many of those fires were really set by human beings, either deliberately to manipulate the environment or accidentally, and how many were the work of nature. This is a subject on which hard evidence is often lacking, and interpretations vary from those who see the fiery hand of aboriginal tribes in every landscape and those who are sure that lightning caused most fires. In any case, historians have joined scientists in asking such questions as, why is Australia the land of the eucalypts, a plant genus hardened to fire? What role, if any, did the Aborigines, who entered the continent from southeast Asia some 40,000 to 55,000 years ago, play in that ecological dominance? Did the English convicts arriving at Botany Bay in 1788 come into a land, "not as God made it," but "as the Aborigines made it"?[16]

I could go on to review the work done by environmental historians on disease and the spread of microorganisms, on demography and human fertility, and on ecological invasions of the many frontiers of European conquest; and could discuss their work on the changing landscape of the American South, of the Gangetic plain, of the Mediterranean basin, and of the world's tropical rainforests. But the point is simple: the natural sciences, particularly environmentally oriented sciences like ecology and climatology, have opened to historians a vast new agenda of research, with enormous relevance to our current global predicament. Most importantly, science can help historians see beyond the framework of culture—can help us appreciate the role of those autonomous material forces, processes, and beings that we call nature. And having learned to get outside the self-reflexive framework of culture and to see the nature that surrounds and constantly impinges on us, we can learn to see the past in a more complete, realistic light.

However, it would be a serious mistake to suppose that environmental historians want simply to become the pupils, or the archival assistants, of the natural scientists. They are not so likely to follow innocently along this new path as I followed Grandpa Ben over the levee to go fishing in Cow Creek. Instead, the historians want to see a convergence of long-divided modes of thought, one that brings about a genuine dialogue and a new openness in all the disciplines. Already, from their brief experience with the dialogue, the historians have concluded that scientists need to absorb a few lessons from their point of view.

In the first place, scientists must acknowledge, as many have begun to do, that the nature they describe in their textbooks often seems unreal and contrived to the historian. Typically, it lacks any connection to human history and all its contingencies, its accidents, its cycles, its ideas and social forces. Too often science seems oblivious to the fact that human beings have been interacting with nature over a long period of time, at least over two million years—some would say four million years—and that what we mean by nature is, to some extent, a product of that history.

That is by no means a new idea, even among scientists, who ever since the eighteenth century have been slowly becoming historians of a sort. Georges-Louis Leclerc, the compte de Buffon, the leading naturalist of pre-Revolutionary France, was historical-minded enough to try to describe the seven great epochs of the earth, beginning with the moment of divine creation and coming down to the present.[17] The geologist James Hutton of Edinburgh, who founded historical geology in the same century, realized that the landscape we see around us has not always looked as it does today but has gone through cycles of decay and renewal. "The earth," he wrote, "like the body of an animal, is wasted at the same time that it is repaired. It has a state of growth and augmentation; it has another state, which is that of diminution and decay. This world is thus destroyed in one part, but it is renewed in another."[18] Those were important anticipations of the historical consciousness, but science had to wait until the next century, when the biologist Charles Darwin came on the scene, to learn to be fundamentally historical in outlook. After *On the Origin of Species* appeared in 1859, science became thoroughly historicized, not only in biology but in almost all the scientific fields, in the sense that natural phenomena came to be studied over time and the so-called laws of nature came to be seen more as historical observations—rather like the observations the social historian makes—than laws that must be obeyed, as Isaac Newton had it. Today, scientists regularly acknowledge that they deal with observations rooted in particular moments, with indeterminate events that may not be repeated, let alone predicted, in the future. Despite all the historicizing of science that has been going on, however, the various disciplines of science have tended to remain, until lately, intellectually isolated from the history that people have made on the planet.

Ecosystems, for instance, have been commonly described in the textbooks as self-contained assemblages of plants and animals, evolving over time but in the absence of any people, ignoring the fact that many of the world's ecosystems have long been the home of people too. Some of those ecosystems have been profoundly, visibly altered by the human presence, while in other places that presence has been far more subtle and hard to discern. If wind has shaped the soil profile of the prairie, if bison have influenced its vegetation, if prairie dogs have dug holes all over the place, then humans have been active too. Historians want scientists to take more seriously the fact that human impact on the rest of nature has always been a possibility and that the impact has been increasingly explosive in the modern era, for deep material and cultural reasons, until now it is as big and powerful as the atomic bomb.[19]

In the second place, historians expect scientists to acknowledge that their ideas of nature, even their most complex scientific ideas, are the products of the cultures in which they live. Ideas of nature have a history, and their history is linked inextricably to the history of culture, whether economic, aesthetic, or whatever. We cannot isolate the study of our views of nature into one division called "science" and into other divisions called literature, the arts, religion, or philosophy, for they all float along together in a common flow of ideas and perceptions.

Historians, like scientists, are acutely aware that the professional papers they read in the scientific journals have dates on them, but may react to those dates differently. For scientists the dates are an index to truth: the more recent the date, the more truthful the paper. For historians, on the other hand, the dates do not necessarily appear that way. They want to make the date itself a subject of analysis. What did an ecologist, writing in, say, 1920, see in nature, and how was his or her experience different from that of an ecologist writing in 1990? Did it matter that the first ecologist was writing in the aftermath of World War I, that he may have voted for Warren G. Harding for President, that he may have lived in Nebraska rather than southern France, that he looked at the landscape through the windshield of a Model T rather than from a covered wagon? Historians are trained to look for personal biography in every idea, no matter how scientifically objective it is supposed to be, and to look for the influence of contemporary opinion on the rise and fall of scientific theories. Giving all due respect to the present generation of scientists who have worked hard to give us the most reliable account of nature they can, historians nonetheless find the scientific ideas of other eras intrinsically interesting, often as interesting as those of our own day, and for all we know, they are as valid in their way.

Words like ecosystem, niche, competitive exclusion, biomass, energy flow, plate tectonics, chaos are all just that—words—and must be appreciated as such. We may hope they indicate facts, but we can only be absolutely sure that they are words, and as words they are only representations of facts. That in itself is a point worth pausing over and considering in depth. Every science that the environmental historian approaches presents him or her with a language, and that language is filled, like any of the world's languages, with metaphors, figures of speech, hidden structures, even world-views—in short, it is filled with culture. The environmental historian wants to learn that language, no matter how uncouth it may seem at first, and use it to improve his understanding of the human past. But as a historian, trained in the modes of thought common to the humanities, where language itself is an important object of analysis, he must insist that the words of the scientist not go unexamined. They are themselves worthy of attention as expressions of culture, which is to say, they are expressions of ethical beliefs. We cannot take science out of its culture, out of the realm of meaning, value, and ethics.

In the third place, environmental historians would argue that scientists need them to answer a very big question that the latter have themselves raised but are unequipped to answer: Why are we in a state of crisis with the global environment? Scientists of many disciplines have described that crisis with impressive precision, measuring, for instance, where the carbon is generated that is causing the greenhouse effect—the warming of the earth's atmosphere by carbon dioxide and other gaseous buildup, acting like a greenhouse suspended over us, trapping solar radiation. They are beginning to track successfully the flow of that carbon from one hemisphere to the other and to make somewhat better predictions of its effects on temperatures and rainfall at the regional level. They can pinpoint with amazing detail the sources of that carbon in the tailpipes and smokestakes of the industrialized, automobilized societies. But having done all that, the scientists still cannot tell us *why* we have those societies, or where they came from, or what the moral forces are that made them. They cannot explain why cattle ranchers are cutting down and burning the Brazilian rain forest, or why the Brazilian government has been ineffective in stopping them. They cannot explain why we humans will push tens of millions of species toward extinction over the next twenty years, or why that prospect of ecological holocaust still seems irrelevant to most of the world's leaders. They cannot explain why the eastern bloc of nations has such serious pollution problems, or why some Western economists believe so fervently that market incentives alone will solve their problems. All those "why" questions are rooted in culture, which is to say, in ethical beliefs. I emphasize the point not to denigrate the achievements of scientists, but only to remind that natural science cannot by itself fathom the sources of the crisis it has identified, for the sources lie not in the nature that scientists study but in the *human nature* and, especially, in the *human culture* that historians and other humanists have made their study.

We are facing a global crisis today, not because of how ecosystems function but rather because of how our ethical systems function. Getting through the crisis requires understanding our impact on nature as precisely as possible, but even more, it requires understanding those ethical systems and using that understanding to reform them. Historians, along with literary scholars, anthropologists, and philosophers, cannot do the reforming, of course, but they can help with the understanding.

So we are making a pathway across the levee that separates nature from culture, science from history, matter from mind. Where we are arriving is not at some point where all academic distinctions or boundaries disappear, where the categories of nature and culture have been completely abolished or subsumed one under the other, but one where those boundaries are more permeable than before. Nature has become less easy to isolate from culture than we once thought, and vice versa. The two realms are linked together in an endless loop of exchanges, interactions, and meanings, so that they keep collapsing into one another. We try to keep them distinct, and sometimes for good reason: We need to try to step outside of culture regularly and to acknowledge, as Henry Thoreau once put it, "our own limits transgressed." On the other hand, we have to realize that what we mean by nature is inescapably a mirror held up by culture to its environment, a mirror reflecting itself. This is a paradox we

humans cannot get out of. The pathway we find across the levee is finally
a passage to that paradox.

We live in a material world, and nature is the largest, most complex,
more wonderful part of that materiality. As an environmental historian,
I want to bring that material world to the attention of my colleagues,
whether they are studying the rise and fall of prices, the policies of kings
and prime ministers, or the causes of war. That material world of nature,
I want them to see, has an order, a structure, and a history of its own. We
historians of every sort need to grant the significance of that nature and
to respect its discordant harmonies, its intricate evolution.

But we cannot then fall back on a simple materialism as an explanation for why societies have behaved as they have. Societies have not been
merely the products of climate, or soil, or disease, or ecosystems, or of an
abundance or scarcity of natural resources. They have also been the products of ideas, dreams, and ethical systems. And it is those latter, distinctly cultural forces that explain how and why we humans have so often
in the past, and almost everywhere today, gotten so badly out of synch
with the material world of nature.

In 1959 the English physicist and novelist, C. P. Snow, described modern academic life as divided into "two cultures," the literary intellectuals
and the scientists. "Between the two," he wrote, lies "a gulf of mutual
incomprehension. . . . They have a curious distorted image of each other.
Their attitudes are so different that, even on the level of emotion, they
can't find much common ground."[20] The literary intellectuals appeared
to him as pessimists about the human condition, turning their back on
their times, seeking refuge in the self or in the past. The scientists, on the
other hand, appeared to be shallow optimists, indifferent to books, indifferent to tradition, yet cosseted by those in power. I'm not sure that we
would describe the two cultures in precisely the same terms today—there
are, for example, a lot of pessimistic scientists around these days—but
the cultural split, and the lack of common ground, that Snow perceived
seems still to be a fact of intellectual life, in the United States as in
England.

Snow proposed that the two cultures find a common ground by
addressing the needs of the world's poor, who were falling farther and farther behind the rich nations. Something like that solution has in fact
come into existence over the past three decades, as scientists, theoretical
and applied, natural and social, have paid a lot more attention to the
problems of poverty, underdevelopment, technical innovation, and training among the poorer nations, while historians and humanists in the
northern hemisphere have expanded their purview to take in people of

color, have addressed the ethical challenges of racism, classism, and sexism, and have come to see the value of all the cultural traditions that lie outside the North. Although we have not closed the gap between the rich and poor, we have made progress together in understanding and addressing it.

Now in this last decade of the century, the 1990s, which some have begun to call the environmental decade, we have an opportunity and a reason to find new common ground between the two cultures. The opportunity appears in the form of the world environmental crisis, which stretches from the once meandering river of Cow Creek to the banks of the Amazon, the Nile, and the Mekong. Scientists, historians, indeed scholars from all the academic disciplines, and from all the various countries too, ought to come together and find pathways across the levees of specialization that divide us, to become aware of our shared life in nature. We ought to do this not only for our own enlightenment as scholars and intellectuals, but also for the good of the earth and all its inhabitants.

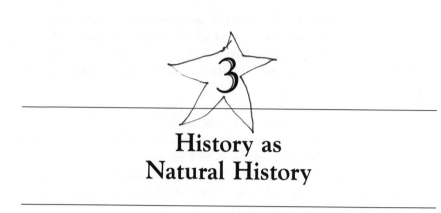

History as
Natural History

◆

CHARLES DARWIN has been moldering in his grave now for a full century. But it is not death with which we associate his name; it is life, in all its abundance and variety. In particular, the argument he made for the natural origin of life, including humans, has been one of the most influential ideas in the world over that century's span. It was accepted a long while back by almost everyone within the reach of modern science, despite the persistent opposition of a raggle-taggle band of creationists. But for all that general acceptance, Darwin's ideas have not yet become working principles among several large groups of scholars. Take history, for example: reading the journals and dissertations in this field reveals the profound, continuing influence of Adam Smith, Karl Marx, and Sigmund Freud, but still there is no Darwin in our history, at least not as a tradition of historical theory. Evolution and history remain, after a hundred years, separate realms of discourse. There is little history in the study of nature, and there is little nature in the study of history. I want to show how we can remedy that cultural lag by developing a new per-

This essay was published in the *Pacific Historical Review,* Volume 53, February 1984.

spective on the historian's enterprise, one that will make us Darwinians at last. It will require us to step back now and then from parliamentary debates, social mobility data, and the biographies of illustrious figures in order to examine more elemental questions that concern the long-running human dialogue with the earth.

The contemporary disjunction between the study of history and of nature has a fairly obvious explanation. In the eighteenth-century world of the English parson-naturalist, there was no such split; antiquities and natural curiosities lay jumbled together in the same country cupboard.[1] As we moved away from that small rural community, the old broad-gauged, integrative "natural history" began to fragment into specializations. History increasingly became an archival pursuit, carried on by urban scholars; there was less and less dirt on it. Recently, however, that drift toward an *unnatural* history has run up against a few hard facts: dwindling energy supplies, population pressures on available food, the limits and costs of technology. A growing number of scholars, consequently, have begun to talk about something called "environmental history." In 1972 the *Pacific Historical Review* devoted an entire issue to this new inquiry, and three years later the American Society for Environmental History formed to promote the study in earnest.[2] If it understands its mission clearly and fulfills it, the new history will re-create, though in a more sophisticated form, the old parson-naturalist synthesis. It will, that is, seek to combine once again natural science and history, not into another isolated specialty, but into a major intellectual enterprise that will alter considerably our understanding of historical processes. What that inquiry involves, what our times have prepared us for, what I wish to propose here, is the development of an ecological perspective on history.[3]

Within the circle of American historians, there have been at least two individuals who earlier took steps towards creating an environmental *qua* ecological mode of analysis. But in both cases they failed to move the profession very far. I mean, of course, Walter Prescott Webb and James Malin. They reached different conclusions at times, but the two had much in common. They both grew up on the Great Plains when that region was still at the edge of white agricultural settlement; they were educated in the frontier, Turnerian school of historiography, which in turn owed something to Darwin's influence; they shared an interest in the problem of aridity and what it has meant for American culture; they were both willing to break down disciplinary fences and range far afield in geography and ecology to get answers to their questions.[4] Webb described his method with characteristic simplicity: "To take a vantage point on the land, and watch the actors approach it, knowing in advance what they will

Webb

meet up with, and having at least some idea of how they may react to it."[5] What he saw was how culture, especially in its material aspects, changes to meet the conditions set by nature; in other words, he saw a process of technological (and to a lesser extent, institutional) adaptation. Meanwhile, James Malin steeped himself in ecological theory, 1930s and 40s vintage, rejected much of it as biased, and applied what remained to his study of the North American grasslands—"not under any illusion," he wrote, "that history may thus be converted into a science, but merely as a way of looking at the subject matter and processes of history."[6]

These two innovative historians still have a few readers today, though their approach was never adequately thought out and the natural science in it is now obsolete. Of the two, Webb wears better, but he often seems to have been a gifted amateur, dealing in metaphors and schematics more than careful research. His work was always marred by a parochial desire to prove that the West was different and to find evidence that its environment made it so; at his worst he was a flagrantly mechanical determinist, at his best, a figure whom other historians have generally quoted more than followed.[7] Malin, on the other hand, was a crusty, unreconstructed Social Darwinist who wanted from nature a justification for free enterprise and economic individualism.[8] Their shortcomings were not all their own fault. They were in part due to their times and their profession's immaturity, in part due to their personal remoteness from a more demanding intellectual milieu. The ecological synthesis I propose ought to acknowledge generously their contribution, then pass on to other exemplars, other issues, and other worlds.

The new history begins where Malin and Webb left off, leaps to the more unfamiliar terrain of the German historian Karl Wittfogel, and from there sallies into the field of ecological anthropology, where we will find a lot going on that is useful. First, the Wittfogel terrain. It is not, I daresay, familiar to many American historians—and it ought to be. Perhaps it is unfamiliar because Wittfogel began with that unwelcome-in-America prophet Karl Marx and his theories of historical materialism and class dialectics. Eventually though, Wittfogel managed the not inconsiderable feat of translating those theories into an environmental interpretation of society and social change that had more of Darwin than of Marx in it. He came to the United States in 1934, an emigrant from Germany, just out of Hitler's concentration camps; he brought with him an established international name in Chinese studies. Before emigrating, he had published an article, "Geopolitics, Geographical Materialism, and Marxism" (1929), in which he emphasized the importance of natural factors in shaping a society's mode of production. The fundamental relation underlying all social arrangements, he argued, is the one between humans and nature. Out of that bedrock interaction comes much of what historians seek to understand: economy, law, political power, social conflict, and so forth. Ignore that interaction, and we have lost the means to explain in the deepest sense what makes history.[9]

Wittfogel arrived at this position in attempting to solve a problem that earlier had baffled Marx: Why were the major civilizations of Asia so different from those of Europe, so lacking in capitalist development, and so unpromising for a Communist revolution? The answer, Marx had vaguely indicated, lay in the advanced water systems built by Asians to provide irrigation for their arid lands; from that base a distinct form of society had evolved in China, India, and the Near East.[10] This much Marx realized, but he was at the same time reluctant to see in nature much more than a passive landscape in which human labor toiled and created. It was Wittfogel who took the argument over and insisted that the natural environment is not really passive but rather is a powerful determining force throughout history. People are forever struggling with the land in an ongoing ecological dialectic: there is the gist of the Wittfogel theory. The earth gets changed in the unfolding dialectic, but so do the people. For example, in the absence of ample rainfall Asian farmers in several places brought water to their fields. Eventually they created what Wittfogel called a "hydraulic society."[11] As their manipulation of water became more and more large-scale, they were forced to reorganize their social structures into elaborate hierarchies of power—into a chain of pharaohs, emperors, bureaucracies, and highly centralized states. There could be no other arrangement of society so long as that ecological pattern, that techno-environmental base, remained in place.

The key question, then, that Wittfogel asked in 1929 was this: How does a society's interaction with nature lead to its own restructuring, to its evolution from one form to another? Later, in his most important work, *Oriental Despotism: A Study in Total Power,* published in 1957, he gave that question his most elaborate and controversial reply.[12] It is a monumental work, impressive in its learning and range, daring in its speculations. Unfortunately, it is also in parts a diatribe against "the communist menace," for Wittfogel had slowly made his way from being Marx's disciple to being a bitter cold warrior. As a consequence of that change in allegiance and the crusading spirit that accompanied it, many other Asian scholars came, somewhat unfairly I think and without sufficient analysis or discrimination, to dismiss his ecological ideas along with his anti-Communist polemics. And there was another unhappy result: those who had never discovered his earlier work—historians like Webb and

Malin, who might have found much in Wittfogel for their own studies of the arid American West and who needed his more advanced theoretical grounding—were not likely ever to do so. Those were sorry outcomes, brought on by Wittfogel himself. Nonetheless, the ecological question he raised is still there, waiting for historians to rediscover it and build on it a broad new interpretation of the past, one that will place human society firmly in, rather than beyond or above, nature.

If historians have tended to overlook or dismiss Wittfogel's work, the same cannot be said for anthropologists. There he has found a more appreciative audience, and to a large extent it is around his work on ancient irrigation that a discipline has coalesced within that discipline, called variously ecological anthropology, cultural ecology, and cultural materialism. So far has this study progressed that now it is the historian's turn to become learner and follower, seeking to apply the anthropologist's approach to the investigation of past societies. In what follows I will briefly review some of the main figures in ecological anthropology and their work, and then I will suggest a few ways in which history can and ought to join in promoting that perspective.

In the 1920s, during the same year that Webb was beginning his studies of the Great Plains, the anthropologist Clark Wissler introduced his "culture-area" concept.[13] It followed the geographic work of Ellsworth Huntington, Ellen Semple, Friedrich Ratzel, and J. J. E. Reclus, all of whom had stressed the importance of habitat and climate in developing cultural diversity. Wissler (and after him, Alfred Kroeber) was thoroughly familiar with diversity; he had made a lifelong study of American Indians, whose artifacts, social patterns, languages, and economics offered a bewildering variety of types. The culture-area hypothesis argued that those Indian cultural diversities formed discrete clusters on a map— and, more important, that those cultural clusters coincided with the spatial distribution of "natural areas," identified mainly by plant and animal food resources. What did that prove? Only that apparently there was some kind of link between culture and nature; nothing more firm than that about cultural causality would Wissler venture. The culture-area idea prompted several researchers to look at groups like the Eskimos and to observe how their environment might have placed limits on their cultural development, or put more positively, might have encouraged them to innovate and evolve in a new direction. After all, if the polar bear showed the influence of its experience with nature, was it inconceivable that Eskimo culture would do the same?

There were, however, problems in jumping from the evolution of bears to cultures. The bear indubitably is part of Darwin's web of life, interact-

ing with other bears, other species, the climate and chemistry of its ecosystem, adapting to that system through natural selection operating on
its genotype. But culture is a more intangible phenomenon; much of it is
carried around in people's heads, with no genetic mechanism involved in
its transmission. Does that distinction make a real difference? A man who
was to become one of the premier American anthropologists, Julian Steward, thought that it does, that as a consequence the concepts used in biological ecology—ecosystem, succession, climax, and the like—are not
meaningful in the study of Eskimo and other cultures. Admittedly, one
could take any group of humans as biological creatures and examine their
diseases, fertility, and genetic makeup; but none of that, Steward
insisted, would further our understanding of how they organize themselves, whom they worship, or what they want for their children. Rather
than treat humans, then, simply as though they are bears, he proposed a
new approach, "cultural ecology," which would deal with the "super-
organic factor of culture which . . . affects and is affected by the total web
of life."[14] His most complete description of cultural ecology appears in
Theory of Cultural Change, published in 1955. Steward had been at work
in the ecology vineyard since the thirties, but with the publication of this
widely influential book, he laid claim to being its foremost representative,
and to being, as one admirer calls him, "the greatest of the synthesiz-
ers."[15]

Steward lifted the discussion of environmental influences far above the
hoary notions of hot climates making hot-tempered, passionate lovers or
a diet of rice producing the *Bhagavad-Gita.* His ecology was not a rigid
climatic or geographical determinism. Nor did he try to explain every
aspect of culture, but only those features that are a part of what he called
the "cultural core—the constellation of features which are most clearly
related to subsistence activities and economic activities."[16] The first step
in his method was to examine the technology that a people develop to
exploit their environment and produce their living—hunting weapons,
water sources, agricultural practices, energy, transportation—and to discover how that technology is influenced by environmental circumstances.
Their dialogue with the earth brings into play certain behavior patterns,
especially work patterns. The second step of the Steward method was to
analyze those patterns. In some cases, the exploitation of resources might
require a large degree of work cooperation, in other cases none at all; in
some situations large masses of workers have to be assembled and
directed, elsewhere small groups organize themselves without coercion or
authority. The third and final procedure in cultural ecology was to ask
what effect work behavior patterns have on other domains of culture,

whether they be political systems, mythologies, or housing designs.[17] There might be only a modest impact on those other aspects, there might be a great deal, but we cannot know unless we ask the question.

Now here is where Steward's anthropology and Wittfogel's history came together. Steward believed that the critical issue was whether similar environments could be correlated with similar cultural cores, similar work behaviors, and similar survival techniques, which meant that cultural ecology must be comparative in its research. Irrigation furnished an ideal test case for that comparative strategy. In 1953 Steward organized a symposium on the archaic irrigation civilizations and included Karl Wittfogel on the program.[18] The intention was to find regularities in the seemingly unlimited diversity of human history. There was, it must be admitted, precious little agreement among the symposium participants as to what those regularities in irrigation were, though Steward and Wittfogel found their own ideas highly compatible. And once again the barebones arid landscape stimulated ecological thinking, just as it had led Malin and Webb, and has continued to lead scores of recent anthropologists, to wonder what hold nature has over the fate of human society.

By the 1950s the ecologists had carved out a secure niche for themselves in cultural anthropology. That achievement has poignant interest for the new environmental history, which is still struggling to be born, laying claim on its own profession to be recognized, and asking for employment. According to Robert Netting, cultural anthropology in the twentieth century has gone through three stages of research focus: first, the study of ideas and ideologies; second, the investigation of social structure and organization; and third, an interest in the ecological roots of cultures.[19] His point is not that ideas and institutions are no longer interesting to anthropologists; rather, it has become increasingly clear that there are basic environmental and technological forces shaping those phenomena and that we will get nowhere in understanding how cultures work if we blithely assume, for example, that a people's ideas simply come from other ideas. Historians, in contrast, have not as a group quite made it down to so basic a view. We are still up on the thirtieth floor, unsure of what goes on at ground level or what makes the elevators run.

Over the past two decades the ecological approach to anthropology has produced a distinguished corpus of monographs and theoretical treatises, which, taken together, have moved the field well beyond both Steward and Wittfogel. One can cite, among others, John Bennett's study of modern adaptation on the Canadian prairie, Harold Conklin's work on Philippine agriculture, Marshall Sahlin's effort to link Polynesian social stratification to land use, Richard Lee's analysis of the Kung Bushman's hunting and gathering economy, and Clifford Geertz's detailed contrast of two Indonesian agro-ecosystems.[20] A common tendency in many of those works has been to erase the line that Steward tried to draw between biology and culture. Virtually no one disagrees with the point that humans are unique in the degree to which they make symbols, acquire values, invent beliefs and tools, and therefore that they are not so limited to inborn ways of satisfying their needs as other animals are. But it is a completely arbitrary act to put culture and nature into separate categories, requiring rigidly separate methods of analysis. The polar bear has claws and a fur coat to cope with its environment; we humans use our cultures to do the same. However distinct they may be ontologically, their function is not so very different. Hence anthropologists have come back to using terms like ecosystem, energy flow, and climax state to analyze the human condition. In the view of Andrew Vayda and Roy Rappaport, the ideal now is to achieve a single unified science of ecology in which students of cultural evolution and of bear predation can talk in the same language.[21]

With the spate of recent environmental disasters and with gathering anxiety over the impending collapse of industrial society, anthropologists have begun to deal more and more with the problem of how different peoples try to maintain themselves in balance (homeostasis) with their habitats. As important as it is to understand successful cases, it is also useful to examine the failures and discover what causes people to fail—inadequate food for a growing population, sudden hazards they did not anticipate, a stubborn blindness to reality, some altogether different reason—and what happens to them when they do. I will single out here the work of only two writing in this vein, though they are two of the most provocative: Roy Rappaport and Marvin Harris. The first likes the small-scale pictures—pigs and islands in the Pacific—as case studies in equilibrium. The second, on the other hand, takes the wide world as his province, reinterprets all of human history and prehistory, and describes the rise and fall of empires, civilizations, and our own "anticivilization." Their perspectives may be quite unlike at times, but both have something to say about contemporary human problems as well as about more primitive existence.

Rappaport's major contribution is to remind us that people are animals with ideas, and that those ideas are not inconsequential. He directs our attention to the formative role that rituals, ideologies, and cosmologies can play in directing our environmental arrangements; they can, among other things, serve a homeostatic end, adjusting population density and land use when they have intensified to dangerous levels, threatening to degrade irreversibly the habitat. This regulatory function depends on how a people understand the world to function. In every culture, Rappaport points out, there is a "cognized model" of nature, which controls how humans behave in their environment. It may or may not correspond to the actual "operational model" of nature. But even where that cognized model is inaccurate by outside scientific standards, as in the case of the New Guinea tribesmen he has studied, it may all the same work wonderfully to restrain the exploitation of resources and keep the earth healthy and productive.

In our own industrial society, Rappaport goes on to say that cognized model, based as it is on a cornucopian vision of nature, is badly maladaptive. Despite our claims to superior factual knowledge and despite our self-confidence that we can manage the natural system skillfully, we do not really have an adequate method of checking ourselves—an effective set of, as he would say, "negative feedback mechanisms." He may be wrong; it can be argued that our recurrent conservation drives and fears of resource scarcity serve as regulatory rituals, keeping us from utterly devastating the globe, much as the New Guineans slaughter their pigs now and then in elaborate religious ceremonies to preserve their valleys. In any case, how people perceive and describe the earth and how they act on those ideas, Rappaport maintains, are not mere epiphenomena; they are powerful ecological components in themselves.[22]

It is Marvin Harris's opinion, however, that differences in how people in various cultures think and act towards nature are trivial and superficial. He finds a transcultural residuum in the human experience at all times and in all places. Briefly, that residuum is this: from the earliest hunters on the African savannah to the atomic era, humans have sought to discover the most rational, efficient way to feed themselves. Every culture, then, is at bottom simply another attempt to answer the eternal calorie problem—how to get the most nutrition out of a situation, what the best cost-benefit answer to the problem is. New cultures evolve, according to Harris, much as new biological species appear, when old answers to the nutrition challenge no longer work. There is in this Darwinian struggle for adaptation and survival no overall progress toward an ultimate, ideal solution, but there is a never-ending process of cycle and elaboration, a branching of the tree of cultural diversity into more and more directions. Old branches drop off the tree, as cultures exhaust their resources; new branches, new cultures, appear to exploit new possibilities. Industrial civilization is only the latest branch to sprout. For a while it was a remarkably effective solution to the recurring pressure to get enough to eat; it produced an unprecedented abundance. Now, however, it has become like the dinosaurs of the Mesozoic, unable to adapt, highly vulnerable through over-specialization, the victim of its own success.[23]

The work of these two anthropologists, Rappaport and Harris, by no means exhausts the possibilities in ecological studies. Nor has their work escaped criticism. Both men have their detractors and refuters: in some cases, they are other ecologists who complain that the models on which Rappaport and Harris depend are outdated; or they are nonecologists who insist that there are better ways of talking about the making of cultures. The chief criticism of Rappaport's anthropology has been that he depends on a too static model of ecology, one that was prominent a few years back but has now been superseded by more dynamic, evolutionary paradigms. When Rappaport undertook his New Guinea studies, the reigning figure in the science was Eugene Odum, whose *Fundamentals of Ecology* (the first edition appeared in 1953, the third in 1971) described natural ecosystems in terms of physics: the quiet, orderly flow of energy through the food chain, life in timeless equilibrium, no struggle or imperfection or failure.[24] Rappaport followed suit, describing a tribal culture in perfect harmony with its habitat, using energy in the most efficient way possible. But, the critics ask, is Odum's really an adequate picture of nature—of its ragged opportunism, its trials and errors, its conflicts? And are human societies, even those living in unspoiled Stone Age isolation, truly so well adjusted to nature? Rappaport's sometime collaborator, Andrew Vayda, has acknowledged the justice of a few of the criticisms of their ecology. It ignored, he admits, evidence of system disruptions and unbalanced relations between people and their environments, and he recommends as better models a new generation of biology textbooks that portray a nature that is unfinished and flawed.[25]

However much truth there may be in those criticisms of Odum and Rappaport, one suspects a hidden agenda. A world full of accidents and misfits, a world that has never been in balance and never known harmony between humans and nature, is a scientific paradigm with many current political uses. It can serve to justify the destruction wrought by contemporary industrial societies: "that is the way history has always been." And it can obscure the unfavorable contrast that Rappaport presents between other "more primitive" people and ourselves. The fact that the textbooks have been rewritten, that there have been revisionists at work here as elsewhere, is no reason to assume that newer is better, that the earlier anthropology is now all wrong. The first rule in borrowing ideas and models from the natural sciences should be to beware of ideologies and fashions that call themselves "truth" and that dismiss yesterday's science as "false."

Ecology, to be sure, must deal with change as well as equilibrium, which means it must not only describe and explain cultures at any given moment in history but also must track the breakdown of adaptation and the process of evolution. In this respect Marvin Harris is a more useful guide than Rappaport. But Harris too has encountered some criticism, and it comes from every direction—from structuralists, sociobiologists, Marxists, idealists. Some maintain that he neglects the genetic basis of cultures. Others say, and I believe they are right, that he reduces complex behavior to an oversimplified, mechanical determinism, much as Malthus did with his food-population ratios.

One of the most telling criticisms, and it comes mainly from Marxists, is that Harris gives us once more the old functionalist creed that runs through much of Anglo-American social science. The functionalist finds rationality wherever he looks. For every institution, every technology, every war, every injustice, every social order, there is a good justification—in Harris's case, the maximization of food benefits over costs, the more efficient adaptation to and exploitation of the earth. But if all cultures are "functional," and all their ways have practical reasons behind them, then, ask some critics, what can be considered irrational, exploitative, or evil? The most outrageous and brutal treatment of one human being by another has a positive survival value, a communal utility, by the logic of functionalism. We can no more object to any society's arrangements than we can object to the teeth of a tiger or the shape of a leaf. But in fact one can draw a distinction between a carnivore's biology and a society's hierarchies and relations. What is missing from a functionalist ecology that blankets everything in sight is an awareness that throughout history some people have had more power than others to define what is rational in exploiting nature. The fact that a culture exists and endures is not proof that it works well for everyone in it—that its efficiency is defined in the interests of all. There is, say Marxist anthropologists, a continuing struggle going on between rival groups in any society as to who will define what is rational, what works, who gets fed and how much. Harris's functionalist explanations do not reflect that struggle and, therefore, distort the processes of change.[26]

There are, it must be said, similarities as well as differences between ecologists and Marxists in anthropology, and hence there are opportunities for a reconciliation. Throughout the development of the ecological school of analysis, from Clark Wissler to Marvin Harris, there has been a persistent bent toward a materialist interpretation of cultures. Even Rappaport, for all his effort to bring cognition and ideas back into the picture, would not insist that ideas can exist apart from or completely independent of the material substratum. In Harris's work, that bent has become militantly positivistic, much as it was in Marx's, and he calls his theory "cultural materialism," a deliberate echo of Marx's economic determinism.[27] The parallels between the two groups go farther. They are alike holistic in their approach to understanding human society; they agree there is more to the shaping of a society than meets the eye; they insist that history is made by people who are creatures of nature, through their work and their modes of production; they are both troubled by the conundrum of where imagination, free will, and consciousness fit into that materialist interpretation. But any reconciliation between the two groups must also come to terms with some profound contrasts in emphasis. They concern the weight anthropologists believe they ought to give forces like climate, population, disease, and biota versus the class struggle, the proletariat, and social relations of wealth and hegemony. And there is another difference: Marxism as a "scientific" theory has a long record now of failing to predict the actual course of events, while the ecologists have just begun to try.

What are those of us in history, especially in environmental history, to do with these examples of ecological anthropology before us? Simply, we must not ignore them or assume that they have nothing to offer the historical researcher. With their aid, it is now time to begin examining specific ways in which an ecological approach to history can be pursued, to ask what it can seek to do, what its limits are, and why its time at last has come.

First, let us be clear about one thing: there is no special new theory that ecological *history* can or should be expected to add to the anthropological models. To believe otherwise is to suppose that history is a self-contained discipline, with its own models of society and its own peculiar epistemology. It is not. History is more a clustering of interests than a discipline, and it has never had a unique, discrete paradigm to work with. As a matter of tradition and convenience, historians agree to deal with certain matters and to omit others. There is nothing odd or wrong about being selective in that way, of course, but the bias of selection ought not to be immune to dissent. For a long while historians tended to limit their purview to the nation-state, to its politics and its relations with other states, and to assume, rather too easily, that culture and ideas were contained therein. A consequence of that assumption was that the field often seemed to have only the vaguest notion of what a culture is and how it works. But that situation is changing rapidly, and as it does, there is less and less reason to insist on an isolated or sacrosanct discipline of "society á la history."

If historians per se have anything special to add to ecological analysis, it is the awareness that all generalizations must be rooted in specific times and places—not a small point when there are avid generalizers like Marvin Harris about. But that is not the same thing as claiming to operate by a peculiar set of theoretical principles and definitions.[28]

The majority of anthropologists, excepting the archaeologists, work among surviving tribal and village societies. Most historians, on the other hand, deal with the dead and their written records, though largely it is the dead of the modern era. These are differences, but they dwindle. Already among premodern historians, there is going on a rapprochement with anthropology; consider, for example, LeRoy Ladurie's *Montaillou: The Promised Land of Error,* in which ecological anthropology figures prominently.[29] It is mainly among modern historians in particular that the gap between the two fields of study remains to be bridged. Let us explore a few of the research areas in which that might be done.

The rise and evolution of industrialism and its close associate, capitalism, is by all odds the central issue confronting modern historians. What would constitute an ecological approach to that subject? In the first place, we would have to understand better than we do now the effect that population increases had on the collapse of feudal society and its techno-environmental base. William McNeill's splendid work on plagues and disease immunities provides some of the foundation for that inquiry.[30] The next step is to discover how increased population pressure on the soil created a demand, and an opportunity, for cultural innovation. At the center of this problem, in other words, is the postfeudal agricultural revolution. What was it? What pushed it along? What impact did it have on natural resources and social relations? As Frank Fraser Darling has put it, "The human ecologist will never neglect the belly of the people."[31] Indeed, that is where ecological history must always begin—with hunger and food, with filling people's bellies. The emergence of the new industrial economy rested on a fresh approach to that problem; it depended on modern agriculture, or factory farming, as it eventually came to be called. If Harris is right, every innovation, industrialism included, reaches at last a point of intensified development that threatens its own destruction. There are plenty of case studies in twentieth-century industrial and capitalist farming where that argument can be tested.[32] We need to understand, then, not only the ecological origins of this mode of production, but also its impact on the land—both on specific ecosystems and on the planet as a whole—and on the land's inhabitants.

A second set of modern experiences where an ecological perspective is called for has to do with that old, familiar theme, the frontier. It is a theme as ancient as *Homo sapiens,* for people have been moving into unoccupied wilderness or invading someone else's territory since Lucy wandered across Ethiopia. And not only have humans been doing it: nothing links us more clearly to other creatures than pioneering. Over the past five hundred years that pioneering process has accelerated remarkably, until the world has become in effect a single country, dominated by a single aggressive species. As a consequence, thousands of plant and animal varieties have disappeared or are on the way into oblivion, millions of humans have died through wars and epidemics, and entire cultures have faded away. This is, as Alfred Crosby and others have demonstrated, a subject that demands, that cries out for, the integration of history and ecology.[33] What we still do not fully understand, despite our Turners and Webbs, is how and why some pioneering cultures succeed while others fail; or what makes one people adaptive and another conservative; or how some recent societies have achieved world dominance through expanding their ecological niche and thus, in the words of Marshall Sahlins, "have shown great capacity to wheel and deal in the face of local natural deficiencies."[34] Global conquest may be a political topic, and it most certainly is an ethical one. But at its roots it is also an ecological event.

I will give one further example of where ecology, anthropology, and modern history could work together: research into the regulation of exploitative behavior, or what Rappaport termed negative feedback mechanisms. Environmental history has already distinguished itself in this area, but there are issues that we have not yet resolved and others that we will never settle. In what ways, for instance, have our cognized models of nature been changed by the rise of an industrial, capitalist order? What contrast does that order make with preindustrial cultures and their regulatory mechanisms? Has the rising scale of social organization in modern times had an adverse influence on people's ability to perceive the limits of their environment and to restrain their demands within those limits? Have our religious and postreligious cosmologies, in contrast to those of animistic cultures, made us runaway successes, or have they undermined our future? Within the past century a number of new social rituals have appeared—the consumer ritual of Christmas is one of the more popular of them—but it is not altogether clear what their cumulative impact on nature has been, or whether in all that innovation there might also be, as hinted earlier, new rituals that have an environmentally conserving function.[35]

The ecological approach cannot alone address all the issues that historians today want addressed. It may, however, redirect their attention to some issues they have forgotten, or never been aware of. I am less ready than Marvin Harris to believe that there is ever likely to be a transdisciplinary science of ecology that will give us, in whatever field we labor, a set of unchanging answers, coldly objective truths, or "laws" of behavior; there is too much of the historicist in me to credit that old positivistic promise. We will always be, I think, the children of our surroundings, unable to see the world through anyone's eyes but our own, always filled with biases, assumptions, passions, and commitments. It is not clear to me why we should want things otherwise. But if the ecological perspective will not make us more scientific, in Harris's sense, if it will not settle every puzzle in history, it may at least open our imaginations and let us look deeper into the past around us. We need that point of view for our continuing enlightenment. And it is now plain that the earth needs it too for its survival.

4

Transformations of
the Earth

◆

FORTY years ago a wise, visionary man, the Wisconsin wildlife biologist and conservationist Aldo Leopold, called for "an ecological interpretation of history," by which he meant using the ideas and research of the emerging field of ecology to help explain why the past developed the way it did.[1] At that time ecology was still in its scientific infancy, but its promise was bright and the need for its insights was beginning to be apparent to a growing number of leaders in science, politics, and society. It has taken a while for historians to heed Leopold's advice, but at last the field of environmental history has begun to take shape and its practitioners are trying to build on his initiative.

Leopold's own suggestion of how an ecologically informed history might proceed had to do with the frontier lands of Kentucky, pivotal in the westward movement of the nation. In the period of the revolutionary war it was uncertain who would possess and control those lands: the native Indians, the French or English empires, or the colonial settlers? And then rather quickly the struggle was resolved in favor of the Ameri-

This essay first appeared in the *Journal of American History,* Volume 76, March 1990.

cans, who brought along their plows and livestock to take possession. It was more than their prowess as fighters, their determination as conquerors, or their virtue in the eyes of God that allowed those agricultural settlers to win the competition; the land itself had something to contribute to their success. Leopold pointed out that growing along the Kentucky bottomlands, the places most accessible to newcomers, were formidable canebrakes, where the canes rose as high as fifteen feet and posed an insuperable barrier to the plow. But fortunately for the Americans, when the cane was burned or grazed out, the magic of bluegrass sprouted in its place. Grass replaced cane in what ecologists call the pattern of secondary ecological succession, which occurs when vegetation is disturbed but the soil is not destroyed, as when a fire sweeps across a prairie or a hurricane levels a forest; succession refers to the fact that a new assortment of species enters and replaces what was there before. In Kentucky, the foremost of those new species was bluegrass, and a wide expanse of bluegrass was all that any rural pioneer, looking for a homestead and a pasture for his livestock, could want. Discovering that fact, Americans entered Kentucky by the thousands, and the struggle for possession was soon over. "What if," Leopold wondered, "the plant succession inherent in this dark and bloody ground had, under the impact of these forces, given us some worthless sedge, shrub, or weed?" Would Kentucky have become American territory as, and when, it did?[2]

Actually, the facts in the case are more complicated than Leopold could explore in the confines of his essay, and they argue for something more than a simple form of environmental determinism, which is what a casual reader might see in his example. Kentucky bluegrass was not a native species, but a European import.[3] Brought by immigrants to the country in the holds of ships, its seed spread through the travels and droppings of their cattle, sprouting first around salt licks, where the animals congregated, then spreading into newly disturbed land like the canebrakes, where it gained ascendancy over its indigenous competitors, much as the colonists were doing over the Indians. The winning of Kentucky was, in other words, helped immensely by the fact that the human invaders inadvertently brought along their plant allies. So, on continent after continent, went the triumph of what Alfred Crosby, Jr., has called "ecological imperialism."[4]

It is with such matters that the new field of ecological or environmental history (most practitioners prefer to use the latter label as more inclusive in method and material) deals. This new history rejects the common assumption that human experience has been exempt from natural constraints, that people are a separate and uniquely special species, that the ecological consequences of our past deeds can be ignored. The older history could hardly deny that people have been living for a long while on this planet, but its general disregard of that fact suggested that they were not and are not truly part of the planet. Environmental historians, on the other hand, realize that scholarship can no longer afford to be so naïve.

The field of environmental history began to take shape in the 1970s, as conferences on the global predicament were assembling and popular environmentalist movements were gathering momentum. It was a response to questions that people in many nations were beginning to ask: How many humans can the biosphere support without collapsing under the impact of their pollution and consumption? Will man-made changes in the atmosphere lead to more cancer or poorer grain harvests or the melting of the polar ice caps? Is technology making people's lives more dangerous, rather than more secure? Does *Homo sapiens* have any moral obligations to the earth and its circle of life, or does that life exist merely to satisfy the infinitely expanding wants of our own species? History was not alone in being touched by the rising concern; scholars in law, philosophy, economics, sociology, and other areas were likewise responsive. It is surely a permanent response, gaining significance as the questions prompting it increase in urgency, frequency, and scope. Environmental history was born out of a strong moral concern and may still have some political reform commitments behind it, but as it has matured, it has become an intellectual enterprise that has neither any simple, nor any single, moral or political agenda to promote. Its goal is to deepen our understanding of how humans have been affected by their natural environment through time, and conversely and perhaps more importantly in view of the present global predicament, how they have affected that environment and with what results.[5]

Much of the material for environmental history, coming as it does from the accumulated work of geographers, natural scientists, anthropologists, and others, has been around for generations and is merely being absorbed into historical thinking in the light of recent experience. It includes data on tides and winds, ocean currents, the position of continents in relation to each other, and the geological and hydrological forces creating the planet's land and water base. It includes the history of climate and weather, as these have made for good or bad harvests, sent prices up or down, promoted or ended epidemics, or led to population increase or decline. All these have been powerful influences on the course of history, and they continue to be so. In a somewhat different category from these physical factors are the living resources of the earth, or the biota, which the ecologist George Woodwell calls the most important of all to human well-being: the plants and animals that, in his phrase, "maintain the biosphere as a habitat suitable for life."[6] Those living resources have also been more susceptible to human manipulation than nonbiological factors, and at no point more so than today. We must include the phenomenon of human reproduction as a natural force giving form to history, and by no means a negligible force, as the last few decades of explosive global fertility have amply demonstrated.

Defined in the vernacular then, environmental history deals with the role and place of nature in human life. It studies all the interactions that societies in the past have had with the nonhuman world, the world we have not in any primary sense created. The technological environment, the cluster of things that people have made, which can be so pervasive as to constitute a kind of "second nature" around them, is also part of this study, but in the very specific sense that technology is a product of human culture as conditioned by the nonhuman environment. But with such phenomena as the desert and the water cycle, we encounter autonomous, independent energies that do not derive from the drives and inventions of any culture. It might be argued that as the human will increasingly makes its imprint on forests, gene pools, and even oceans, there is no practical way to distinguish between the natural and the cultural. However, most environmental historians would argue that the distinction is worth keeping, for it reminds us that not all the forces at work in the world emanate from humans. Wherever the two spheres, the natural and the cultural, confront or interact with one another, environmental history finds its essential themes.

There are three levels on which the new history proceeds, each drawing on a range of other disciplines and requiring special methods of analysis. The first involves the discovery of the structure and distribution of natural environments of the past. Before one can write environmental history one must first understand nature itself—specifically, nature as it was organized and functioning in past times. The task is more difficult than might first appear, for although nature, like society, has a story of change to tell, there are few written records to reveal most of that story. To make such a reconstruction, consequently, the environmental historian must turn for help to a wide array of the natural sciences and must rely on their methodologies, sources, and evidence, though now and then the documentary materials with which historians work can be a valuable aid to the scientists' labors.[7]

The second level of environmental history is more fully the responsibility of the historian and other students of society, for it focuses on productive technology as it interacts with the environment. For help on understanding this complicated level, in which tools, work, and social relations are intermixed, historians in the new field have begun to turn to the extensive literature dealing with the concept of "modes of production," emphasizing (as most of those who use the phrase have not) that those modes have been engaged not merely in organizing human labor and machinery but also in transforming nature.[8] Here the focus is on understanding how technology has restructured human ecological relations, that is, with analyzing the various ways people have tried to make nature over into a system that produces resources for their consumption. In that process of transforming the earth, people have also restructured themselves and their social relations. A community organized to catch fish at sea may have had very different institutions, gender roles, or seasonal rhythms from those of one raising sheep in high mountain pastures. A hunting society may have had a very different configuration from that of a peasant agricultural one. On this level of inquiry, one of the most interesting questions is who has gained and who has lost power as modes of production have changed.[9]

(3) Finally, forming a third level for the environmental historian is that more intangible, purely mental type of encounter in which perceptions, ideologies, ethics, laws, and myths have become part of an individual's or group's dialogue with nature. People are continually constructing cognitive maps of the world around them, defining what a resource is, determining which sorts of behavior may be environmentally degrading and ought to be prohibited, and generally choosing the ends to which nature is put. Such patterns of human perception, ideology, and value have often been highly consequential, moving with all the power of great sheets of glacial ice, grinding and pushing, reorganizing and re-creating the surface of the planet.

The great challenge in the new history does not lie in merely identifying such levels of inquiry, but in deciding how and where to make connections among them. Do the lines of historical causality run from the first, the level of nature, through technology and on to ideology, as a strict environmental determinist would insist? Or do the lines run in precisely the opposite direction, so that nature itself is finally nothing more than the product of human contrivance or desire? This is, of course, an age-old debate over explanation, one that the new history has only inherited, not invented; the debate is too large and complex to reproduce, let alone pretend to resolve, here. Suffice it to observe that most environmental historians seem to have settled philosophically on a position that is at once materialist and idealist; they commonly maintain that the historian cannot rigidly adhere a priori to any single theory of causality but must be open to context and time. In some cases the shifting patterns of the natural order—a sustained condition of severe aridity, for instance, or an abrupt shift from a wet to a dry cycle—have been powerful, forcing people to adapt on both the productive and the cognitive levels. In other cases, however, and increasingly in modern times, when the balance of power has shifted more and more away from nature and in favor of humans, the third level, the sum of people's perceptions and ideas about nature, has clearly become the decisive one in promoting change.

The gathering strength of the human imagination over nature is so obvious and dramatic that it is in no danger of being neglected by historians. What has been neglected, however, or left conceptually underdeveloped, is the second level of inquiry I mentioned. And it is to that middle level, the analysis of modes of production as ecological phenomena, and particularly as they are articulated in agriculture, that the rest of this essay is devoted. The intention here is not to make a definitive theoretical statement about this subject, but to review, especially with nonspecialists in mind, some of the broader themes and to identify areas where more research is needed.

Humans have extracted an extraordinarily diverse array of resources from the natural world, and the number and magnitude of them is growing all the time. But the most basic and revealing of them in the study of human ecology have been the resources we call food. Every group of people in history has had to identify such resources and create a mode of production to get them from the earth and into their bellies. Moreover, it is through that process that they have been connected in the most vital, constant, and concrete way to the natural world. Few of those modes of producing food, however, have been approached by historians from an ecological perspective. If we are to make further progress in understanding the linkages human beings make to nature, developing that perspective and applying it to food production must be one of the major activities of the new field.

To undertake this project, the historian might begin by adopting the scientist's concept of the *ecosystem* and then asking how it might be applied to the agriculture practiced in any setting or period. There is a tall pile of books and scientific papers on the complicated ways in which ecosystems are structured, work, and evolve; but in simplest terms, one might define an ecosystem as the collective entity of plants and animals interacting with one another and the nonliving (abiotic) environment in a given place. Some ecosystems are fairly small and easily demarcated, like a single pond in New England, while others are sprawling and ill defined, as hugely ambiguous as the Amazonian rain forest or the Serengeti plain. Until rather recently, all those ecosystems have been understood by ecologists to have self-equilibrating powers, like automatic mechanisms that slow themselves when they get too hot or speed up when they begin to sputter and stall. Outside disturbances might affect equilibrium, throwing the system temporarily off its regular rhythm, but always (or almost always) it was supposed to return to some steady state. The number of species constituting an ecosystem was believed to fluctuate around some determinable point, the flow of nutrients and energy through the system staying more or less constant. A dominant concern among ecologists has been to explain how such systems manage to cohere, to maintain order and balance, in the midst of all the perturbations to which they are subject.[10]

But historians wanting to undertake an ecological analysis should be aware that lately the conventional ecosystem model sketched above has been coming under considerable criticism from some scientists, and there is no longer any consensus on how it functions or how resilient it is. Are ecosystems as stable as scientists have assumed, the critics ask, or are they all susceptible to easy upset? Is it accurate to describe them as firmly balanced and orderly until humans arrive on the scene, as some of the older textbooks suggested, or is human disturbance only one of the many sources of instability in nature? Even more disputed are these questions: How and when do people begin to produce changes in ecosystems that might be called damaging, and when does that damage become irreversible? No one really disputes that the death of all its trees, birds, and insects would mean the death of a rain forest, or that the draining of a pond would spell the end of that ecosystem; but most changes, induced by humans or otherwise, are not so catastrophic, and the concept of damage has no clear definition or easy method of measurement. Dependent as it is on ecological theory for assistance in analysis and explanation, the new field of environmental history finds itself in a very awkward position—caught in the middle of a revisionist swing that has left in some disarray the notion of what an ecosystem is and how it works, that has even cast doubt on such old intuitive notions as "the balance of nature" and the role of diversity in promoting ecological stability.[11] Historians have long had to deal with such revisionism in their own field and are only too familiar with the resulting confusion. Learning from that experience, they should not rush to assume that the latest scientific paper on the ecosystem is the true gospel or that yesterday's notions are now completely wrong; on the other hand, if they want to work collaboratively with scientists, they must be careful not to borrow their ideas of nature unthinkingly or innocently from outmoded textbooks or discarded models.

Those theoretical disputes should not obscure the fact that ecological science continues to describe a natural world that is marvelously organized and vital to human existence. Nature, in the eyes of most ecologists, is not an inert or formless or incoherent world that awaits the hand of people. It is a world of living things that are constantly at work, in discernible patterns, producing goods and services that are essential for the survival of one another. Microorganisms, for example, are endlessly busy breaking down organic matter to form the constituents of soil, and other organisms in turn make use of that soil for their own nutrition and growth. The science of ecology still reveals a realm beyond our human economies, and beyond the work we do in them, a realm that has been described as a vast, elaborate, complex "economy of nature," an organized realm that is working energetically and skillfully to satisfy the needs of all living things, creating what might be called the indispensable "values" of existence. Without the smooth functioning of that greater economy, without those values that are brought into being by a hardworking nature, no group of people could survive for an hour, and the making of history would come to an abrupt end.

An ecosystem then is a subset of the global economy of nature—a local or regional system of plants and animals working together to create the means of survival. Starting from this understanding, the historian ought to ask how we can best proceed from the ecosystem concept to understand the human past more completely. Taking that next step requires us to adopt still another concept—what some have begun to call an *agroecosystem,* which, as the name suggests, is an ecosystem reorganized for agricultural purposes—a domesticated ecosystem. It is a restructuring of the trophic processes in nature, that is, the processes of food and energy flow in the economy of living organisms. Everywhere such a restructuring involves forcing the productive energies in some ecosystem to serve more exclusively a set of conscious purposes often located outside it—namely, the feeding and prospering of a group of humans. Whatever its place in time, whether its human designers are primitive or advanced, every agroecosystem has at least two general characteristics. It is always a truncated version of some original natural system: There are fewer species interacting within it, and many lines of interaction have been shortened and directed one way. Commonly, it is a system of export, some of the foodstuffs produced being harvested and removed, sometimes only a little distance to a village of folk agriculturists, sometimes a good way off to an international port, in either case leaving the system in danger of becoming depleted and degraded. To survive for very long, the agroecosystem must achieve a balance between its exports and imports, or it loses its productivity and people slide downward into poverty and hunger.[12]

Though something of a human artifact, the agroecosystem remains inescapably dependent on the natural world—on photosynthesis, biochemical cycles, the stability of the atmosphere, and the services of nonhuman organisms. It is a rearrangement, not a repeal, of natural processes. That is as true of a modern factory farm in California or a Douglas fir plantation in Oregon as it is of an ancient rice paddy in China. Whatever the differences among agroecosystems, they are all subject to the laws of ecology, and those same laws govern wild forests, grasslands, savannahs, and heaths, determining just how stable or resilient or sustainable they are as collective entities.

The reorganization of native plants and animals into agroecosystems began long before the modern age. Often it started with a fire deliberately set and fanned into a raging blaze, clearing a patch of open soil; in the ashes of that opening farmers planted their own favored species, maintaining them against the successional pressures of the surrounding vegetation for a few years until the soil fertility was depleted and the agriculturist moved on to new lands.[13] This primitive method of clearance, found among North American Indians, white Kentucky pioneers, and New Guinea tribesmen, is still practiced in many parts of the world today, wherever land is plentiful and there is little pressure to maximize production; it is variously labeled shifting, swidden, slash-and-burn, or milpa farming.[14] In almost every case these early-style farmers introduced plants that were not part of the native ecosystem, that may even have been brought in from remote parts of the planet. Wheat, corn, and rice, the most widely cultivated cereals, have all been carried far from their points of origin and have replaced native vegetation over vast expanses of the earth's surface. As outsiders, they have in many cases thrived exceptionally well in their new settings, freed as they have been from the animal grazers and nibblers and the plant competitors that once kept them in check. In other cases, however, the newcomers have not been so well adapted to their new environment, or at least not so well adapted as the native plants; hence a great deal of effort must be given to securing them against destructive forces, adapting them as well as human ingenuity can, trying to replicate in mere decades or centuries of breeding what it may have taken nature millions of years to evolve, never letting one's vigilance rest. Likewise, the native fauna have been radically diminished, even in many cases exterminated, on every continent by clearance for agriculture, and new fauna—including a plague of insect pests—have appeared over time to thrive in those contrived agroecosystems. Tracing such ecological transformations ought to be the first and most essential step in writing the history of the planet.

Anthropologists and archaeologists are still debating the causes of the Neolithic revolution, which took place some ten thousand years ago in the Middle East (later in other areas), and conclusive support for any theory as to why humans gave up a hunting and gathering life for shifting, or later more settled, farming may always be hard to come by. One of the standard hypotheses starts with a shortage in food supplies brought on by population growth, a situation that may have happened in many places and at different times in prehistory but supposedly always had that same demographic pressure behind it. The hypothesis has plenty of critics, and it is not a matter that historians can pretend to settle, though it may be that historical studies of agricultural change in developing countries in recent centuries can be suggestive. One of the most influential agricultural theorists, the Danish economist Ester Boserup, has followed precisely that strategy and has concluded that population pressure has always been the key force behind land-use intensification, compelling groups to cultivate crops in the first place and then, as the pressure continues, to work harder and harder at the task, developing new skills as they go along and organizing themselves into larger work units. Sheer necessity, in other words, has been the mother of ecological innovation in preindustrial conditions.[15]

All the while they are rearranging the native flora and fauna to produce more food, people are forced to adapt to local conditions of soil, climate, and water. One might even call such conditions the soft determinants of human existence, for they significantly influence how and where people get their living and what kind of living it is.

No people can do without a little soil. Before people began farming on it, topsoil may have required thousands of years to develop, accumulating at the rate of a mere fraction of an inch per century. One of the greatest challenges posed any community is to maintain that fertility under its contrived food system, and the historian must study the techniques by which the community does so, whether through fallowing, green-manuring, legume planting, or plowing human and animal excrement back into the soil, as well as the consequences that follow when it is not done. The second critical factor, climate, has until recently been well beyond human control; therefore the vulnerability of the agroecosystem to natural forces has been greatest here. Water has been less sovereign. It was one of the earliest forces of nature to come under human management, though here too a scarcity or an excess has, at many times and places, put severe constraints on social development.[16]

Unquestionably, all agriculture has brought revolutionary changes to the planet's ecosystems; and, most agroecologists would agree, those changes have often been destructive to the natural order and imperfect in design and execution. Yet as they have gained understanding of how agricultural systems have interacted with nature, scientists have discovered plenty of reasons to respect the long historical achievement of billions of anonymous traditional farmers. As Miguel A. Altieri writes, "Many farming practices once regarded as primitive or misguided are being recognized as sophisticated and appropriate. Confronted with specific problems of slope, flooding, droughts, pests, diseases and low soil fertility, small farmers throughout the world have developed unique management systems to overcome these constraints." One of the most impressive and yet common of such managerial techniques is to diversify the crops under cultivation; traditional Filipino farmers, for example, raise as many as forty separate crops in a single swidden at the same time. The advantages of such diversification include making more efficient use of light, water, and nutrients by cultivating plants of different height, canopy structure, and nutrient requirements, thus harvesting greater total yields per hectare; leaving more nitrogen in the soil from intercropped legumes; and achieving more effective soil cover, pest control, and weed suppression.[17]

The landscapes that resulted from such traditional practices were carefully integrated, functional mosaics that retained much of the wisdom of nature; they were based on close observation and imitation of the natural order. Here a field was selected and cleared for intensive crop production; there a forest was preserved as supply of fuel and mast; over there a patch of marginal land was used for pasturing livestock. What may have appeared scattered and happenstance in the premodern agricultural landscape always had a structure behind it—a structure that was at once the product of nonhuman factors and of human intelligence, working toward a mutual accommodation. In many parts of the world that agroecosystem took thousands of years to achieve, and even then it never reached any perfect resting point.[18] Rises and falls in human numbers, vagaries of weather and disease, external pressures of wars and taxes, tragedies of depletion and collapse, all kept the world's food systems in a constant state of change. Yet, examined over the long duration, they had two remarkably persistent, widely shared characteristics, whether they were in medieval Sweden or ancient Sumer, in the Ohio River valley or the Valley of Mexico, whether the systems were based on maize or wheat or cassava. First, traditional agroecosystems were based on a predominantly subsistence strategy in which most people raised what they themselves consumed, though now and then they may have sent some of their surplus off to cities for the sake of trade or tribute. Second, subsistence-oriented agroecosystems, despite making major changes in nature, nonetheless preserved much of its diversity and complexity, and that achievement was a source of social stability, generation following generation.

So it was, that is, until the modern era and the rise of the capitalist mode of production. Beginning in the fifteenth century and accelerating in the eighteenth and nineteenth centuries, the structure and dynamics of agroecosystems began to change radically. I believe the capitalist reorganization carried out in those years and beyond into our own time brought as sweeping and revolutionary a set of land-use changes as did the Neolithic revolution. Despite its importance, we have not yet fully understood why this second revolution occurred nor asked what its effect has been on the natural environment. I submit that the single most important task for scholars in the history of modern agroecology is to trace what Karl Polanyi has called "the great transformation," both in general planetary terms and in all its permutations from place to place.[19]

We do not yet have a thoroughly researched picture of just how and where ecological factors may have played a causative role in the great transformation. Since almost all studies of the rise of capitalism have been written by social and economic historians, those factors have not received much attention. Did the old medieval peasant life, we want to know, break down because it was degrading the environment? Was it falling hopelessly behind the pressing demands of population growth? Was it stretched to the point of collapse, until people were ready to heed the solutions offered by a new generation of rising capitalistic entrepreneurs? Or, quite the contrary, was the new capitalist mode of production forced on peasants who had been living in equilibrium with their environment and were reluctant to change? The questions are admittedly overly broad and need refinement, while the evidence collected so far is too spotty to suggest which explanation is right. We may be in a position to ask better questions and form a coherent response when we have gained a clearer understanding of how the transformation is proceeding in Third World countries today, undermining traditional farming just as it was once undermined in England, France, and Germany.[20]

When I speak of the capitalist mode of production in agriculture I mean something broader than Marxists do when they use the phrase. For them, the crucial distinguishing feature of the new mode has been the restructuring of *human* relations: the buying of labor as a commodity in the marketplace and the organizing of it to produce more commodities for sale.[21] In my view, the buying of labor is too narrow a feature to cover so broad, multifaceted, and changing a mode as capitalism, even considered in merely human terms. It would leave out the slave-owning cotton planters of the American South, who bought people, not merely their labor; it would not include the agribusiness wheat farmers of the Great Plains, who have seldom had access to hired hands and have invested in technology instead; and today it would have to omit from the realm of capitalism the California grower who has just bought a mechanical tomato harvester to replace all his migrant workers. In order to define capitalism more adequately, some have extended it to any organization of labor, technology, or technique for producing commodities for sale in the marketplace. If few agricultural producers have been capitalists in the strict Marxist sense, it is said, more and more of them have become "capitalistic" over the past four centuries, and nowhere more so than in the United States.

But this looser definition will not quite do either, for it is so imprecise that it could describe agriculture in ancient as well as modern times, in Africa, Central America, and Asia as well as Europe—wherever men and women have set up markets to trade their produce for goods and coin. Most important here, it does not incorporate the perspective of the environmental historian: it does not acknowledge that the capitalist era in production introduced a new, distinctive relation of people to the natural world. The *reorganization of nature,* not merely of society, is what we must uncover.

An adequate definition of the capitalist transformation of nature is a larger order than I can here undertake to fill, but a few preliminary thoughts may clarify what is meant. In the first place, a distinction must be made between markets and the market system or economy. The new order was not a matter of the existence of isolated markets here and there, but of an entire economy designed according to a simplified, idealized model of human behavior: the meeting of a buyer and a seller for the purpose of freely maximizing personal wealth. The most satisfactory definition of that market economy, one that captures its underlying moral essence, is Polanyi's:

> The transformation implies a change in the motive of action on the part of members of society: for the motive of subsistence that of gain must be substituted. All transactions are turned into money transactions, and these in turn require that a medium of exchange be introduced into articulation of industrial life. All incomes must derive from the sale of something or other,

and whatever the actual source of a person's income, it must be regarded as resulting from sale. . . . But the most startling peculiarity of the system lies in the fact that, once it is established, it must be allowed to function without outside interference.

As Polanyi explains, capitalism was distinctive in that it was unabashedly based "on a motive only rarely acknowledged as valid in the history of human societies, and certainly never before raised to the level of a justification of action and behavior in everyday life, namely, gain."[22]

Capitalism introduced still another innovation, one that would change profoundly the way people related to nature in general: It created for the first time in history a general market in land. All the complex forces and interactions, beings and processes, that we term "nature" (sometimes even elevate to the honorific status of a capitalized "Nature") were compressed into the simplified abstraction, "land." Though not truly a commodity in the ordinary sense, that is, something produced by human labor for sale on the market, land became "commodified"; it came to be regarded as though it were a commodity and by that manner of thinking was made available to be traded without restraint. Whatever emotional meanings that land had held for the self and its identity, whatever moral regard it had engendered, now was suppressed so that the market economy could function freely. The environmental implications in such a mental change are beyond easy reckoning.[23]

What actually happened to the world of nature, once it had been reduced to the abstraction "land," is one of the most interesting historical problems presented by the capitalist transformation and will require a great deal more research by environmental historians. There are many possible lines for that research to take, but among the most promising is an inquiry into the restructuring of agroecosystems that capitalism promoted. First in England and then in every part of the planet, agroecosystems were rationally and systematically reshaped in order to intensify, not merely the production of food and fiber, but the accumulation of personal wealth.

Despite many variations in time and place, the capitalistic agroecosystem shows one clear tendency over the span of modern history: a movement toward the radical simplification of the natural ecological order in the number of species found in an area and the intricacy of their interconnections. As markets developed and transportation improved, farmers increasingly concentrated their energies on producing a smaller and smaller number of crops to sell for profit. They became, in short, specialists in production, even to the point of producing virtually nothing for their own direct personal consumption. But that is not all: the land itself evolved into a set of specialized instruments of production. What had once been a biological community of plants and animals so complex that scientists can hardly comprehend it, what had been changed by traditional agriculturists into a still highly diversified system for growing local foodstuffs and other materials, now increasingly became a rigidly contrived apparatus competing in widespread markets for economic success. In today's parlance we call this new kind of agroecosystem a *monoculture,* meaning a part of nature that has been reconstituted to the point that it yields a single species, which is growing on the land only because somewhere there is strong market demand for it. Although farmers in isolated rural neighborhoods may have continued to plant a broad, multispecies spectrum of crops, the trend over the past two hundred years or so has been toward the establishment of monocultures on every continent. As Adam Smith realized back in the eighteenth century, specialization is at the very heart of the capitalist mode of production. It should not be surprising then that it would eventually become the rule in agriculture and land use as it is in manufacturing.[24]

In Smith's day, however, the trend in the new agriculture toward a massive loss of ecological complexity was not easy to foresee. On the contrary, it was obscured for a long while by the discovery and colonization of the Americas by the European nations, which suddenly made available to farmers a dazzling array of new plant species to try out in their fields: maize, potatoes, tobacco, to name some of the more valuable among them. On both sides of the Atlantic, agroecosystems might now contain more kinds of plants than ever before. That outcome was part of a more general process of global biological exchange, migration, and mixing that occurred with the great discoveries and the subsequent migration of Europeans all over the globe, reversing, as Alfred Crosby has written, the effects of continental drift and geographical isolation that has obtained for millions of years.[25] Thomas Jefferson's enthusiasm for introducing mulberry trees and silkworm cultivation from China into Virginia was only one example of what seemed, in the early days of modern farming, to be the possibility of a new plentitude in production. There was more variety in the modern agricultural market economy, considered as a whole, than in each of the scattered traditional economies of the past—a broader base for consumers than even the Philippine farmer enjoyed with his dozens of varieties growing in the forest clearings. Ironically, however, the individual producer had less biotic complexity to deal with on a given acre than before; his fenced and deeded lands became, in ecological terms, depauperate environments.

Another reason for the long obscurity in capitalistic agriculture's trend toward radical simplification was the near-simultaneous rise of modern science, both practical and theoretical, and its application to the problems of agriculture. The "agricultural revolution" that began in England during the eighteenth century was a double-sided phenomenon: one half of it was capitalistic, the other scientific, and the two halves have never been altogether compatible. In the early years of their relationship, scientifically inclined reformers taught traditional English farmers, faced with declining soil fertility and low output, to rotate their fields between arable and grass to improve livestock husbandry and augment their manure supplies, and to cultivate root crops such as turnips to feed their cattle and legumes such as clover to add nitrogen to the soil.[26] Today those innovations would be viewed as sound ecological practices—real improvements over archaic methods. Unquestionably, they also improved productivity and added to England's economic growth. For a while, they held considerable appeal for profit-seeking entrepreneurs, who preached the gospel of turnips and clover across the English countryside. But in later periods most farmers in England and North America drifted away from those reforms, for example, replacing nitrogen-building root crops with chemical fertilizers. A biology-inspired system of farming, based on careful field rotations and striving for a better balance between plants and animals, failed to establish a secure, lasting, dependable hold on the imagination of capitalist landowners. The reason was that, over the long run, such farming too often interfered with the more compelling system of the market economy. There have been, in other words, two kinds of logic in modern agriculture—that of the scientist and that of the capitalist—and they have not agreed much of the time.[27]

My own research into the restructuring of ecosystems by capitalistic farming has dealt mainly with the raising of wheat on the western plains of North America in the twentieth century. Like any single case, it can afford only a partial understanding of ecological tendencies in the capitalist mode; but wheat provides much of the world's basic nutrition, and patterns of growing and consuming it may be taken as symptomatic of the whole modern mode of food and fiber production. The history of the Great Plains region followed a familiar line of development: It began with a rapid and drastic destruction of ecological complexity and the substitution of a single marketable species (indeed, a single variety of that single species in many instances) over a wide acreage. In their preagricultural state the Plains, though seeming bare and monotonous to many travelers, were in reality a highly diversified environment, containing hundreds of grasses, forbs, and sedges, some of them annuals, some perennials, together with large and small herbivores, and further up the trophic ladder, populations of carnivores and decomposers, which consume the herbivores and return their matter to the soil. From Texas northward into Canada that ecosystem, or more accurately, that series of ecosystems, gave way to wheat and a scattering of other crops. Not everything of the older order disappeared, but a large portion of it did, and some of it may have disappeared forever.[28]

wheat on the western plains

The process of rigorous environmental simplification began among the sodbusters who first appeared on the Plains in the 1870s, looking for a crop they could raise and ship back east on the railroads. The process took a great leap forward during World War I when markets in wheat boomed, and it continued into the late 1920s. Most striking was the fact that livestock—the principal remaining fauna in most agroecosystems—were from the outset a minor, and diminishing, part of the Plains farmstead. Cattle, pigs, sheep, and chickens were seldom found in more than token numbers on those farms or soon disappeared if they were. They were a distraction from the main business of raising grain. Of course, they did show up in other places, including livestock ranches in the region, but in spectacularly large numbers, in gatherings of thousands of animals, all one species again. The most important result of that severing of agro-ecosystems by the sharp knife of economic specialization was to make the maintenance of soil fertility and stability harder. Plains and prairie topsoils are deep—one to two feet on average—and they could grow a lot of crops before productivity began to decline. Eventually, though, the farmer must put back in what he took out; if there were no bison or cattle or prairie dogs to do that for him, he must buy some other sort of fertilizer on the national or world market; in effect, he must buy fossil fuels, for modern synthetic fertilizer is made from natural gas.[29] When the Plains farmer was forced to do that, he came to depend on an often remote, impersonal network of credit suppliers, manufacturers, and trading corporations, and he could only hope that what he could buy from them would be as good for the soil as the bison's great splats of dung had been.

The vulnerabilities inherent in modern monoculture now have a long history to be studied and understood. They include an unprecedented degree of susceptibility to disease, predation, and pest population explosions; a heightened overall instability in the system; a constant tendency of the human manager to take risks for short-term profit, including mining the soil (and in the American West mining a limited underground water resource); an increasing reliance on technological substitutes for natural plant and animal services; a reliance on chemical inputs that have often been highly toxic to humans and other organisms; a depen-

dence on imports from distant regions to keep the local system functioning; and finally, a demand for capital and expertise that fewer and fewer
individual farmers could meet.[30] This last characteristic is one of the earliest to show up and has been widely studied in rural history, though seldom from an ecological point of view. Farming communities reflect the
biological systems they rest on. A society cannot radically diminish the
diversity of natural ecosystems for the sake of maximum crop production,
nor keep the land regimented for profit, nor augment the flow of energy
through the system by introducing fossil fuels without changing the
rhythms and diversity and structure of power within its various communities. An ecological approach helps explain why capitalistic agriculture
has had its peculiar social effects as well as its managerial problems.

I have not yet mentioned what turned out to be the most serious vulnerability of all in Great Plains farming: its susceptibility to wind erosion
and dust storms of the kind that wracked the region in the 1930s, storms
that followed hard on the extension of wheat farming into high-risk areas
in the preceding decades. The dirty thirties were an unmitigated ecological disaster for the Plains; in fact they were one of the worst environmental catastrophes in recorded human experience. In part, of course, the
disaster was due to drought, the most severe drought in some two hundred
years of the region's climate. But it was also the result of the radically
simplified agroecosystem the Plains farmers had tried to create. What
they demonstrated in the 1930s was that reducing the land to the single
species of wheat did not provide an adequate buffer between themselves
and drought. Wheat was a splendid species for making money, but taken
alone, planted on immense expanses of plowed acres from which so many
other, better-adapted forms of life had been eliminated, it proved to be a
poor defense when the rains failed.[31] And therein lies one of the most
important lessons we can find in the history of the new mode of production: it had the capability of making the earth yield beans or corn or wheat
in quantities never before seen, and of creating more wealth and better
nutrition for more people than any traditional agroecosystem could boast.
But the other side of that impressive success was (and is) a tendency to
bet high against nature, to raise the stakes constantly in a feverish effort
to keep from folding—and sometimes to lose the bet and lose big.

Neither ecology nor history, nor the two working together, can reveal
unequivocally whether modern capitalistic land use has been a success
or a failure; the question is too large for an easy answer and the criteria
for judgment too numerous. But they can make the point that scholars
ought to begin to address the issue and also that the conventional
answers, which have generally been laudatory and narrowly focused on

economic or technological efficiency, need to be supplemented by an eco-logical perspective. From that vantage the historical interpretation of the past few centuries is likely to be a darker, less complacent one than we have known.

This blooming, buzzing, howling world of nature that surrounds us has always been a force in human life. It is so today, despite all our efforts to free ourselves from that dependency, and despite our frequent unwilling-ness to acknowledge our dependency until it is too late and a crisis is upon us. Environmental history aims to bring back into our awareness that sig-nificance of nature and, with the aid of modern science, to discover some fresh truths about ourselves and our past. We need that understanding in a great many places: for instance, in little Haiti, which has been under-going a long, tragic spiral into poverty, disease, and land degradation, and in the rain forests of Borneo as they have passed from traditional tribal to modern corporate ownership and management. In both of those cases, the fortunes of people and land have been as inseparably connected as they have been on the Great Plains, and in both the world market econ-omy has created or intensified an ecological problem. Whatever terrain the environmental historian chooses to investigate, he has to address the age-old predicament of how humankind can feed itself without degrading the primal source of life. Today as ever, that problem is the fundamental challenge in human ecology, and meeting it will require knowing the earth well—knowing its history and knowing its limits.

5

Arranging a Marriage: Ecology and Agriculture

◆

WE hear these days a repeated call by scientists, agricultural reformers, and environmentalists to effect a marriage between agriculture and the science of ecology—to create a new agroecology and a new ecologically based agriculture. Each party needs the other, it is said, but agriculture in particular needs this marriage and this spouse, if it is have a more secure, less environmentally destructive future. So far we have heard mainly the views of ecologists, who might be described as the bride pursuing the groom, who is agriculture. We don't, however, really know what agriculture thinks about the idea, whether he thinks about it at all, or whether he is really the marrying kind. Those of us who are mere observers to the marriage proposal, including this historian, may support the idea of matrimony on general principles but confess to being a little nervous and uncertain as to whether such a union would work or not.

Who is this potential groom, agriculture, and what has been his past? A very complicated fellow, he is the farmer in the field, of course, but also the rural banker, farm implement manufacturer, pesticide salesman, international grain merchant, and food processor. He is modern agribusiness in all its manifestations. He works hard, is full of self-confidence, and wants no interference with his work. Yet these days he is a ward of the government, unable to function alone. He is full of contradictions, not only between his insistence on free enterprise and his simultaneous demand for public support, but also between his ancient memories of stability and harmony and his modern drive for wealth and power. The first and most difficult task for the bride is to convince this fellow that he needs a mate. Before he will come to the altar, he must be brought to understand that his life is incomplete as it is, that in fact it is a mess. He must see that he needs to reform himself if he has any hopes of surviving and that the proposed marriage with ecology can be the first step toward that reform.

The history of agriculture in North America provides the best argument I know for a marriage with ecology. Over the past three hundred and fifty years, since the Europeans began taking control of the continent away from the first native agriculturists, we have had a record of failure as much as success. The first commercial agricultural venture in the New World was the tobacco plantation system established in the sixteenth century around Chesapeake Bay, and scientists have marked that advent from the increased mud deposits that show up in sediment cores taken from the floor of the Bay. Soil erosion and depletion plagued that regime nearly from the start. Another beachhead for European agriculture was New England, and it too did not show much stability. By 1850 most of southern New England had been deforested and planted to corn, wheat, English hay, and other crops. The landscape was as open as Kansas. The region was virtually self-sufficient in food, and farmers would have scoffed at anyone warning it would all end soon. By 1900, however, extensive acreages had returned to brush and many farmhouses had been surrendered to the field mice and porcupines. Today, two-thirds of the state of Massachusetts is covered with forest once more, and old stone walls that once marked the edges of fields are now lost in the trees. Over 80 percent of the food is imported. The bears have returned, and so have the beaver, deer, and an occasional moose. Is New England a success or a failure agriculturally? If you think about the long term, about establishing rural communities that endure, traditions that last, human and ecological relationships that are stable, then the region is very nearly a failure. Our first efforts to farm this continent started off profitably, but within a century or two they began to self-destruct.

So goes the history of agriculture westward across the continent. Americans boasted of winning a permanent empire, but they lost about as much as they gained. Every decade since the late nineteenth century the cotton belt of the Deep South has had to take in a few more notches, until

today it is a shrunken version of its former self; some of the largest producers of cotton are now located out in west Texas, Arizona, and the Central Valley of California, while large expanses of the old cotton kingdom
have gone back to grass or forest. And because the new cotton fields in the
West have an uncertain water supply, they may in turn go out of production soon.

The Great Plains, which we once prophesied would be the garden of the
world, is still our most failure-prone agricultural region, as it has been
throughout the twentieth century. Take away the underground water
reserve of the High Plains aquifer, and the area would lose a considerable
portion of its farm economy. Take away federal relief and price supports,
and it would lose even more. The exhaustion of the aquifer within another
half-century is now pretty certain, and the drying up of federal monies is
more and more a distinct possibility. Consequently, over much of the
region we soon may be back to a condition of dry-land farming in a free
market economy—a condition that in the 1930s gave us the Dust Bowl
and, in some counties, a population loss of nearly 50 percent. Recalling
those facts from the past ought to sober up the potential groom and bend
his thoughts toward reform of character, marriage, and settling down. He
has been living a hard life, if he only knew it, and it is getting harder.

Agriculture does not have to live this way. In other parts of the world,
at least until very recently, there have been plenty of examples of rural
communities that have existed in the same place, with little change in
population or techniques, for a thousand or more years. Why have we
Americans had so much difficulty in achieving something similar? It is
not because we have lacked scientific know-how or capital or time. No, the
reason is that the American agricultural sector has been unwilling to
accept the social and ecological restraints needed to have such communities.

A stable, enduring rural society in equilibrium with the processes of
nature cannot allow much freedom or self-assertiveness to the individual.
Typically, such societies hedge the individual about with a complex array
of rules, regulations, and traditions: for instance, he or she cannot buy or
sell land without community approval, cannot marry or start a family
before reaching a prescribed age and achieving an adequate holding, cannot plant or harvest before others, must follow the group in the herding of
livestock, marketing of cheese, or selecting of seed. The whole community, and often all the ancestors too, are involved in the single individual's
decisions. A farmer acts within a severely constraining network of duties
and obligations that allow little personal initiative. That is the best way,

people all over the world have understood, to avoid too much risk and preserve the rural community in harmony with the soil.

Of course, all those restraints put a ceiling on the amount of private wealth that any one person in the community can accumulate. They limit creativity. They make rural life conservative and hidebound. But they prevent most of the failures caused by misjudgment, egotism, ignorance, ambition, experimentation, excitement, and fantasy. Why have we in North America rejected that way of thinking? Why is our potential groom, the American agriculturist, so very different in temperament?

The historian replies that our agriculture has, from its beginnings in 1607 or 1620 (depending on whether you start with the settlement of Jamestown or Plymouth), been shaped by the market economy and its culture of economic individualism. Or to put it another way, much of our agriculture began with a capitalistic, market-oriented ethos and has adhered to it ever since. It is radical in its rejection of traditional rural community patterns. It is revolutionary in its elevation of the individual over the group. American agriculture has taken as its first principle the idea that the pursuit of unlimited private property and private gain ought to decide all questions of plowing, herding, planting, reaping, all rearrangements and manipulations of nature. Whatever the individual conceives, he should be free to do with the land. Every one of the successes we proudly celebrate in our agriculture—high production, comparative great wealth, diminishing labor requirements—are the clear result of that determination to establish a free, individualistic, market-directed approach to decision making. But then we must admit, when we have finished being celebratory and boosterish, that we have a long list of failures too, failures that have been rooted in the same commercial mentality.

So is this American agriculturist, long devoted to his freedom to play around in the grain and wool markets of the world, now chastened and mature, ready to enter into the bonds of matrimony? That is the first question a historian brings to this scene of proposal.

The bride to be, or the bride that wants to be, is the science of ecology, or more accurately the bride is a growing number of ecologists who have a personal interest in agriculture and want to see it saved from itself. They are like a young earnest schoolmarm, full of piety and learning, eager to land this husband and make him a pupil, instilling in him the virtues of reverence, responsibility, and scientific reason. A historian must admire the intention but wonder about the bride's preparation for such an undertaking. Can this good soul succeed in her desires?

Ecology promises to bring to the marriage an informed, expert understanding of how nature works, a knowledge that agriculture does not have on its own but needs from others. It is a promise backed up by impressive credentials. Over the past few centuries science has accumulated a vast knowledge of the processes and structures of the natural world; for example, it can tell the farmer much about the methods plants themselves have developed to combat their insect enemies or survive drought. Most of this knowledge was unavailable to farmers of the last ten thousand years, and the fact that it is now available is one of the indisputable blessings of modernity. Any one in agribusiness who does not appreciate that knowledge and seek to take advantage of it is foolishly blind to scientific progress.

But the knowledge offered by ecologists is deceptive in one vital respect: it does not afford a general or comprehensive measure of what it means to be successful or unsuccessful in agriculture. Science is excellent in addressing particulars but vague and indecisive in recommending general policies for a society to follow. And it is too much a product of its culture to be the broad, independent, all-wise oracle that agriculture needs. All of ecology's models of nature derive at last from culture. The ecologist finds it very difficult to step outside of her moment in history, her place in society, to reveal some general authoritative truth about the order of nature and to insist that agriculture adapt itself completely to that order.

The historian sees immediately in all the shifting scientific models of nature the fickle but powerful hand of a changing culture. One generation of scientists invents the idea of the ecosystem and, worried about the environmental transformations going on in the world, holds it up as a measure for all to follow. Another generation, however, looking for verification of the model and perhaps less worried about those transformations, decides to throw the ecosystem idea out of the textbooks. None of those scientists is truly independent of her times or culture so that she can talk about nature in some final, oracular way. Each is influenced by the world of current events. In all of our scientific ideas of nature there has been a great deal of history.

Even what the ecologist knows for certain often proves difficult to apply in practical situations. She may understand in minute detail the folly of our pesticide practices, for instance, and recommend other methods or ends. But the farmer may feel trapped by his own past and have to ignore her advice. He is not, in truth, a completely free agent, able to adjust instantly to a rush of scientific advice. He may have debts to the bank that have to be paid on schedule and in full; his crop decisions may, therefore, be made according to the prospects of high market return, not primarily on moral or ecological grounds. He may see the danger in letting the marketplace determine all land use but feel that circumstances give him no choice but to risk those dangers.

In short, the farmer and all his associates in the agricultural sector are people who cannot live outside of history either. They commonly think in the ways their age sanctions and cannot realistically be expected to do otherwise without a great deal of pressure, persuasion, and community support. They often feel they must live with the economic institutions they have inherited, despite their obvious faults, until in some distant future other and better institutions may have evolved. They may talk a great deal about asserting their individuality, but they also tend to accept the notion that no freedom, even in a marketplace economy, is ever really complete. To be sure, the heavy weight of economic history and tradition can be lifted, but it will not be easy.

Thus the plea from a prospective bride to "come and let me teach you how to be ecological" must appear a little utopian at times to such a groom. Science is not in any position to find for any part of society, agricultural or not, a perfectly rational, coherent, comprehensive, objective, or lasting design. It has not done that for itself. How could it do it for farmers?

Agriculture in the United States has become more and more deeply embedded in the market economy over the past several centuries. Now it cannot be expected suddenly to go in radical new directions until and after it has confronted and dealt with that history and that economy. Does the ecologist fully realize those truths? Does she know what she is up against in the case of the groom, and does she have a realistic sense of her task as a tutoring wife? That is the second question that the historian brings to this scene of proposal.

Speaking as a third-party observer, I support such a marriage and hope it takes place soon, even if it has to be helped along by others instead of flowering as a spontaneous private romance. What is needed in that marriage, however, is a common dedication to a larger ideal than each other's welfare. Both bride and groom, before they take another step, need to agree on a shared idea: namely, that nature is a pattern and a set of processes that we humans did not invent, cannot altogether replace, and must learn to respect. Nature, they must both grant, is more than a field to be exploited by the human mind and its technology. It is more than a pile of commodities to be bought and sold for gain. It is more than an intellectual puzzle to be taken apart by curious minds. It is more than whatever it is we want it to be. Nature is a whole greater than we can understand or manipulate or control. A marriage that does not begin with that common understanding by both parties is unlikely to go very far and will flounder soon. Furthermore, both science and agriculture must acknowledge that they cannot teach that awareness to each other. Such thinking must come from outside the relationship, from ethics and philosophy, from politics and social discourse, from the community at large trying to discover a new relationship to nature. In short, for this marriage to happen we require as a people another way of seeing from the one that has dominated both science and agriculture over the past few centuries. I mean our tendency to see nature only in pieces, not as a whole—our habit of being so analytical, so focused on particulars, that we lose sight of the very order and harmony of nature, even lose confidence that such a harmony exists. That has happened, I believe, to an agriculture ruled by the market mentality, which cultivates the ability to see opportunities for personal profit but not a sense of harmonious interdependencies. The same loss of vision has also plagued science since the seventeenth and eighteenth centuries; science may have begun with a glorious vision of a harmonious nature, but now in many cases it has reached the point of seeing only fragments from the larger picture.

A marriage that merely united two narrow, technical ways of seeing would produce more, not less, blindness. On the other hand, a marriage that was informed by a broader moral purpose, integrating our lives more fully into the circle of nature, might one day bring forth a rural community better than any we have known.

6

A Sense of Soil

◆

"The soil, too—let others pen-and-ink the sea, the air, (as
I sometimes try)—but now I feel to choose the common
soil for theme—naught else."
                    WALT WHITMAN, *Specimen Days* (1882)

LAST year marked the fiftieth anniversary of a landmark event in American agricultural and conservation history, and few seem to be aware of the fact. In April 1935, Congress passed the Soil Erosion Act, the first effort in the United States to establish a nationwide, comprehensive program to preserve the very earth on which farming and rural life depend. That act committed the nation to a permanent program of research and action to stop "the wastage of soil and moisture resources on farm, grazing, and forest lands." Describing erosion as "a menace to the national welfare," it promised action on private as well as public lands, even to the point of condemning and purchasing private properties when inducements to good practices proved ineffective. And the act established within the Department of Agriculture a new agency, the Soil Conservation Service (SCS), to carry out the work.

Now, after fifty years, it is appropriate to ask what cultural forces produced this 1935 commitment and to speculate about what our attitude, our commitment, is today. What have we as a people done with our soil

This essay first appeared in the *Forum for Applied Research and Public Policy,* I (Spring 1986).

since the act was passed? What have we learned about preserving the soil and what have we forgotten?

The South, soil-conscious and erosion-plagued beyond other regions, played an extraordinary role in preparing the way for the 1935 act. It furnished both lessons in consequences and leaders for reform. From an earlier period, a succession of southern leaders had warned of the dangers of soil depletion and erosion. Thomas Jefferson, for example, wrote in 1819 of a land carelessness that, if not ended, would force planters to abandon their Virginia fields and "run away to Alabama (*sic*), as so many of our countrymen are doing, who find it easier to resolve on quitting their country, than to change the practices in husbandry to which they have been brought up." After him, men like Edmund Ruffin preached the gospel of lime, of "calcareous manure," up and down the land, earnestly calling for stability, conservation, and a permanent agriculture for the region.[1]

In Jefferson's day, the worst abuses were found among tobacco planters in the tidewater and piedmont South, especially around Chesapeake Bay. Then as now, tobacco was an intensive crop that drew heavily on the soil. Its great appeal, outweighing its undeniable damages, was its immense profitability. It gave higher returns, by far, than almost anything else a farmer could grow, and that was an appeal any hard-headed, rational, calculating man found irresistible.

In that fact lies the continuing nub of the Southern, and the American, problem of living with the earth. A people whose economic culture has long been oriented to, if not controlled by, the world marketplace—a people whose values and ways of calculating have been based heavily on market success—has never found the idea of soil conservation very easy to accept. In other places and times, the destruction of this vital resource may have gone on too, but usually for other reasons—the pressures of population, for instance. But in this region and this nation, the main degrading force, as Jefferson and many others have recognized, has been an entrepreneurialism driven by a powerful, often very distant, market economy.

One Southerner who saw the connection between his region's slow, fateful decline and its much-abused landscape was Hugh Hammond Bennett, the man who more than any other was responsible for the 1935 act and who became the first director (the "Chief," as he was familiarly called) of the Soil Conservation Service. Born in 1881 in Wadesboro, North Carolina, and growing up on a soil-impoverished cotton farm there, Bennett grappled in a most immediate and personal way with this legacy of resource exploitation. Eventually he escaped his rural trap by going to the state university in Chapel Hill, and then by taking a position in Washington as a scientist in the Bureau of Soils.

He came to government service in the first decade of the twentieth century. The so-called Progressive conservation movement was at its peak. Large numbers of Americans both in and out of government had begun to take seriously the notion that the nation might run out of the raw materials of prosperity. But as yet, few Americans, even among the conservationists, paid much attention to soil. In 1909, Bennett's own agency, the Bureau of Soils, announced: "The soil is the one indestructible, immutable asset that the nation possesses. It is the one resource that cannot be exhausted; that cannot be used up." For the next five decades, until his death in 1960, Hugh Bennett worked zealously to correct that misconception.[2]

In 1928, after much travel and investigation, Bennett and W. R. Chapline published, as a United States Department of Agriculture circular, their pathbreaking paper, "Soil Erosion as a National Menace." Their surveys had led them to see the full extent of the long-festering agricultural problem, reaching well beyond the Southern piedmont into the Ohio and Mississippi and Missouri valleys, into Texas and Oklahoma, reaching all the way to California. "As a Nation," they wrote,

> we are doing very little to abate the evil effects of erosion. Every one who knows anything about it admits the problem is a serious one, but few realize how very devastating is the wholesale operation of erosion. There is necessity for a tremendous national awakening to the need for action in bettering our agricultural practices in this connection, and the need is immediate.[3]

They pointed out that some places had lost their topsoil entirely, a topsoil that had taken five to ten thousand years to build and accumulate. Under cultivation, it had washed downhill and piled up along fence rows, had aggraded stream bottoms, and caused flooding. They estimated that erosion had rendered some 15 million acres utterly useless for agriculture. Though writing in a decade of widespread agricultural distress and farm failures, they insisted, that when viewed from the long run, soil destruction was "the biggest problem confronting the farmers of the Nation over a tremendous part of its agricultural lands."[4]

Congress was moved far enough by Bennett's report to set up a few soil stations around the country, but it was not yet willing to be moved very far. It spent $100,000 to address a billion-dollar problem. And with the onset of the Great Depression, it soon had on its hands a more immediately pressing, preoccupying calamity. The expansionary, entrepreneurial culture of America, the old market-driven culture, had ways other than soil erosion to bring about its self-destruction. That culture and its institutions could put its city as well as farm people at risk through its intense drive to produce, sell, and pile up private wealth, through its willingness to take chances with the future, to put short-term gain and individual advantage ahead of the common welfare. Seeing that fact and fearing it, Congress, led by President Franklin D. Roosevelt, began in the 1930s to search for ways to reform American society. Though in the first part of the decade soil conservation was not a matter of priority, it eventually became so. In fact, without the Depression and a general disillusionment with laissez-faire capitalism, the Soil Erosion Act of 1935 might never have been passed.

The Depression thus boosted concern for the nation's soil. And so did the most dramatic ecological disaster in American history, the Dust Bowl of the 1930s. In April 1933, weather stations on the Great Plains reported 179 storms of blowing dust, raging over fields where plows had destroyed the native vegetation and drought had killed young crops. One year later, a storm carried dirt from Montana and Wyoming all the way to Georgia and New York. Enroute, it dropped 12 million pounds on Chicago—four pounds for each person in the city. The dawn of May 11 found western dust settling over Boston, Washington, and Atlanta. Savannah's skies were hazy all day on the 12th, the last city to report dust conditions. As the storm moved out to sea, ships in the Atlantic (some of them 300 miles off the coast) found dust on their decks during the next day or two.[5]

Unable to rouse much Congressional interest in piedmont gullies and in river sediment, Bennett at last found his moment of vindication in the dust storms. The worst single period of the Dust Bowl years was April of 1935, as legislators were considering a comprehensive soil legislation package. While on his way to testify before a Congressional committee, Bennett learned that another great storm was blowing in from the western plains. Stalling and dawdling, he managed to keep the committee in session until a copper gloom settled over the capital city and blotted out the light. "This, gentlemen," he announced with an impresario's flourish, "is what I have been talking about!" Congress saw and Congress acted. Without the Dust Bowl's potential for theater, there most likely would not have been such a large commitment of money and federal personnel to protect the soil. Wind erosion accounted for only a small part of America's soil losses. By 1934, 262 million acres—an area 2.5 times the size of the Dust Bowl—had been severely damaged or destroyed by erosion, for the most part by water runoff.[6] But wind erosion was the calamity that moved people to act.

The Dust Bowl, like the Depression with which it coincided, like the long heritage of soil erosion going back to Jefferson's time and before, was largely the outcome of an economic culture. That culture had turned a continent into wealth, had created vast fortunes, had made American agriculture more of a business than a way of life, had taken immense chances with fragile environments, and had left many bills to be paid by the next generation.

The old thinking created, but it also destroyed. It made many people rich, but it also made others poor, made their way of life much harder than it had to be, and made them search endlessly for fresh unspoiled lands. Behind legislation like the Soil Erosion Act was a national groping for a new social and environmental ethic to alter that culture. In place of the old emphasis on private good, the new ethic began with defining the collective good, and the good not only of those now living, but of those to come.

A new ethic then, but at bottom it was actually to be a profoundly conservative ethic—conservative in a way that Americans had not previously imagined. It was an ethic devoted to stability, order, and continuity, as well as to equity and commonwealth—all values lost or jeopardized by the restless entrepreneur. The program of soil conservation initiated in 1935, along with the larger idea of rural conservation of which it was a part, was expected to be one of the clearest expressions of this social ethic. Henceforth, each generation was to leave the earth in as good shape as it had found it, or in even better shape: that, in short, was the cultural imperative emerging in the troubled 1930s.

So much for American culture and its emerging soil consciousness of fifty years ago. Since then our society has moved this way and that, now trying hard to remember the dark days of the past and their lessons, now trying to forget them in a euphoria of expansionism. But generally it has kept faith with the ethic of soil preservation more in words than in deeds. We have remained at heart an entrepreneurial people, a people with eyes intently fixed on the marketplace and profitability and world economic demand. Although we have accepted the fact that there will be no fresh land left when we wear out the existing stock, we have come to hope that technology can be an effective substitute for the old frontier.

What we destroy, we like to think, we can fix up with a little know-how. Therein lies the persistent hope of the past half-century in American agricultural conservation: that technology will relieve us of the difficult task of changing our social philosophy, our ethic toward others and the land. Put another way, the hope now is that modern chemistry and modern apparatus, not institutional or attitudinal reform, will save us from our deeply rooted habits of land exploitation and abuse.

The SCS has itself been heavily responsible for the post-Depression effort to think technologically, not socially or ecologically. It has boasted repeatedly that it offers "scientific" solutions to land problems. What that increasingly has come to mean is that SCS is an agency of engineering. It offers a spectrum of techniques that can help farmers get the highest return from the land, not in a single boom year perhaps, but over several years of technically proficient management. Disasters like the Dust Bowl have been interpreted as evidence that technique was lacking. Remedy the western plainsmen's incompetence, and their entrepreneurial farming could be saved, rationalized, and set going again. Greater output and greater productivity, the economic forces behind the destruction of sod on marginal acres, can still be our social purpose. As long as SCS advice is followed, the risk of destroying the capital in land can be eliminated. Within a few short years of its founding, the Service came to speak the old, familiar language of the marketplace, of private gain, and of technological solutions to cultural problems. And so, the critics say, it speaks today.

This drifting back into well-worn cultural ruts has been due to the fact that the SCS, like other New Deal agencies, is a bureaucracy, and the first law of bureaucracies is to survive. Men who had been frightened by the specter of unemployment now had government jobs and wanted to make them as secure as possible. They also wanted to see their mission grow and prosper, to see others like themselves hired, and to see their agency become a permanent fixture on the American landscape. That is a difficult, perhaps impossible, set of ambitions to hold if one is also trying to challenge persistent habits of mind. Since the 1930s, the surest way to power and success in the American political complex has been the way of accommodation to powerful interests and prevailing notions of success: in short, to endorse the economic culture, not to criticize it.

An illustration of this self-protective strategy lies in the eventual disappearance from the SCS agenda of an effective land purchase program. Section One of the 1935 act specifically authorized the agency "to acquire lands, or rights, or interest therein by purchase, gift, condemnation, or otherwise, whenever necessary for the purposes of this Act." Lands that were manifestly unsafe to cultivate under any methods—steep slopes in heavy rainfall areas like Appalachia, loose sandy soils in high wind areas like the southern plains—should be removed permanently from farming and from pressures to produce. Such purchasing, however, was rarely done by the federal government, and most was the work of the short-lived Land Utilization Project of the Bureau of Agricultural Economics, not the SCS.[7]

Bennett, it is true, unlike some of his associates, went on insisting that sizable portions of the Great Plains ought to be put back into grass, even arguing the point with state-college agriculturists who were vociferously opposed to placing any land beyond the reach of the plow (putting their trust, instead, in better farming techniques). But all the same, Bennett was an economic expansionist too, a believer in the creed of more as he revealed in statements made during the 1940s. There was a wide, hungry world out there, his message went, and it was waiting for American plenty. "By increasing the per-acre, per-farm, and per-nation supply of food and fiber," he promised in 1947, "conservation technology can provide the basis for an improved standard of living and simultaneously reduce the hunger and discontent among peoples which so frequently leads to discord, dictatorships, and war."[8]

Social bureaucrats may have been social optimists, believing, as Alistair Cooke once put it, that the common American citizen was a person who could "take up contour plowing late in life."[9] That simple reform, however, became the limit of their optimism and ambition. They approached the farmer with an array of techniques now familiar to all of us: contour plowing, terracing, residue management, gully control, and a nationwide system of soil conservation districts to get such measures into local practice. In drier areas, the most popular part of the SCS agenda was water, not soil, conservation. The agency spent a great deal of money constructing small dams for water storage, developing irrigation, and building water-spreading earthworks. All were structural or engineering solutions. Their main appeal to the farmer was that they increased production and improved income without requiring change in economic culture; whether they also preserved the soil for the next generation was increasingly incidental.

In the postwar years, the SCS program appealed in particular to the young, the well-to-do, the educated, and the entrepreneurial farmer—all those in the forefront of American agribusiness. Soil experts repaid those enterprising farmers' confidence with solicitation. Contrary to Alistair Cooke's witticism, they had little patience with the poor, dull-witted, unambitious farmers who were slow to innovate. Eventually, the experts hoped their clients would all be efficient businessmen quick to understand and take up new, more profitable methods of production. Bennett made it clear whom the SCS vision of abundance through conservation technology was meant to help: "Farming," he predicted, "will become an expert profession; the inexpert and inept will be forced off the land."[10]

In his 1952 work, *The Politics of Agriculture,* the political scientist Charles Hardin noted and criticized this creeping reduction of the soil conservation problem to engineering strategies. The Service, he argued, was treating "the symptoms of erosion instead of the disease."

> Economic instability of farming, unfavorable man-land ratios, educational disadvantages, rural poverty, insufficient amounts of the right kinds of credit, unfortunate tenurial arrangements, and a culture which tends to reinforce the establishment and maintenance of these conditions and of the farming practices and customs that go with it—these are the kinds of things alone and in combination, which are often reflected in eroded land.[11]

Hardin should have added to that etiology the most fundamental of all cultural causes—the market economy and its tendency to overwhelm local, traditional, conserving judgment. He did go on to point out that concentrating on engineering rather than social programs was what made the Service attractive to many people. "These people," he observed, "are anxious to identify themselves with a noble cause, but preferably one without 'radical' connotations. SCS can be supported without risking the social displeasure of the respectable."[12]

The evasive formula was an immense success politically. The Service became a federal fixture, had secure budgets year after year, spread its money and personnel broadly over the land, and convinced many Americans that soil erosion was a problem of the past. In every state one could find the neatly painted green and white signs along roadsides identifying the proliferating soil conservation districts—signs that reassured the passing motorists that the land was now being well cared for. In fact, they were limited and illusory symbols of progress toward agricultural reform and permanence—not signs of a cultural transformation in rural America, but only mechanisms to promote the technician's tools, methods, and narrow view of the land.

By 1981, there were 2,925 districts organized in the United States, and they covered over two billion acres. Not all land within the districts, however, was protected from erosion by SCS-approved practices; in fact, only 48 million acres nationwide followed all the official technical advice available. Tennessee counted 95 districts extending over 26 million acres, though there were slightly less than 500,000 acres with full protection. On paper, these achievements seemed impressive. And to an extent they were. So they should have been, for over the half-century life of the Service they had cost American taxpayers more than $15 billion.[13] But harder questions remained: Had the money been well spent? Had it been concentrated where it might have done the most good? Had the broad social ideals of the 1930s been realized? Was serious soil erosion truly a thing of the past?

The SCS itself had some of the answers to those questions, and they were at once honest and disturbing. In 1947, Bennett had estimated that the country was losing three billion tons of soil each year to water and wind erosion. In 1977, the *National Resource Inventory* arrived at precisely the same figure: three billion tons again. By the present decade that total may have gotten even worse, as many soil scientists believe that erosion has become as bad, or almost as bad, as it was in the dirty thirties. According to the *Inventory,* updated in 1982, almost half of the cropland in the United States now is losing more of its soil than is being replenished.[14]

Erosion is, of course, a fact of nature—the wearing down of mountains, the building up of plains and deltas. Soil creation is also a fact of nature— the work of geological and biological forces acting on bedrock. Life and human prosperity hang somewhere in the balance between those opposing energies. We can throw our weight to one side or the other, can speed up erosion or slow it down, can make the earth a desert or a garden. Lacking the ability to see far into the future and discern what our needs will be at some distant point, the better part of land wisdom, most soil conservationists have believed, is to leave the natural balance pretty much as we have found it. That principle, as we have seen, was the essence of the emerging land ethic of the 1930s.

Now it is clear from the SCS's own figures that we are not close to meeting that natural equilibrium ideal. Following the scheme of one of its great leaders, Walter Lowdermilk, the SCS distinguishes between "geologic" (or "normal" erosion) and "accelerated erosion," which comes from the "artificial disturbance of factors which controlled the development of soil profiles."[15] On an average acre of land, five tons of new soil are created each year through natural forces replacing normal erosion losses. The Service calls this figure its T (for tolerance) value, and though the national average is set at five tons, it may decline to a low of one ton per year on the thinnest, most fragile soils. Though there are scientists who argue that these values are too generous, and there are some economists who maintain they are too strict, we may take them as the best, most widely accepted standard available to us for measuring soil erosion. And the stark fact they indicate today is that we are undermining rapidly the foundations of our rural life and food supply.

Taken acre by acre, the harmful consequences of soil erosion are too diffuse, even when it is on as large scale as ours is, for farmers to take much notice. What farmers have trouble appreciating, city folks may never see at all. For people who fear the escape of poisonous gas from a chemical plant or the instantaneous annihilation of all life by nuclear

war, the slowly accumulating impact of soil loss is an easy catastrophe to
yawn away. A ton of topsoil removed from a field represents a mere fraction of an inch. If the topsoil is commonly six or seven inches deep, the
accelerated erosion may take several decades to have a significant effect.
In geological terms, and for that matter in terms of a nation's history, decades are mere moments. The critical point to keep foremost in mind is
this: a fertile soil is the work of millennia, and it can be destroyed in a
mere hundredth, a mere thousandth, of that time.

Indifference stiffens into disbelief when a people have been schooled,
as we have been, to believe in technological panaceas. Over the past 50
years, the soil engineers have been joined by many resource economists
and fertilizer salesmen in preaching that sermon of easy remedies: the
constructing of a few more terraces here and there, a shifting of fields
downhill where the soil is going, and above all, the injecting of a lot of
NPK—industrial nitrogen, phosphorus and potassium—injected like
vitamin pills into the depleted or eroded soil body. For those who believe
in such panaceas, there is no need for more costly or culturally difficult
strategies, no need to take erosion-prone lands out of continual production, no need to maintain shelterbelts or cover vegetation, no need to plant
a less profitable but safer crop, and no need to rethink our devotion to
profit maximization.

Carry the faith in technological answers far enough, and the SCS could
become only a hollow shell of New Deal thinking. It then could be altogether abolished, and farmers could be left to find their own free-market
solutions to soil maintenance—just as they were in the 1920s and all the
way back to Tidewater Virginia in colonial days. This is a genuine possibility these days. That the abolition of the SCS is the serious goal of
some men currently in Washington is no secret. The most recent federal
budgets show that they have some way to go before that goal is achieved,
but also that they are making progress. In the 1984 budget, the present
administration authorized $622 million for the SCS; now they are asking
for only $453 million, a cut of 25 percent in two years. They will cut con-
siderably more if they can do so without political damage. Whether the
Service has been doing the job it should have been doing, whether more
of its funds might have been spent on real needs and less on pork barrel,
are not the questions prompting these cuts—the motive is rather to
diminish the idea of collective responsibility for the soil.[16] And that is
where we are, where we are heading, fifty years after the passage of the Soil
Erosion Act.

One of the near-mythic heroes of twentieth-century America, though
he seems out fashion these days, was a tall, humble farmer who dwelt in

the Tennessee hills. His name was Alvin York, though he was better known as Sergeant York of World War I fame. The movie celebrating his life was released in 1940 and starred Gary Cooper as York. In that film, filled with passion for rural simplicity and virtue, York does something that few of us modern Americans have ever done or would even want to do. One night he brings into his rough cabin a handful of soil and dumps it onto his dinner plate, spreads it out, and scrutinizes it. He has before him the makings of his sustenance, the stuff of his dreams—a dark mound of rich Tennessee bottomland. Poor and desperate as he is, York understands that his prospects depend on access to that soil. He tilts the plate back and forth, smells and fingers the mound, and imprints it on his mind. It has for him a powerful meaning that it cannot have for those whose material existence does not depend so directly on it—whether they be resource experts, industrialists, or poets. For most of us the soil has become dirt. For York it is the revered means, indeed the only means, to a future in harmony with the past, to personal security, to a home.

We have lost that intimacy with the soils, and with that loss has come a diminution of the feeling, the reverence, the folk wisdom of long-enduring rural cultures found all over the world. But if we have lost, we have also gained. It is possible for us to find values in that handful of topsoil that York missed. Modern science reveals for us a world under our feet that has an astonishing complexity and order that is part of nature. Spread this world on our plate and we can find in it not only possibilities of enrichment, of community, of social permanence, but also the qualities of natural beauty, integrity, and harmony. Some of these qualities are visible only under a microscope. Others strike the eye immediately as a rich mosaic of blacks, reds, yellows, and browns. For a scientist, at least for one who has made an effort to understand this part of nature, the plate is not filled with mere undifferentiated, inert, unclean dirt. It is filled with life and relationships, with the stuff and fabric of life.

In its simplest terms, the soil is, of course, a supplier of the minerals needed for plants to grow. It is a derivation of granite or limestone, of volcanic lava or shale, an assortment of fine or large particles of the basic chemical elements. But as any ecologist knows, there is much more to a soil than this. There is the humus, the organic residue of roots, carrion, feces, bone, and leaves mixed through the mineral components. On this humus there is an incomprehensibly large number of bacteria working away, decomposing the dead, fixing nitrogen, forming nitrates to feed the living. The soil is fungi, too, and earthworms, moles, burrowing insects—over a thousand different animal species in all, aggregating more biomass below ground than above it. Soil is the water, the gases, the solar energy that all these living things need to keep going as they plow and add their carcasses to the whole. The English writer Edward Hyams speaks of "the soil community." "All components of a soil," he writes, "are bound together in an association, a symbiotic relationship so close that none of them would have the significant attributes which belong to it as a part of a soil, were it not for the others." Some scientists might want to qualify this emphasis on cohesion or to substitute the world "ecosystem" for "community." Few, nonetheless, would deny that the topsoil is an organization of life, fundamentally akin to a mountain forest, a coral reef, or a school of minnows. As in all these organizations of living things, humans may enter and live as cooperating members, or they may disturb. "If the men be few and the (soil) community large," Hyams writes,

> this disturbance need not be disastrous. But if or when the men become numerous relative to the size of the community, the result may be very terrible: it may by the destruction first of the soil balance; then, as a consequence, of fundamental soil fertility; and this being the basis of life of the soil in question, all living members of it perish, including in the end, the community of men which has brought this death about by turning from a contributing, cooperating member of a delicately adjusted organism, into a parasite upon it, and a parasite which is not constructed to endure.[17]

Like all ecosystems on the planet, the topsoil has marvelous powers of recuperation, but they are not beyond our capacity to exhaust.

A scientist who has spent a lifetime studying this living community of nature is Hans Jenny, emeritus professor at the University of California at Berkeley, and past president of the Soil Science Society of America. What Professor Jenny has learned through his long, distinguished career is, in his words, a "reverence for the soil body," a reverence that makes him "automatically a preservationist of natural, undisturbed soil." "I grant soils the right to exist," he declares, a view that admittedly may seem at first to be hopelessly utopian but can be eminently practical. With Hyams, Jenny would have us see that thinking too narrowly about the soil, regarding it only as an economic commodity, can do us very great damage.[18]

Put next to these modern, biologically informed perceptions of the soil ecosystem, the common American confidence in technological remedies for erosion must appear dangerously naive. We can no more manufacture a soil with a tank of chemicals than we can invent a rain forest or produce a single bird. We may enhance the soil by helping its processes along, but we can never recreate what we destroy. The soil is a resource for which there is no substitute. Like the earth itself, it is a network of activity that we cannot yet understand, let alone replicate. Yet it is more than a resource, which is to say, more than an instrument of production. Any patch of soil, whether we use it or not, is not so much a value that we have defined as it is a value we have begun to discover.

Thought, it has been said, grows in the interstices of habit. Over the past few decades as old habits of commodity-thinking, economic rationality, and individualistic ethics have reasserted themselves, these new thoughts about soils and our relation to them have simultaneously begun to appear in the interstices. I have suggested that these thoughts, for want of a better label, might be called ecological. They have arisen in part out of the work of scientists who are unhappy with traditionally reductive ways of perceiving the soil—ways found in their own ranks sometimes as they are elsewhere. The new ideas come from an advance guard of environmental philosophers who are looking beyond the entrepreneur's short horizon and even beyond thirties-style thinking about resources and communal needs—who believe that our best hope for a permanent agriculture requires above all the maintenance of biological diversity and complexity in all our environments, the soil included. We have before us now these new thoughts as we have some old, still vigorous habits left over from past dealings with the earth. A few choices have to be made.

7

Good Farming and the Public Good

◆

RAIN is a blessing when it falls gently on parched fields, turning the earth green, causing the birds to sing. But when it rains and rains, for forty days and nights, as it did for Noah, then the waters rise and destroy. Life is everywhere like that. Too little is a curse, too much is a plague.

For thousands of years, the philosopher's task has been to discover an optimum point where men and women can live modestly and securely, avoiding the extremes. The philosopher may seek a point of environmental balance where there is neither too little nor too much of nature's gifts. Or he may try to define the point where private ambitions and collective needs are in harmony, where individual appetites do not overrun the commonwealth and society's demands do not cut too deeply into individual freedoms. When philosophy is applied to the definition of a society's welfare, we call that point the "public good." Farmers, more than most people, ought to be responsive to that philosophical quest for a harmonious,

This essay was published earlier in the book *Meeting the Expectations of the Land,* edited by Wes Jackson, Wendell Berry, and Bruce Colman (San Francisco: North Point Press, 1984).

balanced good, for it has been their aim over a long history to seek moderation from nature and cooperation from their neighbors.

Yet it has been a while since American agriculture, as a whole, has enjoyed a feeling of balance. The problem has not been in nature so much as in our society. We have not had a feeling of balance because we have come to hold extravagant ideas of what agriculture should contribute economically to the nation and the farmer. These days we are not a people noted for moderate thinking, so perhaps we have no reason to expect the idea of moderate farming to thrive. The most serious consequence of an immoderate culture, I will argue, is that the public good will not be well understood and therefore will not be achieved—in agriculture or in other areas. Another consequence is that farmers in the aggregate will suffer immensely and so will the practice of farming.

That has indeed happened in America, and we can blame it on our extreme dedication to the goal of maximizing agricultural productivity and wealth. In turn, that goal stems from a larger cultural conviction that wealth is our main aim in this nation and that wealth is an unlimited good. Almost everything we have celebrated as our success in farming has been defined in terms of those ends. It has now, however, become clear that our ends have been our undoing. We wanted more rain, unlimited rain, and we got a flood. It has left American farmers drowning in dreary statistics: crop reports, production charts, mortgage rates, energy bills, land and commodity prices.

For the past century or so, the nation has had to deal repeatedly with gluts of farm production, particularly in the cash grains. In 1981, a U.S. Department of Agriculture study declared an end to that nemesis; farmers, it predicted, would see no more price-depressing surpluses because we were at last able to peddle all the excess overseas.[1] World population and demand had caught up at last with the American farmer. The study admitted that selling all our glut abroad would make the life of domestic producers more unstable than ever, that they would find themselves on a wild roller coaster ride, plunging up and down the track of international markets. But the old problem of recurrent overproduction had now been licked. There would never again be mountains of grain piled up and waiting for boxcars, never again be oranges or cotton or sugar cane going to rot.

Things have not worked out quite the way they were supposed to. In the summer of 1982, the old surplus problem appeared again: an all-time record wheat harvest of 2.1 billion bushels; not enough American buyers to absorb it; the Russians emerging once again as the main hope of salvation, but acting unpredictably as usual; crop prices declining; real farm income the lowest it had been in fifty years. Angry Colorado farmers, fighting against foreclosures on their farms, were tear-gassed by the sheriff, a replay of the turmoil in the 1920s and 1930s. Consequently, doubt begins to creep into our farm policy assumptions. Is there possibly something wrong with our approach to agriculture? How else can we explain the fact that farming, after so much attention, continues to be in so much trouble?

There can never be a perfect equilibrium in farming or any other sphere; existence might be unbearably dull if there were. But when you are flooded again and again, you are not in any danger of boredom. You naturally look up and ask, What's making so much rain? Can we turn it down a little? In America we have seldom accepted excess in nature; on the contrary, we have put our best talent and energy to work getting rid of it, making what is dry wet and wet dry. Why then do we accept excess when it is our own doing? Simply because powerful elements in our society do not allow us to recognize that there is such a thing as too much productivity, too much chasing after wealth. Despite overwhelming evidence that the idea is not working, good farming continues to mean *more*. We have not yet come to see that more of any good may, after a point, wash us away.

In the depressed 1930s, when times were even harder for farmers than they are today, American political leaders took counsel. They listened to ranchers, growers, sharecroppers, agronomists, soil experts, and marketing specialists; a few of those leaders raised basic questions of value. What, they asked, is agriculture for? What is the ultimate moral reason behind the pursuit of abundance, new farm technology, and an expanding economy—or is there one? Are our farm policies improved means to unimproved or unexamined ends? Whose ends should farming serve, those of the rich and powerful or those of the poor? How much of nature should we spend on human desires? What are rational limits to our demands? What is the public good in agriculture and what kind of farming will most likely achieve it? Those questions are as relevant today as they were fifty years ago.

To begin a reappraisal, let us consider what the public good has come to mean in the standard discussions of agricultural policy. "Cheap and plentiful food" is the most common theme. The public deserves to eat at the lowest possible cost, so we are told, and then they will be able to spend the rest of their wages on an automobile or at the movies or on college. This, in fact, is what our policy persistently has assumed to be the chief public interest. Agriculture is supposed to contribute mainly to the wealth of Americans generally, to make possible an ever-higher level of personal consumption.

Such has long been a typical farm expert's definition of the public good. But is it what the American public really wants? According to scattered public opinion polls, people say they prefer having lots of small farms around rather than a few big ones, more little dairies and truck gardens, not so many giant agribusinesses.[2] It might be that encouraging smaller farms would be worth more to people than saving a nickel on cheese or lettuce; a choice between the two options, however, is not clearly presented to them when they walk into a supermarket. The farm experts merely assume, on the basis of marketplace behavior, that the public wants cheapness above all else. Cheapness, of course, is supposed to require abundance, and abundance is supposed to come from greater economies of scale, more concentrated economic organization, and more industrialized methods. The entire basis for that assumption collapses if the marketplace is a poor or imperfect reflector of what people want. And it is. In matters of national defense, education, health care, and old-age assistance, we do not assume that the marketplace would be an adequate basis for public policy. Why then should we make that assumption in agriculture?

A corollary, and sometimes a rival, to the notion that good farming is farming that makes America richer through mass production, is the belief that farming is successful when it makes farmers as a special group more affluent. A common belief among policy makers is that swelling prosperity down on the farm immeasurably benefits society. No other sector of the economy has managed so fully as this one to identify its private fortunes with the public good—not dentists, not teachers, not even defense contractors. Billions of tax dollars have gone into scientific research and innovation to promote higher production, lower costs, and greater income on the farm. Heavily subsidized irrigation water flows to some very wealthy growers in the western states. Price-support programs, which have raised consumer prices by as much as 20 percent, have put money into agricultural pockets.[3] A huge department in Washington, as well as agencies in every state, looks out for the welfare of this group. Hardly anyone begrudges the farm sector all of these gifts, though it is well established that most of them go to the wealthy few. We have been taught from Thomas Jefferson's day on down that what is good for the farmer is good for America.

That doctrine has survived some revolutionary changes in the conditions of rural folk. Currently only about six million people live on farms, and only a small fraction of them (one in ten) now falls below the poverty line.[4] Contrast those numbers with the eleven million who were unemployed at the depth of the recent recession, roaming city streets, standing in bread lines, dreading the day their unemployment benefits ran out, or consider the several million more who have given up looking for work. Although farmers, like the unemployed and destitute, have at times experienced the indifference of other Americans to their plight, by and large they have retained an unusually sympathetic audience. When the man or woman on a tractor is in economic trouble, there is widespread worry; something, the newspapers agree, must be done. Farmers, particularly the better-off ones, maintain powerful friends and well-financed lobbyists to plead their case for governmental aid—unlike the city welfare mother who is roundly berated by the president and legislators in Congress, told to economize further on her food budget, to find a cheaper slum to live in, to forget a "handout" from Washington, to get off the public dole. In other words, the welfare and profit of this rather small group of largely middle- and upper-income farmers and ranchers have become identified with the public good in agriculture.

What is wrong with that identification? Do modern, business-oriented farmers not deserve our compassion when they go through hard times and are threatened with the loss of their assets and even their entire farms? They do, and they deserve our respect for their intelligence, hard work, fortitude, and skill. But respect and compassion should not be confused with favoritism or the private welfare of a single group with the larger welfare of the American commonwealth. When that confusion occurs, farmers are hurt; their welfare depends on a clear, reasoned concept of public good. What is good for all Americans, we must understand, will in the long run be good for farming, too.

The source of our difficulties is not a lack of popular concern for farmers or such superficial things as stagnant overseas markets or expensive credit. Rather, it is an inadequate idea of what truly constitutes the agricultural good of this nation.

The predominant idea of the public good in agriculture takes two forms: first, forever increasing the gross farm product and, second, forever seeking to augment the wealth of the farm sector (even if it means losing most of our farmers). Both programs are tied to the ideology and pressures of the marketplace. When pushed to the extreme as we have pushed it, that market mentality becomes seriously destabilizing to rural communities. It produces a perpetually crisis-ridden farm economy. Worse, it embitters people because it cannot deliver what it says it will: a general contentment and happiness. When the marketplace is made the main idea, it diminishes other values, leads to a degrading of personal independence, social bonds, virtue, and patriotism—for those qualities cannot thrive in an unbridled culture of acquisition, which the mentality of market maximization leads to.

In an earlier America of extensive rural poverty and poor living conditions more could be said for the vigorous pursuit of wealth in the marketplace, just as more may be said for it today in Bangladesh or Haiti. But when that pursuit persists beyond the point of material sufficiency, when it becomes a dream of unlimited economic gain, troubles follow. That is what has happened to American farmers and indeed to this country in general. Farmers must run their machines nonstop to keep up with the self-aggrandizing industrialists. The faster farmers go, the more crops they harvest, the more secure their position in the marketplace may be, the more they can buy—so they hope. But what they win in that way lasts only for a brief while. A continual uncertainty is their fate in this society.

The average farmer is not altogether responsible for this predicament. He did not set up the race, and he is not leading in it but is somewhere back in the pack, straining to catch up with corporate presidents, athletes, lawyers, movie stars, and engineers. The modern farmer lives in an intensely high-pressure world of many wealth maximizers. In that milieu, growing food becomes his only defense, his sole means of competing for social position. Unfortunately for him, food has been a comparatively poor basis for income growth, for it quickly saturates its market: humans can eat only so much lettuce or beef. Unlike others in the race, the farmer must always confront the biological limits of the consumer. He cannot make more money without finding more mouths and bellies to feed. Agriculture, by its very nature, is a productive activity that deals primarily with real human needs, not the contrived wants around which the game of maximization revolves. That difference must inescapably put the farmer at a disadvantage.

In another respect agriculture is not unique. It cannot evade the bitter disappointment over shrinking promises that is endemic in marketplace societies. All individuals cannot maximize their wealth; some people have to give up something in order for others to get all they want. The social philosophy of private accumulation is a lot like Calvinism: an elect few are chosen to live in paradise, while the rest can go to hell. The number of the elect is not fixed once and for all; it decreases steadily to the vanishing point. Especially since World War II that outcome has been a familiar experience in American farming. In 1900, there were 5.7 million farms in the United States, averaging 138 acres apiece. By 1978, the num-

ber had dropped to 2.5 million, and their average size was 415 acres. Over
the past thirty years the typical American farm increased its spread by 20
to 30 percent each decade, and all of the increase was taken from a neighbor's side of the fence.[5] At that rate the promise of unlimited farm riches
will someday soon be made only to a tiny privileged remnant.

Any farmer must look in the mirror each morning, like an anxious Puritan on his way out to church, and ask, "Am I to be among the saved or
not?" Do what he will, the odds are clearly running against him. And if
the promise of the land will tingle the ears of fewer and fewer people, if
eventually it will belong to an oligopoly—and it is naive to believe agriculture alone can forever escape the corporate takeover—then the offer of
unbounded wealth for farmers will turn out to have been a fraud.

The public good cannot be realized in agriculture, therefore, by the
untrammeled workings of the market economy and the endless striving
for private profit that it institutionalizes. The market creates wealth all
right, but its wealth cannot satisfy; it holds up an ideal that is never really
achieved, receding indefinitely before our eyes. A farm policy defined only
in market terms inevitably must destroy the agricultural community to
make it prosper. It must lead to disillusionment and frustration, uproot-
ing and alienation, wearing farmers out, then casting them off.

That is not to say there are no benefits at all in the free-market
approach; rather, the arguments on its behalf can take us only a short way
toward locating the optimum good of our social life, and then they become
immoderate and illusionary. It is now time in the United States to try
another tack, to search beyond the marketplace to serve the public good.

Suppose we begin by simply asking what it is that we as a society want
out of farming in the future. Are there significant human values that agriculture can help us to realize? Once we have answered that large question,
we can call in the farmers, along with the agronomists, the economists,
and the fertilizer salesmen, to make the ideal real. By that strategy we
might establish better control over where we are going, decide where we
want to end up, and stop the drift toward rural chaos. Good farming, by
that approach, would be understood as the art, the science, and the wisdom of growing values in the soil—and no calling can be more honorable
than that.

Slowly, several worthy answers to that large question of the common good
in agriculture have begun to emerge in public discussions. They are familiar in one form or another to us all. The task now is to make them as compelling as possible and move them out from under the deadening shadow
of profit maximization.

1. *Good farming is farming that makes people healthier.* It does so by creating and delivering food of the highest attainable nutritional quality and safety. Agriculture fails in its most obvious mission when that quality of healthfulness is missing or when it becomes corrupted by such things as toxic chemical residues. One of the most serious calamities to befall modern industrial farming is that it has turned food into a suspect, potentially dangerous commodity. When people begin to bite gingerly into apples, wondering whether cancer might be lurking there, or when they hesitate to drink a cup of milk, remembering that heptachlor has been found in the dairy's cows, or when they are unsure whether chemical growth-stimulants are lingering in a chicken-salad sandwich, then agriculture has created for itself the most serious possible problem. After all, the essential point of farming is to keep people alive. No gain in export earnings or farm profit, no ease of harvesting or freedom from pests can justify risking human life, can excuse putting the public's health in danger; to act or think otherwise ought to violate ethics as much as the willful practice of bad medicine. Yet the willingness to risk life and health has become daily news in contemporary food processing and agriculture. The problem is compounded by the fact that farmers may conscientiously harvest crops that meet the strictest standards of nutrition and safety but then must turn them over to numerous processors who, for the sake of profit, have been known to take most of the nutrition out, put additives in, turn wheat into Twinkies and corn into breakfast-table candy.[6] The more complex and powerful the system of farm production, the more sensitive and strict must be the moral consciousness behind it and the more elaborate and expensive the system of public control overseeing it. There is no cheaper, simpler, easier way to realize this value.

2. *Good farming is farming that promotes a more just society.* For a long time in America, the land was where most people expected to go for their start in life, where they hoped to find opportunity and secure a living. The land, always the land: if not in this place, then farther west. Our society's thinking about fairness and democracy reflects even now a reliance on the land as an available, inexhaustible resource. Today, however, we are telling the majority of rural people that there is not enough farmland for them, that they will have to go someplace else for their livelihood, although it is never precisely indicated where that "someplace else" is. If agriculture passes the buck, where will it stop? Does agriculture not have an obligation to the poor and landless in its midst? An obligation to pay decent wages to its laborers and to make room for new farmers, rather than expecting the besieged, depressed cities to take the unwanted? Agriculture, through both private and public agencies, can and should give

assistance to struggling racial minorities across the country: to black
farmers who are living as tenants on worn-out land, to Indian farmers who
need irrigation water, to small Hispanic growers who seek a fair share of
attention from county extension agents, to Hawaiians who want land for
taro and cultural survival. The agricultural community should work to
lop the top off of the rural pyramid of wealth, which is reaching stratospheric heights; today a mere 5 percent of the nation's landowners control
almost half the farm acreage, while in the Mountain West a minuscule 1
percent owns 38 percent of all agricultural land and, in the Pacific states,
that same percent owns 43 percent of the land.[7] Agriculture, however, is
not doing any of these things. On the contrary, it is everywhere retreating
rapidly from a commitment to justice and democracy. Meanwhile, several
other nations are managing, despite the pressure of the world marketplace and industrialization, to hold onto the democratic principle; the
Danes, for example, have long pursued the ideal of a rural world where few
have too little and even fewer have too much.[8] When our own farm experts
and leaders rediscover that moral value, American agriculture will be
stronger and more successful than it is today.

  3. *Good farming is farming that preserves the earth and its network of
life.* Obviously, agriculture involves the rearranging of nature to bring it
more into line with human desires, but it does not require exploiting, mining, or destroying the natural world. The need for agriculture also does not
absolve us from the moral duty and the common-sense advice to farm in
an ecologically rational way. Good farming protects the land, even when
it uses it. It does not knock down shelterbelts to squeeze a few more dollars from a field. It does not poison the animal creation wholesale to get
rid of coyotes and bobcats. It does not drain entire rivers dry, causing irreversible damage to estuaries and aquatic ecosystems, in an uncontrolled
urge to irrigate the desert. It does not tolerate the yearly loss of 200 tons
of topsoil per acre from farms in the Palouse hills of eastern Washington.[9]
Those are the ways of violence. American agriculture of late, pushed by
market forces and armed with unprecedented technology, has increasingly become a violent enterprise.

  Good farming, in contrast, is a profession of peace and cooperation with
the earth. It is work that calls for wise, sensitive people who are not
ashamed to love their land, who will treat it with understanding and care,
and who will perceive its future as their own. Many farmers and ranchers
are still like that and can give us all advanced lessons in ecological ethics.
But most preservation-minded farmers are now old men and women, preparing for retirement. There is great danger that they will sell out to less
informed, less careful individuals or corporations, who may acquire more

earth than they can know intimately and farm well. Somehow we must avoid that outcome. Agriculture's future must be oriented toward using land according to the principles of practical ecology—toward a conserving ethic and intelligence. That orientation is essential if we want to leave our children a planet as fruitful as the one we inherited.[10]

Other public goods I have not mentioned include creating beauty in the landscape, strengthening rural families, aiding the world's hungry—especially helping them produce their own food, diverting investment capital into other sectors of the economy that now need it more than agriculture, and preserving the rural past and its traditions. All of them require us to make policy, not merely make more food. These common goods do not assume that the lot of farmers can be bettered without also considering what the entire human community requires.

Americans are often accused of being a privatizing people. We take the question of public good and break it into millions of little pieces, into every individual's private wants, and then reduce it further by trying to put a price on those pieces. This is my property, we say, and no one can tell me how to farm it. These are my cows, and I will graze them where I like and as hard as I like, until the grass is dead if I like.

There is another America, however, one that has been more open to ideas of the common welfare. That America usually can be found today in less progressive corners, often in rural neighborhoods where there is still a long memory running back to a time when farm folk got their living together and worked more as partners with the land. The future of agriculture will be determined by whether that community thinking can be nurtured and grown more abundantly. It is easily the most important crop we can raise and harvest in the United States.

Those who have forgotten what the sense of rural commonality was like in earlier periods can find it again in the pages of history and literature: in a novel, for example, like O.E. Rölvaag's *Giants in the Earth,* which depicts the settling of the Dakota prairie by a group of Norwegian immigrants.[11] They brought little into that grassland besides themselves and their old-country habits of mutual aid. When nature gave them more than they wanted—gave them plagues of grasshoppers, droughts, and blizzards—they struggled together and came through to more moderate times. They endured and even prospered, but they did not become rich. They made homes for themselves, but they did not conquer that hard land. What they achieved was a wary peace with the prairie, an affectionate and understanding peace, a peace that reflected the fact that they were at peace among themselves. Each family had its own property and fences, its own way of doing things. Occasionally they competed against one another in friendly rivalries. But the overarching principle of their lives, as Rölvaag describes it, was the maintenance of a social bond, which finally became a bond with the strange, foreign land where they settled. Communalism of that sort, in real life as well as in fiction, is receding today, but it has not yet altogether disappeared over the horizon.

The challenge now is to retrieve that commitment to community from the past, from scattered pockets of rural life, and to find a modern expression for it in this new age of industrial agriculture.

At the heart of any nation's agricultural policy must be its ideal of a good farmer. For a number of years we have told farmers, through our colleges, agricultural magazines, government officials, and exporters, one clear thing: get as much as you possibly can out of the land. We have not told them how many farmers would have to be sacrificed to meet that instruction or how much it would deprive the few who remained of their freedom, contentment, or husbandry.

But sooner or later the prevailing ideals wear out, giving way to new ones or to new versions of even older ones. The American ideal of good farming, and the agricultural policy we have built on it, may be ready for a shift in the directions suggested here. In the not-too-distant future, farming may come to mean again a life aimed at permanence, an occupation devoted to value as well as technique, a work of moderation and balance. That is a shift in which we all have a stake.

8

Private, Public, Personal: Americans and the Land

◆

I SAT down the other night to do something I had not done in a long time: read the United States Constitution. Though a short document, only some twelve or thirteen double-columned pages in most printings, it was writing I had not looked at for over a decade. Yet I am an historian of this country. My excuse is that there is not enough time to read most things even once, and twice or more is out of the question. It is a poor excuse; some things we really ought to read more than once in a lifetime—ought to read every year, like Emily Dickinson's poetry or Henry Thoreau's book about that pond in Massachusetts. The Constitution is a piece of writing I would recommend reading no more than once a decade. It hasn't got much of a plot. The language is clear and easy, but lacks eloquence. Its single great virtue is its plain sensibleness, a virtue that has, with many glaring exceptions, stayed with us and become one of our most attractive national qualities. We like to think we are a level-headed people and that this document epitomizes our level-headedness. In a world that often seems to have gone plumb crazy into one fanaticism or another, the Constitution reassures us with its good sense. We can look back to it with relief that our political system was framed by wise, far-sighted people;

and unsure today whether we could improve on their wisdom, we usually leave it alone. Now and then we take the document out and actually read it.

There is, however, one glaring omission in the Constitution, so immense and damaging that I believe we ought to try to repair it. Nowhere in all the sections, articles, and amendments is there any mention of the American land and our rights and responsibilities pertaining thereto. I find the word "land" appearing only once, and then it refers to rules governing the capture of prisoners "on Land and Water." Otherwise, the subject is never mentioned: no reference to any role the government has in acquiring, holding, or regulating the use of land; to any rights of the people to land or a productive and healthy environment; to any obligations the land lays on us as citizens. The consequences of that omission have been greater than we can describe.

Of course, there are lots of important things not mentioned in the Constitution. It says nothing about television sitcoms or AK-47's or pizza parlors or red LeBaron convertibles. Such things did not exist at the time the document was written in 1787, and its authors and signers could not have imagined them. But the land did exist in that year and was a vital part of the people's daily experience; over 90 percent of Americans at the time were farmers and planters or their servants and slaves, and the rest owed their livelihood to the land in some way too. Europeans had been confronting the North American land for two centuries before the Constitution was drawn up. They had chopped down forests, cleared fields, gone fishing for cod and whales, navigated the rivers, explored the vast and howling wilderness, trapped beaver, watched ice form on their lakes, and noted the birds migrating through the seasons. In the two hundred years following the drafting of the Constitution, they would acquire an immense land stretching all the way to the Pacific and Arctic Oceans, would move west to settle it, would build an industrial society with the resources it provided. One would have thought that land was a subject worthy of some attention from the men gathered in Philadelphia, thinking about the country's future. But they did not think about it. They thought about elections, roads, taxes, armies, free speech, separation of powers, slavery, bail, presidential terms, and bribery; and their successors who added the Constitution's amendments thought about race, gender, elections again, and booze—but never about the land as part of the fundamental law and reality of the nation. Why was that?

Part of the answer is suggested by a line in one of Robert Frost's poems: "The land was ours before we were the land's."[1] Through war and independence we came to possess a territory that for a long time had belonged to the English Crown (and before that to the aboriginal inhabitants). We now possessed it, but it did not yet possess us—it had not quite entered the circle of our affections. That was certainly true of land lying beyond the Appalachian Mountains, but it was also true in older places like New York and Virginia, where there had been a century or two of occupation but by successive waves of immigrants, each wave coming in and taking a while to get its bearings, each not quite sure whether they wanted to stay or not. Many people in those places did not have a sense of belonging, and many never would.

Another part of the answer is that the framers of the Constitution did not believe that the land was a proper subject for the federal government. It was strictly a private and local matter, like marriage or religion. The ownership and management of land ought to be left entirely in the hands of ordinary individuals, acting informally among themselves. Connected to that view was the assumption that the power of individuals to affect the land was severely limited. No species of plant or animal could ever be made extinct; everything in nature was put there forever by divine decree, and all that any person could do was temporarily rearrange things here and there. In such a stable, enduring world, there was no need for the government to bother with issues of land and land-use; it had quite enough to do raising armies to defend against foreign aggressors, finding money to pay for those armies, and making sure the mail got from one part of the country to the other.

I have said that, in traditional European society, land had ultimately belonged to the Crown. No individual could assert absolute, total authority over any part of it as long as it was in a final sense the Crown's, and the Crown was supposed to hold it as representative of all people living through all time. In the Middle Ages land was held in a complex system of reciprocal obligations extending from the sovereign through various lords and ladies all the way down to the lowliest peasant. To get access to land was to incur duties that had to be met—work that had to be done, crops that had to be yielded up, taxes that had to be paid to the sovereign. Such a grant of access, on the other hand, also brought rights to the plain folk to collect the fruits of the land (or "usufruct rights"). Throughout the Middle Ages and even into the early modern period in Europe the land was harvested collectively: farmers went out together into communal fields and plowed and gleaned in concert, townspeople went into nearby communal forests to gather fuel. All rights to the land had been hallowed by ages of tradition, and no one, not even the king, could interfere with them.

The men who wrote our Constitution called this system of land tenure "feudalism" and thought it hopelessly wrong-headed. It did not allow enough freedom of enterprise, they said; it led to a tragedy of overuse or to political repression or to laziness and low economic return. Though some of those Old World notions were brought over to the New World and set up here in the first towns and rural villages of Puritan New England, by the time the Constitution appeared, they had been largely abandoned. The old feudal ideas had fallen into disrepute and modern liberal, individualistic ones had taken their place.

Americans did not want to see any new figure of authority emerge to reassert control over them. They did not want any government to stand between them and their property. Reflecting that changed way of thinking, the men in Philadelphia avoided any mention of the word land in the Constitution. They dared not even suggest that the federal government might replace the Crown as the ultimate owner of the country's farms and forests. Nor did they consider the idea that citizens, in possessing and using the land privately, might have duties of stewardship or care.

Private property in land more or less appeared and grew up as America did, and we Americans have believed in that institution more than any other people on earth. In fact it may be our most cherished institution. The Constitution does not mention land anywhere but it does mention private property in the Fifth Amendment, which reads that no citizen shall be deprived of property "without due process of law; nor shall private property be taken for public use, without just compensation." Note in those words that there is still something recognized as "public use"— that is, a use defined by and for a public, a use not reducible to private interest. But realize too that the Fifth Amendment was deliberately added to the Constitution to make as explicit as possible the idea that land belongs first and foremost to individuals, not the state, and that their private rights to possession are not casually to be set aside.

Five years before the Constitutional Convention a book appeared under the title *Letters from an American Farmer* that passionately expressed this American desire to privatize land. It was written by a French immigrant, J. Hector St. John de Crèvecoeur, who had acquired a large estate north of New York City, and from that vantage he explained:

> The instant I enter on my own land, the bright idea of property, of exclusive right, of independence exalt my mind. Precious soil, I say to myself; by what singular custom of law is it that thou wast made to constitute the riches of the freeholder? What should we American farmers be without the distinct possession of that soil? It feeds, it clothes us, from it we draw even a great exuberancy, our best meat, our richest drink, the very honey of our bees comes from this privileged spot. No wonder we should thus cherish its pos-

session, no wonder that so many Europeans who have never been able to say that such portion of land was theirs, cross the Atlantic to realize that happiness. This formerly rude soil has been converted by my father into a pleasant farm, and in return it has established all our rights; on it is founded our rank, our freedom, our power as citizens, our importance as inhabitants of such a district.[2]

This passage is worth recalling because it expresses why Americans became so determined to make the land over into private property. Owning a piece of it gave one a feeling of utter independence and freedom from powerful, arbitrary forces. It gave its owner some pride of rank that formerly had been denied to the vast majority of people. Those were seductive benefits, and no government would be permitted to intrude upon them.

In Crèvecoeur's book we find two distinct ideas about the land, both of them part of the mentality of the Constitution-makers:

First, to keep America a decent, virtuous nation the land ought to be owned by as many individuals as possible.

Second, to make the nation grow in richness and power the land and its products should be treated as commodities, put up for sale to the highest bidder in the marketplace.

Much of our country's history deals with the unfolding of those two ideas, their influence over our land policies, and their inevitable conflict with one another. If we examine that history in more detail, we can appreciate better the current situation we are in regarding the land and environment in this nation.

Many of our founding fathers, historians have discovered, were motivated by an intense fear of strong centralized power, a fear that was almost paranoid in intensity and was the other side of their Constitutional common sense. They would have agreed completely with the axiom that concentrated power corrupts those who hold it and hurts those who don't. A society with too much power gathered at the center is a society that will eventually weaken and degenerate, the rot spreading outwards from the center to the peripheries. That corruption from the center, they were sure, was precisely what had happened in England: too much money and power placed in too few hands had led to idleness, debauchery, vice, tyranny, and base self-interest. Americans had been forced to take up arms to free themselves from that corruption, and now, following the success of their effort, they were faced with the challenge of making sure that America would never fall back into decadent English ways. The surest means of doing that, it was widely believed, was to put the bulk of the population securely on their own farms where they would raise their own food and other necessities. Thus the masses would be free of dependence on the powerful few and could not be corrupted by them.

In other words, just as America had declared its national independence from England, the great harlot festering with immorality and corruption, now each American citizen must declare his or her independence from any and all forms of power, so that the corruption, if it did spread across the Atlantic, would not have much of a chance to spread here. Our forefathers thought of power as a kind of social disease and looked for ways to prevent its communication through quarantine, dispersal, and isolation. Cities are the prime source of infection, they warned; stay away from them. Stay away from people in general, if you can. A piece of private property in the country, with only a few clean neighbors around you, is the safest place to live.

The man we most commonly associate with this plan of living independently on the land, free of contaminating influences, is, of course, Thomas Jefferson. His most famous words on the subject are these:

> Those who labor in the earth are the chosen people of God, if ever he had a chosen people, whose breast he has made his peculiar deposit for substantial and genuine virtue. It is the focus in which he keeps alive that sacred fire, which otherwise might escape from the earth. Corruption of morals in the mass of cultivators is a phaenomenon of which no age nor nation has furnished an example. It is the mark set upon those, who not looking up to heaven, to their own soil and industry, as does the husbandman, for their subsistence, depend on it for casualties and caprice of customers. Dependance begets subservience and venality, suffocates the germ of virtue, and prepares fit tools for the design of ambition.[3]

Put more prosaically, Jefferson is saying that it is impossible to corrupt an entire nation so long as the majority of its citizens are small landowners, dispersed across the landscape, dependent on no one but themselves for their livelihood. Does this philosophy still seem to us wise and practical? Or does it sound too antisocial, too fearful of other people and of human nature?

In truth, of course, we never quite believed Thomas Jefferson or altogether wanted his rural, decentralized, self-reliant utopia. Americans may have feared contamination all right and been eager to avoid it, but they were not willing to live quite so far apart, so self-contained, on the land. After all, most of them had come to this continent not only to find virtue but to find wealth. They soon understood that one cannot get wealthy by living in isolation from others; wealth *requires* other people, requires lots of them, requires people living in cities and trading constantly with one another, requires people who can suppress their fear of contamination at least long enough to make a buck.

From the very beginning of settlement, therefore, Americans commonly assumed that the land is a form of capital and must be used to turn a profit. At times it was Jefferson's own view. He owned several hundred acres of Virginia farm land, worked them with an army of black slaves, and sold tobacco raised by their labor in the ports of Europe. He was a sincere man but, like the rest of the nation, he had confused and contradictory ideas about what the land was for. Somehow he hoped the land could simultaneously free people from their susceptibility to vice *and* augment their bank accounts. But the land cannot serve both of those ends and serve them well.

Apparently this is a very hard fact to face, and the country has not fully done so yet. From the President on down, millions of us are still searching for some piece of the earth located well away from the noise and corruption of our fellow man, some bit of land where we can be clean and pure again; but all the while we are searching just as earnestly for a way to get in on the money and corruption. Sooner or later we all must make a choice between which of those two ends we most want the land to serve. Jefferson made it when he went into tobacco production and slaveholding. The rest of the country generally followed his choice and, when pressed, said it preferred using the land to gain wealth rather than virtue. Americans as a consequence, despite their strenuous effort to secure independence from Old World corruption, began to look very much like the people they had fought to free themselves from.

The federal government might have worked to prevent that outcome and tilt the choice back toward virtue, but it would have had to outlaw the sale of all land in the United States, distribute it freely to all citizens, white, red, and black alike, and put strict controls on all commerce. The government did none of those things. On the contrary, it quickly became the single most active agency in treating land as a commodity, as a thing to be bought and sold for a profit. It did so despite the fact that it had no express legal authority under the Constitution to buy or sell a single acre. From the 1780s to the 1850s the federal government acquired, through state cessions and Indian treaties, hundreds of millions of acres. In addition, the government bought land from foreign states, the largest single such purchase occurring in 1803, when Thomas Jefferson was President, unsure of whether he had the power to carry out such a transaction but unwilling to pass up a sweet deal. Jefferson paid the French $23 million for the whole Louisiana Purchase, an area of over 500 million acres, extending from New Orleans through Kansas to the Dakotas. He paid four cents an acre, not a bad price for so much potential virtue. His successors in office went on buying and buying, though still with no clear constitutional right to do so. Often they simply took land first and paid for it later, and often they paid on their own terms. With the acquisition of Alaska in 1867 they finished putting together a continental real estate package of over 2.3 billion acres.[4] For the portion that was or is in the public domain they spent a mere $175 million, about what the Pentagon now spends between breakfast and lunch each day. That price averaged out to a mere ten cents per acre. Here was commodification of nature on a grand scale, far grander than any private citizen or corporation would ever be capable of doing. The U.S. government has been, in a sense, our biggest accumulator of capital, and its capital has been land.

Soon after it began purchasing land, the government also began selling it off at a profit to raise funds for its day-to-day operation. In the century and a half that followed the drafting of the Constitution officials sold or otherwise disposed of approximately one billion acres. A large part went to those who had the cash to buy it, and usually it went in enormous chunks, mainly to speculators who then turned around and resold it to farmers, miners, and timber companies. With so much land to move on the market, it made sense to move it wholesale and move it fast. In 1836, to take one of the more active years, approximately twenty million acres of land were sold at an average price of $1.25 per acre. Possibly it could have fetched more, but given what had been paid for it, that was a staggering profit. Over ninety million acres (an area the size of California) were given free to the railroads as a public investment in the future wealth of the country. Jefferson's small family farmers, the people chosen by God to be repositories of virtue, acquired 287 million acres, but then many of them turned around and sold out, taking themselves off to the city or farther west.

Buying and selling the land of this continent has been the great American way to wealth. It is what we have all done, big man and little alike. Moreover, it has furnished one of our principal criteria for evaluating citizenship: Those who have accumulated lots of land have been hailed as the best citizens, while those who have preferred to let it alone or have not become landowners have usually been regarded as failures. And all along it has been the government that has made it possible, through its territorial expansion and sales offices, for private citizens to treat the land in this intensely acquisitive way.

After the land had been disposed of to private owners, with deeds signed and fences erected around it, it was put it to work producing something to sell. In two centuries we have made it produce a sum of wealth that is little short of incredible. Even the sterile deserts of the Great Basin have been made to produce countless flocks of bleating sheep, on the range and in the casinos. All that wealth has been possible, free-market economists tell us, because in this country we have given owners a wide margin of freedom to use the land as they see fit. The economists may be right; certainly they have plenty of expertise on what it takes to maximize wealth. What they have not realized though is that with the wealth comes some costs that we cannot separate out or avoid, among them, an endangering of democracy and a ravaging of the land. We have paid those costs again and again in our two centuries of national existence. Our democracy, which started off with such bright hopes, has given way to a class-divided society in which a tiny elite control most of the private land, take most of the profit from it, and largely run the government to suit themselves. As for the land, few of those 2.3 billion acres acquired from the Indians and others is today free of toxic substances, soil erosion, and ecological degradation. We have made the land pay off, all right, but we have paid a big price.

You may want to argue that the wealth was worth getting and therefore, despite the costs, the land has been put to good use. But you cannot maintain in all honesty that we have left the environment in as good a shape as we found it. Privatizing the land and putting a "For Sale" sign on it has nearly worked its ruin. And by many measures, it has nearly worked our ruin too.

For a long while now those costs have been growing more and more obvious, more and more serious, prompting citizens to begin looking for some alternative to a strictly individualistic, private property ideal. Such an alternative has appeared and has grown to have a significant influence. We call it "conservation." Though there is some disagreement on what is implied in the term, this much is clear: The conservation movement emerged out of discontent with an intensely private approach to land ownership and rights. It has been an effort to define and assert broader communitarian values, some idea of a public interest transcending the wants and desires of a strictly individualistic calculus.

Beginning about a hundred years ago, the conservation movement began to take form in the United States, focusing at first on establishing a community interest in our forested lands, particularly in the western states and territories. Under private exploitation, abetted by the old federal land disposal policies, American forests were disappearing at an alarming rate, threatening the long-term security of the nation. Similarly, wildlife, considered merely the private property of whoever killed them, were being slaughtered wholesale by market hunters and landowners. The most dramatic moment in the early conservation movement came in 1872, when Congress was persuaded to set aside Yellowstone National Park as a permanently public property, providing sanctuary to the last remnants of the great buffalo herds. In 1891 it withdrew an additional thirteen million acres from the public domain and set them aside as the first national forest reserves, forbidding any private citizen from entering and exploiting them without express permission. More national forests, wildlife preserves, parks, and grasslands would be added to those initiatives, and many states would follow suit with their own parks, forests, and biological and mineral reserves.

Today, an astonishing 40 percent of the land in this country is publicly owned in some fashion, and that percentage continues to increase slowly, as various agencies go on acquiring new land for highways, parks, and military bases.[5] The federal government alone holds 34 percent of the nation's land, though its share ranges from a mere 0.3 percent of Iowa and 0.6 of Kansas to 60 percent of Alaska and 85 percent of Nevada. Most of the publicly owned land lies, of course, in the western states, where an arid climate limited agricultural settlement, but by no means is all of it here. In eastern states like Massachusetts there are still a few town forests and commons dating back to the archaic seventeenth century, mixed among twentieth-century national seashores and Nike missile sites. Again, nothing like this system of publicly owned lands that has grown up and out and around in all directions is explicitly mentioned anywhere in the Constitution as a legitimate function of government. But the American people have voted for that system, paid for it, wanted it, used it, in large part because they have lost some of their early faith in private property as a universal ideal. We may *say* that individualized ownership is still our sacred creed, and as far as a family homesite is concerned that is certainly so; but all the same we acknowledge the limits of that creed when we demand or expect or tolerate the evolution of an alternative system of government ownership on state, federal, and local levels.

Without our quite realizing it, we have put together an entirely new kind of commons—*an American commons*—where individuals may go to find natural resources but which no one can take into his or her exclusive possession. What is most interesting about this American commons is that there is nothing feudal about it; it is the achievement and patrimony of a modern nation that, in some measure, still believes in the dream of democracy and realizes that it cannot be fully achieved through the institution of private property. Indeed, one of the most effective ways our democracy has devised to rescue itself from near extinction at the hands of holders of great private wealth has been through public land ownership. That discovery has been part of the legacy of the American conservation movement.

After looking at the long-term historical patterns in the United States, we have to conclude that the system of public lands are here to stay, probably forever. Every effort to get rid of them, to go back to a lost world of John Locke and Adam Smith, when privatization was the ruling passion and laissez-faire the dominant ethos, has failed. President Herbert Hoover tried to get rid of the federal lands in the late 1920s, tried to turn them into state lands. Cowboy capitalists of the 1940s and '50s strenuously demanded that the western public lands be put in their control (and pockets), but they failed too. In the 1970s a new generation of itchy-handed stockmen and miners, the sagebrush rebels, didn't get a single acre handed over to them. Eventually, after so much failure, one would think that reality might break through at last and the rebels would say, "Well, shucks, it looks like those lands are going to stay public." They may get shifted from one category of management to another, from harvested forest to wilderness, from wildlife refuge to oil field; from cattle country to bombing range; they may get shifted from one branch or level of government to another. They may, and probably will, go on increasing in acreage for a long while. They will not disappear.

That is not to say there are no problems with the system of public lands or no way in which they might be better managed. Quite the contrary, the system is full of problems. In the eyes of some economists, the lands have never been managed very efficiently or rationally; in their opinion, we could get more dollars out of them if we made them compete more vigorously in the marketplace.[6] I don't happen to share that particular opinion. It seems to me that if the economists need an efficiency project to work on, they have plenty available in General Motors, Silicon Valley, the savings and loan industry, the Pentagon, or agribusiness. We are, apparently, losing our shirts in the international marketplace because of the sloth, greed, and inefficiency in our corporate circles and because of a bloated military-industrial complex. Squeezing a few more bucks out of our public lands will do precious little to change that greater pattern of national non-competitiveness. We might be better advised to try selling high-priced electronics rather than our last old-growth forests, the last pristine wildlife habitat we have left in Alaska, or the soils of our western range, all at giveaway rates to Japan and other countries.

But to their credit the economists have, over the years, raised some thoughtful criticisms of public lands management that we have not yet fully addressed. Do bureaucrats, they ask, have the same incentive to give close attention to land that resident private owners do? And just what kind of thinking, what kind of expertise, should the managers of the public estate, working for and representing the real owners who are diffused across the nation, bring to their jobs? How we answer those two questions may be among the most significant things we do in this generation, for they will largely determine what our relationship to the land, to the natural world, will be.

Can a bureaucrat in, say, the Forest Service or Bureau of Land Management provide as good a stewardship of the land as a private owner would? Before tackling that question, we ought to admit that the real choice on the public lands is not, in most cases, between individual private owners and public bureaucrats. That choice disappeared a long time ago. Almost all of America is incorporated these days, and all our forms of work and management have been bureaucratized. The vast majority of us, even in the wild and rugged West, are working for someone else, or for *something* else. Therefore, the relationship of a federal forester or Bureau of Land Management employee to the public lands does not differ from an Exxon pipefitter's or executive vice-president's to his company's equipment and lease holdings. If employees in large organizations cannot take care of property as well as individual private owners would do, then we had better start making some big changes all over the place. We had better bust up Exxon, IBM, Weyerhaeuser, Toyota, Sony, the whole incorporated, multinational economy and put all property back into the hands of single owners. Of course that is not going to happen anytime soon; maybe, in light of our tremendous global population, it will never be possible to live that simply, directly, self-reliantly again. Somehow we must learn to make the best of a world where ownership has become highly collectivized and corporatized, where individual responsibility has become harder to find.

The employees in charge of managing our public lands have been unique only in the degree of confusion they feel as to what is expected of them in their work. In part that confusion comes from serving an employer as faceless and dispersed as the American nation. What does the boss want out of this place, they ask themselves, and who really is the boss? But also in part the problem began a long time ago, in the era of Gifford Pinchot, our first Chief Forester, with the fuzzy definition of expertise that his era created and we have followed ever since. A forester, it was said, must be an expert working in the name of the public good. But precisely what was she or he supposed to be expert in? What was the body of knowledge required for that work? "Economics" was one reply: the public lands professional must be an applied economist, managing a specific resource commodity—trees, mineral ore, game, scenic resources for tourists—and must know how to maximize the economic returns from that commodity over the longest possible term. Although academic economists may not find the public lands expertise quite up to snuff, they must admit that economics has been part of the required training from the earliest point. But economics is not the only kind of expertise expected; there has been another, completely contradictory kind—training in the science of biology. The manager of public lands must know how nature lives and is organized—how ducks mate and migrate, how bunch grass regenerates, how fire changes a forest community—and must protect those processes from destructive human exploitation. Throughout this century almost all of our controversies over public lands management have stemmed from disagreement over which kind of expertise— economic or biological—ought to dominate. In the case of the National Park Service or Fish and Wildlife Service, we have come to believe that biology ought to be the dominant expertise, while in the case of the Forest Service and Bureau of Land Management, economics has been emphasized, especially during the last four decades. Nothing, however, is settled in these expectations, and the resulting confusion, the uncertainty about the kind of expertise needed, continues. How can any man or woman do a job well when it is so ambiguously defined?

As an historian, I think I can discern through all the past confusion and ambiguity a strong trend in what the nation is coming to expect from its public lands managers, and it is not one that will make the economists happy. The nation is, by fits and starts, moving through a second conservation revolution. The first revolution, to repeat, was the inventing of the American commons. The second is what we might call the "ecologizing" of land use in America, public and private alike. More and more, we have begun to look at the land not merely as a storehouse of economic resources but as an interconnected, interdependent community of living organisms on which our survival depends. We are listening to ecologists, we are adopting an ecological perspective, and increasingly we are demanding that the public land managers become applied ecologists no matter which agency they work for.

To be sure, ecology is a far more uncertain guide to policy than economics. The economists are all agreed that land is supposed to be used efficiently to increase the gross national product. Ecologists, on the other hand, don't quite know what their expertise is for: Is it to help the economists with raising GNP or is to save nature for its own sake? Ecology lacks the ends consensus of economics, the devotion to a common social vision. But if the science of ecology does not furnish a clear policy direction, the public is gradually moving to furnish it; ecology, the public indicates, ought to show land managers how to preserve the flora and fauna of our commons in as healthy, self-renewing a state as possible. The public may want plenty of lumber and wood products extracted from its forests too, but it is also coming to demand that the snowy owl be preserved; it wants the timber wolf back, it wants more bobcats, more bighorn sheep, more blackfooted ferrets, more golden eagles, more native prairies. Ecology, therefore, not economics, will likely be the dominant kind of expertise on all the public lands of tomorrow.

If Gifford Pinchot was the leader of the first revolution, then the great leader and prophet of the second one was Aldo Leopold. He was born in 1887, just as the first conservation movement was beginning to take shape, the son of German immigrants who had settled on the banks of the Mississippi River. Like others in the movement, he came to believe strongly in the need to establish an alternative system of public land tenure and management, and he devoted much of his professional life to that goal, working first as a U.S. forester in the Southwest and later as a wildlife scientist in the state of Wisconsin. But by the 1930s Leopold was beginning to have a few criticisms of the conservation movement and its public land program. The movement, he feared, was still based on a narrow economic attitude toward the natural world; it started from the same premise that the old private property approach did, namely, that the role of the land is to make us rich. Though we had moved toward a more collective method of deriving that wealth from the soil and of distributing it to people, there still remained the danger of ecological degradation. In the first place, the new public managers could feel just as pressured as the old private ones to make the land produce to the maximum, and they could destroy land just as readily. Then there remained outside the public domain millions of acres, most of them farmlands, that were still part of the private realm and vulnerable to heavy-handed exploitation. On all those lands, public and private alike, Leopold insisted, we must "quit thinking about decent land-use as solely an economic problem." It was time to apply broader ethical principles to the relationship.[7]

Thus was spawned the single most important new idea about land we have had since we created the institution of private property, even more important than the invention of the American commons. It grew out of the conservation movement but required an imaginative leap beyond anything conservation had previously meant. Leopold called his idea "the land ethic." Briefly, it says we ought to acknowledge that we belong to the land as much as it belongs to us. It is part of our community—all the trees, insects, parasites, waterfowl, the whole collective organism. And the prosperity and health of this community ought to become our concern, just as the prosperity and health of the human community is. We owe personal obligations and duties to the land, as well as enjoy opportunities and advantages from it.

Leopold was worried that, in setting up a new American commons under official auspices, we might neglect the need to make the land's welfare an individual moral issue. He wanted to instill in the ordinary farmer and hunter as well as in the federal employee an ethical awareness, a personal responsibility. Himself a private landowner of some extent, Leopold believed the institution of private property might be necessary to developing that new land ethic. In fact he feared the prospect of federal control over all the land, for it might lead to a loss of personal responsibility. Government, he feared in a manner reminiscent of Thomas Jefferson, might be too large and impersonal to become an effective, reliable moral force.

> At what point [he asked] will governmental conservation, like the mastodon, become handicapped by its own dimensions? The answer, if there is any, seems to be in a land ethic, or some other force which assigns more obligation to the private landowner.[8]

Thus, he called for a new ideal of the "voluntary practice of conservation" by individuals acting on their own lands.

Leopold died over forty years ago, and since that time we have not yet resolved the dilemma he saw in our tenure of land. We founded our country on an ideal of private property, an ideal that proved in many ways to work against democracy as it has worked against environmental well-being. We have moved somewhat away from that ideal in the direction of a public system of ownership and centralized government management. Yet we remain fearful that government cannot be automatically depended on to own and manage land in the most virtuous way, removing all obligation from the rest of us. Thus we must also seek a personal ethical relationship with the land, which for Leopold depended on personal contact and direct accountability.

This is a real and difficult dilemma, but I don't think it will be resolved by trying to turn the last hundred years around, going back to Thomas Jefferson's individualistic yeoman landowners. Remember that the origins of private property involved elevating the individual above the community. How can one expect a land ethic, with its strong emphasis on ecological community, to emerge where the institution of sacrosanct private property exists? How can one expect people living with such an institution to develop broader moral ideals than the self-interest of the individual? They can only do so by becoming *bad* property owners. Once a farmer or rancher has put other values ahead of acquiring personal wealth, he or she has ceased to have a good reason for exclusive, sovereign ownership. Private deeds and private fences can simply get in the way of the land ethic.

I suppose Aldo Leopold might answer that private ownership is necessary, or at least is useful, to developing the love and concern needed in a land ethic. But history suggests that people do not have to possess something as private property in order to love it. On the contrary, possession has often led to alienation of affection, to exploitation and indifference. No North American Indian needed to own the land in fee simple in order to feel empathy with its creatures. Generally, a system of exclusive private possession has encouraged an ethos of domination, precisely the evil that Leopold was seeking to overcome—of trying to conquer the land rather than living on it as a mere citizen cooperating with all its inhabitants.

Before people can be expected to think cooperatively about their place in nature, they must first be trained in the habits of thinking cooperatively about the society in which they live. I submit that means they must live in a country where most of the land is held under some form of communal ownership or control, not only the forests, mountains, and deserts of the American West, but the farms and ranches, the waterways and woodlots all over the place. That land need not be put wholly into federal hands; a more localized, decentralized kind of communal ownership and management might be pursued instead, including ownership by nonprofit land trusts and environmental organizations. But if we are ever to move forward in our land thinking, if we are ever to become Leopold's "plain citizens of the land," practicing an ethic informed by ecology, we will surely have to make a few more changes in the way Americans own and use property.

Already, we are creeping towards those changes; at least we more or less practice communalism 40 percent of the time, if you take the current size of the public estate as an index. Where we have an opportunity to speed up that cultural evolution is on what are presently held as private lands, both urban and agricultural. And there too changes have been in process for more than five decades, beginning with the soil conservation program of the 1930s and including recent sodbusting laws, pesticide regulations, and groundwater control legislation, all of which have established public controls over private lands. All are evidence that we are awakening to other values in land use than maximizing personal wealth. All across the nation we now have a substantial body of laws restricting the free market in land: laws, for example, that zone some acres as agricultural, or laws that allow the buying of development rights. These laws, like the public lands in the West, are not going to disappear; in fact they are likely to grow in number and power. In the most affluent parts of the country towns have purchased outright a considerable amount of endangered farmland and other open space and hold it communally. This is obviously a strategy that can work only where there is lots of local money; state and federal funds must be provided for areas of limited population and economic distress. Someday we may be ready to divert the money we now spend on crop production controls or on military procurement to buying prime agricultural and urban land in the public name all over the nation. And citizen groups like the Nature Conservancy, the Audubon Society, and more than a hundred community land trusts nationwide may add significantly to that public estate.

So far all this shifting of ideas about the land, from the eighteenth century to the dawning of the twenty-first, has gone on without any effect on the Constitution and its clauses. Maybe that has been for the better. People might have been more reluctant to do that shifting if they had had to explain it in writing. On the other hand, amending the Constitution has often promoted dramatic changes in our social behavior, as the civil rights movement, which has drawn heavily on the Fourteenth Amendment for authority, demonstrates. The same might be true of a Constitution that spoke outright of our obligations as citizens to the land we own and inhabit.

I can see the possibility in the not too distant future of a revised Constitution that school children will learn about and adults will sit down to read now and then. It will declare that all the lands of these United States belong in a final sense to all the people and that present occupants have the use of them for their fruits only. It will demand that any use of the land not leave any lasting impairment, or diminish its beauty, or endanger public health. That new document will affirm, in the spirit of Aldo Leopold, that all forms of life, nonhuman and human alike, are henceforth to be considered as citizens dwelling together in this great and virtuous republic. That is a Constitution I sense is coming—a Constitution that the course of our history suggests is coming—and a Constitution that anyone ought to stay up late to read.

9

The Kingdom, the Power,
and the Water

◆

AMONG the truly outstanding books written in this century about the American frontier—and the shelf of such books is rather small—is *Great Basin Kingdom* by Leonard J. Arrington, published in 1958. When it appeared, it had only a few rivals either in scholarship or ideas. There was Henry Nash Smith's work on the West as symbol and myth, Bernard DeVoto's vigorous account of explorers and imperialists, Paul Horgan's saga of the Rio Grande valley, Wallace Stegner's biography of John Wesley Powell, and Walter Prescott Webb's sweeping survey of Europeans on the global frontier.[1] All of those books appeared in the 1950s within a few years of each other. All were well researched and brilliantly written, in many cases by accomplished novelists whose talents in creating plot and character recruited a wide audience for frontier and western history. Arrington's study of the Mormon frontier was different from the others in that it was the work of an economic and social historian who was interested in how institutions took shape in one small part of the West and how they differed from those in other parts of the region and in the East. Like the other historians, he gave his story a compelling plot and filled it with arresting, complex characters; but for him the chief interest was how a vague, half-articulated set of ideas had migrated to Utah and taken shape there as a thriving, distinctive economic order. Better than any of his contemporaries, moreover, and better than most of his successors, he understood how powerful the drives of capitalism had been in developing the West, how thoroughly those drives had entered into the region's overall sense of purpose, and how fiercely the battle had been waged, at least in Utah, to prevent that from happening. As romance, his story may not have been able to compete with DeVoto's lusty adventurers or Horgan's brown-robed padres preaching among the Indians, but in its implications it may have been the most important story of all.

Arrington's thesis was that nineteenth-century Mormon Utah was at once an intensely materialistic society, intent on achieving wealth, and a determinedly anti-capitalistic one. It repudiated many of the economic attitudes that the rest of America was coming to live by: self-seeking individualism, Social Darwinist ethics of ruthless competitiveness, hostility toward all government and all ideas of public responsibility. In the midst of the period Vernon Parrington called "the Great Barbecue," when gluttony became the national style, the Mormon pioneers tried to live according to a different ethos.[2] They sought public control of natural resources. They held fast to the nearly obsolete idea of the "commonwealth," which is one of public, not merely private or individual, welfare. They insisted on controlling prices and regulating incomes, so that there would be "neither rich nor poor" in their midst. In contrast to other parts of the nation, they did not enter fully into the marketplace economy but held themselves aloof, setting up home-based, cooperatively owned industry and agriculture to supply their needs.

The origins of this anti-capitalist ethos appear to lie primarily in the Judeo-Christian religious tradition, and in New England Puritanism in particular. According to Arrington, the Mormon people adhered to a set of economic ideas that had once been common among the Puritans, including the idea that political or moral leadership ought to exercise some control over individual economic behavior and give direction to it. "Unquestionably," he wrote, "traditional American thought and practice sanctioned the positive use of public agencies to attain given group objectives."[3] By the second quarter of the nineteenth century, when Mormonism was getting founded and hounded from state to state, those ideas no longer had much acceptance; they were being extinguished by the secular capitalist revolution. What had once been common understanding was now widely viewed as subversive and threatening.

Thus, the collectivist spirit was central to Mormon identity well before their trek into the Great Basin to escape their persecutors. But once arrived there, Arrington and a number of other observers have argued, they seem to have found that spirit intensified significantly by a local environmental condition—the arid climate. Aridity forced them to resort to the unfamiliar technique of irrigation to raise food for themselves, and irrigation, at least in its primitive stage of development, reinforced their traditional, collectivist thoughts and habits. It was not an agriculture that gave much play to Social Darwinists. How that exactly worked, however, is a complicated and murky problem in the relations among environment, technology, and society.

As undoubtedly every bright young child in Utah knows, the Mormons first attempted irrigation in the year 1847 on the banks of City Creek, within the bounds of present-day Salt Lake City. Church leader Wilford Woodruff later recalled:

> We pitched our camp, put some teams onto our plows . . . and undertook to plow the earth, but we found neither wood nor iron were strong enough to make furrows here in this hard soil. It was like adamant. Of course we had to turn water on it . . . We went and turned out the City Creek. We turned it over our ground. Come to put our teams on it, of course they sank down to their belleys in the mud. We had to wait until this land dried enough to hold our teams up. We then plowed our land.[4]

From this crude beginning the Kingdom expanded and grew. By 1850 they had put some 16,000 acres under irrigation, raising on them over 120,000 bushels of grain, as well as potatoes, hops, vegetables, and tobacco. And by 1895 the irrigated lands had increased spectacularly to a total of 417,000 acres.[5] Every major river and many, many minor streams—virtually everything but the deeply intrenched, inaccessible Colorado River—had been harnessed by century's end to produce a bounty of crops.

Out of the muddy fields came the necessities of life, but also came wealth—wealth that was promptly reinvested to build up manufacturing, increase the labor supply through sponsored immigration, and improve transportation. By 1860, Utah was the most prosperous of all the western territories. Its improved farmlands were valued at over $1 million, its manufacturers at $0.9 million, and its real and personal property at nearly $5.6 million. It had but one case of suicide reported, only a single pauper drawing relief, and only eight convicted criminals.[6]

If their economic success derived in large part from their irrigation system, that system in turn derived from the concentrated power of the Church, which was the chief organizer of labor, the chief supplier of capital, the overall planner of construction, and ultimately the owner of all water in the name of the community. In Brigham Young's words, "There shall be no private ownership of the streams that come out of the canyons, nor the timber that grows on the hills. These belong to the people: all the people."[7] And for him the Church was the people; the Church decided what the people wanted and needed, and it carried out their will. It was the Church, through its active leadership in promoting the unfamiliar technology of water control, that made Utah more successful than its neighboring societies. "The Church," writes Arrington, "was expected to play the central role in erecting and maintaining an improved economic system for its members."[8] However suspicious they were of the far-off, national government in Washington, the Mormons trusted their local religious government completely and looked to it for material progress.

Arrington does not describe that pioneer Utah economy as socialistic, for the land was still held privately and no one was interested in communalizing it completely. But he does speak of "the partial socialization of investment" that occurred in the early years of settlement when the Church taxed the population and put some of that revenue into water development and other enterprises.[9] Certainly, the Church-sponsored irrigation system must be considered a more or less socialistic investment. The hydraulic apparatus was a critical means of production, the people owned it collectively, and that, after all, is mainly what we mean by socialism. Perhaps the early Mormon economy should be labeled a hybrid: a modified socialism or a "third way" (resembling, say, modern-day Sweden), an economy in which men held their land as private property but put their other resources and a great deal of their money and power into the hands of the ruling authorities to use for the benefit of all.

Having set up in Utah an attractive, strong, successful rival to the capitalistic American West—which Arrington calls "the economy of Babylon"—the Mormons then had to defend themselves constantly against invasion. They had to live as a besieged people. For a number of years they held their ground firmly, but then, with the entrance of the first transcontinental railroad into the Great Basin in 1869, their defenses began to crumble. Outside secular money, technology, and corporations, all backed by the might of the federal government, entered and gradually wrested control away from the Church and the local community. "Eventually," Arrington points out, "the leviathan of American finance capitalism . . . ruled Utah as it had long ruled Montana and other Western states and territories."[10] The water system continued to function, but what was raised on the irrigated fields was heavily traded with Babylon to get more and more of its goods and services.

By the twentieth century Mormons had become part and parcel of the mass consumer society, hardly different at all from non-Mormons in their economic beliefs or practices. "Individualism, speculation, and inequality—once thought to be characteristics of Babylon—were woven into the fabric of Mormon life." This outcome Arrington terms, in a tone of regret and nostalgia, "the great capitulation."[11]

But having told us of the great capitulation, Arrington then presents a surprising conclusion. In the long run and despite severe setbacks, he insists, Mormon communitarianism did manage to win the hearts and minds of the West after all. Under the continuing pressure of the arid environment, and the imperative to make the most efficient use of every drop of water, the rest of the West learned to follow the Mormon example. Specifically, he mentions the establishment of the Bureau of Reclamation, a federal agency created to do for the region what laissez-faire capitalism could not or would not do—build an irrigation-based agriculture. The Bureau, he suggests, is a secular equivalent of the Mormon Church, one put to work demonstrating, as the Church once did, "the effectiveness of central planning and voluntary cooperation in developing a large semiarid region."[12] Through the Bureau and similar agencies, the federal government, so it is argued, has in this century assumed considerable responsibility for the public welfare, has invested in hydraulic technology in the interests of all, and has distributed the surplus of production broadly through the society. The capitalistic West may *think* it defeated the Mormons, but in truth it has been forced, by the demands of the harsh environment and the technology of water control, to adopt Mormon collectivism and brotherhood after all. Beginning in the 1930s, when the New Deal undertook the massive development of western river basins, that final triumph of Mormonism might be said to have commenced.

The magic of irrigation, it would seem from this conclusion, is supposed to have done more than merely make Utah's pioneers and other westerners well-fed and prosperous. It has also made them virtuous. Such a notion stems from the fact that constructing dams, digging ditches and canals, and distributing water were all tasks requiring a great deal of coordinated labor. Out of such labor, we are asked to believe, came a culture of cooperation. Nels Anderson, for example, has written: "The settlers had to work together on their ditches and dams. They had to use their irrigation water cooperatively to get from it the maximum benefit."[13] Sociologist Thomas O'Dea has made a similar conclusion: "It was in the cooperative control and management of water—the urgent prerequisite of life in Utah—that Mormon co-operation found its most impressive expression."[14] The economist George Thomas, writing in 1920, also found that cooperation had been the dominant social pattern in the institutions associated with irrigation in Utah history, from the beginning to his own time.[15]

And still another economist, Richard Ely, noted early in this century that "the agriculture pursued [by the Mormons] was irrigation agriculture, which for its success is dependent upon a compact society, well knit together. Individualism was out of the question under these conditions, and in Mormonism we find precisely the cohesive strength of religion needed at that junction to secure economic success."[16] What is being claimed here is nothing less than a regeneration of human character through the processes of irrigation. Morality, it would seem, as well as prosperity, was somehow produced by the technique of water control and management and the social relations it required. People learned to put aside their selfishness and greed, found themselves arriving at a more organic sense of community, felt more brotherly toward their neighbors than they had done back east where they had depended on rainfall to water their crops.

At this point in the history of the American West we leave the land of factual, objective, verifiable description, the land of economic statistics and crop reports, and enter the more spacious, intriguing land of myth. By myth I mean, in the words of the *American Heritage Dictionary of the English Language,* "any real or fictional story, recurring theme, or character type that appeals to the consciousness of a people by embodying its cultural ideals or by giving expression to deep, commonly felt emotions." The specific myth I refer to is one of forming an irrigation-based community—call it "the irrigation myth." The central theme in that myth, the plot in its story, is that the work of redeeming the desert from its sterility is simultaneously a work of self-redemption for humanity. Call it then the myth of human redemption through irrigation technology. A powerful moral force, we are told, operates in this material world of dams, siphons, ditches, and canals, and it has produced a more virtuous community of Americans than can be found in humid areas where the technology is not needed. The myth has been a persuasive one even for seasoned scholars.

The West is our most myth-shrouded region, so much so that we often cannot say where its actual physical boundaries are. But of all the myths associated in the popular mind with the West, far and away the most appealing, at least to white American males, and the most long-lived and persistent, has been quite a different myth, one associated with very different cultural ideas and emotions. It is the myth of the lone individual going off to confront a howling wilderness or a savage people with his bare hands, or at least he is armed with nothing more than a single gun. In that encounter he fights, wins, is personally redeemed by his bloody courage, and thereby, through his violence, redeems his people, who come following after to inherit the land in innocence and righteousness. Richard Slotkin has referred to this dominant American myth as one of "regeneration through violence."[17]

By the middle of the nineteenth century, this myth of the frontiersman had begun to serve, openly and emphatically, the capitalist ideology and way of life. That was so largely because the myth was sited in the West, and it was in the West where many of the aggressive new class of entrepreneurs were most active—in mining, railroad building, cattle ranching, and land speculating. But even before that merger, going back well into the eighteenth century, the folklore of the westward-moving frontier had served to prepare people for the emerging capitalistic view of the world. Its heroes were men like Daniel Boone, who had blazed a path into the wilderness to prepare the way for a real-estate scheme, and those legendary Rocky Mountain fur trappers, who were in truth part of the workforce of a global haberdashery. The world such heroes inhabited, or imagined they inhabited, was a hard, cruel place much of the time where they had to fight constantly for survival. They could never relax their vigilance. Nor could the frontier hero depend on his fellows for much aid, because in this competitive environment, each man was mainly interested in his own welfare and the only dependable moral principle was self-reliance. Thus, through the elaborations of myth, the early West came to symbolize the dog-eat-dog world that capitalism was building; supposedly, it revealed in the clearest way that the law of nature was one of cutthroat competition. The myth of rugged individualism on a western frontier has long been our largest and most compelling national myth, and it has helped teach Americans the ideas of a laissez-faire economy and reinforced, however subtly or blatantly, its ethos.[18]

All those great historians of the 1950s I have mentioned had to deal in some way with that mythic West, either accepting it or repudiating it. Some of them believed in it to a great degree and could not escape its power (I have in mind DeVoto and Webb, two passionate believers in the cult of individualism). Others tended to look for an alternative set of ideas outside the West (as did Smith and Stegner, both of whom celebrated the counter-mythic career of John Wesley Powell, a federal scientist and planner). Still others tried to discover some alternative within the West itself and make a countermyth of it (Horgan, for example, with his Hispanic Southwest).

Arrington, I submit, adopted this last strategy. Like Horgan, he searched within the West for an alternative mytho-history to that of the rugged hunter-explorer-entrepreneur and found it in a traditional religious community—in this case his own—situated in that arid terrain where religion and technology had merged into a single myth of collective redemption. "Making the waste places blossom as the rose," Arrington writes, "and the earth to yield abundantly of its diverse fruits, was [for the Mormons] more than an economic necessity; it was a form of religious worship."[19] His book was at once a reasoned analysis of that mytho-history and a believer's celebration of it.

The irrigation myth had been around almost from the very beginning of arid land settlement, but perhaps its most extravagant statement was published by the non-Mormon journalist William Smythe in his book, *The Conquest of Arid America.* In Smythe's view, Utah was "our classic land of irrigation," the archetype where not only new techniques of water control had first been tried out but also where a better type of American was emerging. This control over nature constituted, he claimed, nothing less than the realization of "man's partnership with God." After a long wandering in a darkness of corruption and self-interest, man had at last come to the sun-filled desert and there was driven by "the club of necessity into a brotherhood of labor." In typically rhapsodic style, Smythe continues: "To proceed in the making of your farm, in the development of a great region, in the formation of institutions, by knowledge rather than chance, is a profoundly religious thing. Irrigation is a religious rite. It is the fortune of Arid America," his last sentence reads, "to be so palpably crude material that it can not be used at all, save upon the divine terms."[20]

Still another passionate believer in the religion of irrigation was the Mormon scientist and educator John A. Widstoe, and one could hardly find a more distinguished proponent. From 1907 to 1916 he served as president of Utah State Agricultural College, then until 1921 as the president of the University of Utah, and finally, in his last three decades of life, as a member of the Church's Quorum of the Twelve Apostles. Here is where he saw the great story concluding:

> The destiny of the man is to possess the whole earth; and the destiny of the earth is to be subject to man. There can be no full conquest of the earth, and no real satisfaction to humanity, if large portions of the earth remain beyond his highest control. Only as all parts of the earth are developed according to the best existing knowledge, and brought under human control, can man be said to possess the earth.

Widtsoe may be talking about the future, but he is also drawing on a powerful myth taken from the past. The duty of mankind on this earth is to achieve absolute mastery. Now that the easier, more temperate regions have come under human management, there are only the vast arid spaces still unpossessed. These unconquered areas now summon people to a last great effort of pioneering, and it will be in such places, and in their subjugation by irrigation, that the human species will reach its highest moral achievement.[21]

Here then is the myth that animated a large part of the American West from the nineteenth century well into the twentieth. It begins with a symbolic landscape or environment in which heroic deeds can be done, a landscape that looks a lot like a rural Utah. There are tall, powerful-looking mountains on the horizon, where the snow is packed deep and white and from which the rivers run down to the plain. In the lowlands there are level fields, green with the promise of prosperity. Row upon row of fences organize that prosperity, divide it up, suggest its dimensions, and acknowledge its limits. Smooth, straight canals carry water to those fields, carry it gurgling and racing along the fences, and then feed innumerable smaller ditches and furrows, all of them as smooth and straight as the canals. Small frame or adobe houses cluster together in village centers, from which the inhabitants walk out to their fields. Orchards of peach and apple trees scent the air in this landscape, while bees hum and small herds of livestock low and bleat.[22] Everywhere there is order: no mishaps of nature, no unforeseen disasters, no waste or inefficiency, no random meanderings. All nature has been made productive, and the productivity contributes to the increase of humankind and its welfare.[23]

The irrigation myth is a story, as I have said, of creating a better social as well as environmental order. The people who have wrested that ideal landscape from the wasteland have done so because they have learned to put aside their jealousies and quarrels, their differences and idiosyncracies. They have become one. Together they clear their ditches and bring the water down to their seedbeds, sharing it equitably among everyone in the group. They do not go to court against one another. Their fences, it is true, denote private property, but all the ditches and canals are public property, and between the two systems of ownership there is no disharmony, no sense of cross-purposes, so closely have the public and the private welfare merged into one. It is the technology of irrigation that has bound these into so powerful a unity. Through labor and technique, they have learned it is possible to establish common goals and rely on one another to reach them. All around them they see clear, unmistakable evidence of what such a collective effort can achieve. Beyond the oasis, however, beyond the ditches and fences, there stretches the unreclaimed desert, a desolate wilderness, without order or human meaning or material value. No one wants to live there, except for a few poor outcasts and misfits.

This irrigation myth, like the myth of the lone heroic hunter dressed in buckskin, originates far back in the dim recesses of history; long before it appeared in the American West, it found expression in Mesopotamia, Egypt, and China. But, above all, it has been the Judeo-Christian peoples who have handed it on and on, creating a literary tradition that reaches from the Book of Genesis to the Book of Mormon. Much of the literature of Judaism and Christianity, as well as that of Mormonism, is filled with images of gardens and oases that have been wrested from barren deserts by concerted, righteous human labor.[24] What the western part of the United States did for that tradition was to suggest that a mythic paradise could now be regained, in this age, by people like you and me; that at the very heart of the West lay a real desert out of which could materialize at last a real, Christian, sanctified Eden. And when nature there had been restored to productive order, when it was at last providing an economic abundance for all, then humanity too would be restored to its original innocence and peace.

At the very heart of the irrigation myth is an affirmation of technology as a divinely ordained instrument of domination over the natural world. Technology, especially agricultural technology, has come to be invested with an intensely religious potential, as have its products. The myth says that God dwells in machinery—in the water pump, the irrigation dam, all the instruments of desert reclamation.

As late as the 1950s, the myth of human redemption through technology was still alive and active in the minds of Americans, western and eastern alike. The West was standing at the dawn of a whole new era of massive reclamation projects, and within a short space of time those projects would bring every major river basin in the West under human domination. In the terms of the irrigation myth, those projects were needed to complete the noble dream of conquest begun in 1847. If Richard Slotkin's lone hunter in the wilderness served to legitimate the capitalist economy and its expansion, then the irrigation myth helped give legitimacy to the entire postwar program of intensive, large-scale reclamation.[25] It also gave support to the federal agencies engaged in that work, notably the Bureau of Reclamation.

Today the attitudes of Americans have begun to change perceptibly, and the irrigation myth has lost some of its credibility. It is no longer so clear that the domination of nature it urged and celebrated carries any promise of mankind's moral redemption. On the contrary, such domination now seems to more and more people to be a source of great evil in this world. The drive for domination has been accused of subverting, not supporting, a democratic social order by creating elaborate hierarchies of greed, power, and expertise which dominate the masses of people. It has also come to be regarded as diametrically opposed to, and immensely dangerous to, any ethic of environmental stewardship. Such a drive must end, many fear, in the exploitation and degradation of the environment—the creation not of paradise but of a man-made wasteland.

Furthermore, the materialism that Arrington argues was pursued so avidly by the Great Basin pioneers has come to be understood more and more as the very antithesis of a genuine morality. Few among us confidently believe today, as our ancestors did, that producing more wealth of every kind is the highest way to serve God; indeed, that old materialism often looks nowadays like the quickest way to decadence and impiety. And as all those changes in thinking have occurred, the irrigation myth has lost much of its hold over people's imaginations.

Deep, complicated questions remain unresolved. If the story of desert conquest does not reflect our cultural ideals to the extent it once did, then what of the long Judeo-Christian religious and moral tradition that once supported it? Is it too losing its hold over our feelings and convictions? Do we still believe in that tradition as it once existed? And if not, do we have another one, a better religious and moral tradition, to put in its place? These are some of the hard questions a new generation of western and Mormon historians will have to address.

Critically examining some of the views held by historians thirty years back should not be confused with rejecting their example as scholars and engaged citizens. The lasting, and the inspiring, achievement of Leonard Arrington's book of 1958 was that it offered the public a challenging, and I would say a radical, analysis of western history. Indeed, it was far more radical than most of the historical writing we have seen since then. In view of the conformist temper of its times, it was the work of an independent, courageous mind. In its pages Arrington called his people back to the memory that they had once stood forth and opposed coercive American values. He recalled for them what their own native religious tradition had once been and told them of a past set of values they had forgotten. We may hope that a newer generation of historians will do as much.

10

Thinking Like a River

◆

WHEN we drive by a modern farm, we still expect to see green plants sprouting from the earth, bearing the promise of food or cooking oil or a cotton shirt. Pulling up one of those plants, we are still prepared to find dirt clinging to its roots. Even in this age of high-tech euphoria, agriculture remains essentially a matter of plants growing in the soil. But another element besides soil has always been a part of the farmer's life-water. Farming is not only growing crops on a piece of land, it is also growing crops in water. I don't mean a hydroponics lab. I mean that the farmer and his plants inescapably are participants in the natural cycle of water on this planet. Water is a more volatile, uncertain element than soil in the agricultural equation. Soil naturally stays there on the farm, unless poor management intervenes, whereas water is by nature forever on the move, falling from the clouds, soaking down to roots, running off in streams to the sea. We must farm rivers and the flow of water as well as fields and pastures if we are to continue to thrive. But it has never been easy to extract a living from something so mobile and elusive, so relentless and yet so vulnerable as water.

This essay was published earlier in the book, *Meeting the Expectations of the Land,* edited by Wes Jackson, Wendell Berry, and Bruce Colman (San Francisco: North Point Press, 1984).

If there is to be a long-term, sustainable agriculture in the United States or elsewhere, farmers must think and act in accord with the flow of water over, under, through, and beyond their farms. Preserving the fertility of the soil resource is critical to sustaining it, of course, but not more so than maintaining the quality of water. In many ways, the two ideals are one. And their failure is one, as when rain erodes the topsoil and creeks and rivers suffer.

But there are differences between those two resources, differences we must understand and respect. Unlike soil, water cannot be "built." It can be lost to the farmer, or it can be diverted, polluted, misused, or over-appropriated, but it can never be deepened or enhanced as soil can be. There is only so much of it circulating in nature, and then there is no more. A sustainable agriculture is one that accepts and works carefully within the firm limits of the water cycle. It is one that exercises restraint in the demands it makes on the cycle. It is farming as close as possible to the nature of water, flowing with the current rather than opposing or obstructing it, as the Taoist philosophers of China recommended a long while back.[1]

Throughout history, the water cycle has served humans as a model of the natural world. Early civilizations saw in it a figure of the basic pattern of life, the cycle of birth, death, and return to the source of being. More recently, science has added to that ancient religious metaphor a new perception: the movement of water in an unending, undiminished loop can stand as a model for understanding the entire economy of nature. Looking for a way to make the principles of ecology clear and vivid, Aldo Leopold suggested that nature is a "round river," like a stream flowing into itself, going round and round in an unceasing circuit, going through all the soils, the flora, and the fauna of earth.[2] Another scientist, Robert Curry, has argued that the watershed (the area the river drains, its body, as it were) is the most appropriate unit for thinking about and dealing with nature.[3] The watershed is a complex whole, uniting biota, geochemistry, and energy in a single, interdependent system, in a dynamically balanced set of countervailing forces-erosion and construction, productivity and grace. Each watershed has its own peculiar shape and its own way of moving toward an elegant equilibrium of forces. The language of these scientists may be novel, but the insight is old and familiar. In water we see all of nature reflected. And in our use of that water, that nature, we see much of our past and future mirrored.

The first commandment for living successfully in nature—living for the long term at the highest possible level of moral development—is to understand how that round river and its watershed work together and to adapt our behavior accordingly. Taking a purely economic attitude toward water, on the other hand, is the surest way to fail in that understanding. In a strictly economic appraisal, water becomes merely the commodity H_2O, bulked here as capital to invest some day, spent freely when the market is high. It comes to be seen as a "cash flow," no longer as the lifeblood of the land. And then we begin to do foolish things with our streams and rivers. We fail to see that the meanderings of a creek across a meadow exemplify not chaotic or wasted motion but a fundamental rationality, that those meanderings make sense. Government engineers, confident that they know better, straighten the creek with bulldozers so that it will carry off floodwater faster, and in the process they destroy all the wild riparian edges that express a rationality that is different from economics, one we have not yet fully understood. The elementary need in learning how to farm water effectively, Leopold would have said, is to stop thinking about the problem exclusively as economists and engineers and to begin learning the logic of the river.

The oldest river in the world in terms of sustained human use is the Nile. Any modern farmer or agricultural expert would be well advised to study the natural history of that usage from its earliest times (about 5000 B.C.) to the present.[4] It is a history with good and bad lessons: an extraordinarily long symbiosis between people and river, a recent set of cataclysmic environmental changes, a persistent tendency toward concentrated political power based on water management, a rich accumulation of river lore given to Egyptian life. Beginning in the time of the pharaoh Menes (about 3200 B.C.), the valley farmers constructed a series of ditches and dikes to direct the annual floods to their fields. For thousands of years thereafter, Mother Nile fed the Egyptians with undiminished abundance, as the water and silt from the floods enriched the narrow strip of green land that lies between the river and the desert. When the river was low for lack of highland rains, there were poor harvests and famines. Eventually the Egyptians learned how to store the surplus of barley and pulse from the better years in order to feed themselves in the leaner ones. It was not dumb luck that gave their agriculture a durability unmatched anywhere else; they respected the river, learned to use it without violating its order, and thereby achieved an advanced level of civilization.

The Egyptians developed a technically simple basin system of irrigation that had little adverse environmental impact and was manageable under most circumstances by the ordinary fellaheen in the villages. Even so, historical evidence indicates that now and then local management proved inadequate. Government experts thereupon entered the scene, and on the foundation of their more unified, sophisticated program of water control, Egypt created a powerful, despotic state, which exercised life-and-death authority over the masses. More intensive, centralized control over the river became a means for some men to dominate others, giving rise to what Karl Wittfogel has called a "hydraulic society."[5] Egypt is one of history's outstanding examples of that socioecological order in which a concentrated power structure emerges out of large-scale water engineering and coordinated irrigation.

In the early nineteenth century, Egypt was invaded by British and French armies, whose engineers sought, as agents of empires, to convert that country to Western-style agriculture. Egyptians could raise more crops, they argued, and sell them at a good profit in the world market-place, if dams and storage reservoirs were constructed along the river. Then began a long process of environmental transformation that, most recently, has led to the High Aswan Dam, a gargantuan chunk of concrete that has created Lake Nasser, one of the largest artificial bodies of water in the world. Now the silt that for so long fertilized Egypt's fields accumulates behind the dam. Downstream, new irrigation canals have stimulated an epidemic of snails, which carry the disease schistosomiasis into agricultural settlements, while the once productive delta fisheries are disappearing. In place of the old pharaonic hierarchy, the nation has substituted a powerful modern bureaucracy, which alone has the trained competence to design and maintain the hydraulic apparatus. What will be the life span of this new water regime? Not, assuredly, so long as that of the old one. Egypt has put economic calculation in the place of ecological rationality, short-run maximum production in the place of sustainability and the round river. The result may be a long-lasting decline of the Nile valley as an agricultural resource.

Americans have followed much the same course with rivers in our arid lands. Over the past century virtually every major western river has been dammed, diverted, and siphoned off to distant places, until the natural drainage of water has been obliterated over large parts. (A good many eastern rivers have also been altered, especially those under the Tennessee Valley Authority's administration.)

One of the more substantial achievements of that river control . . . has been the industrialization of American agriculture. Wherever intensive, large-scale irrigation has appeared, farming has quickly become a factory operation, mass producing for a mass-consuming market. Since at least the 1930s, the irrigated farms of the Southwest and the West Coast have led the nation in adopting the industrial mode, and they have forced farmers elsewhere to keep pace or drop out. Irrigation farming is expensive, requiring large amounts of capital investment; where there is no subsidy, only a small number of farmers can afford it. Once agriculture has started down that industrial road, it is not easy to stop: waterworks are followed by pesticides, chemical fertilizers, armies of stoop-and-pick laborers, and a high degree of mechanization.[6] The western river thus ends up becoming an assembly line, rolling unceasingly toward the goal of unlimited production. After basic human needs have been satisfied, there appears to be no deeply considered purpose justifying this production; water comes to have merely an international-trade value, abstracted from its natural milieu and made to serve the industrial imperative of growth as a self-justifying end. When we can "drink" no more irrigated oranges or corn or rice, world marketers tell us, we can sell our rivers (sell, that is, the products they water) to Japan or Germany. In that outcome is the final alienation of a people from their land and its stream of life—when both are sold to the uttermost parts of the planet for a mess of gadgets.

Alienation is an abstract, though completely real, outcome. Thirst is more concrete and measurable, and it is staring us in the face. The irrigated factory farms of the West are likely to drink the region dry. Irrigated crops currently use about one-half of this country's annual withdrawal of water.[7] But in western states with low rainfall that proportion is much higher: 80 or 90 percent. According to the U.S. Geological Survey, California withdrew in 1970 some thirty-three billion gallons of water per day for irrigation, or one-fourth of the national total, from surface and groundwater sources. Idaho was the second largest agricultural user, with a daily withdrawal of fifteen billion gallons; Texas came next, with ten billion gallons. Thirteen other states—all but one of them (Florida) located west of the Mississippi—used at least one billion gallons a day for irrigation.[8] In some places most of the water comes not directly from rivers but from long-accumulated underground deposits. Each year farmers pump from the Ogallala aquifer of the Great Plains more than the entire flow of the Colorado River. That resource, left over from Pleistocene times, once the largest natural storage system of its kind anywhere, now has a life expectancy of about forty years.[9] Irrigated farming, carried on in so grand a fashion, has become an extravagance this nation cannot afford and which many states cannot much longer sustain.

Even if there were enough water to last forever, in many cases there might not be enough energy to make it available. Modern irrigation involves the drastic reorganization of the hydrological cycle, and that task can succeed only with plenty of cheap energy. In the United States, it has taken an abundance of artificial energy to make our rivers move in unnatural ways, in ways that are less efficient in terms of their own dynamics.

For in nature, Robert Curry explains, a river constantly seeks the most energy-efficient path to the ocean.[10] Wherever an obstacle appears, the river goes to work to remove it or find another route. Put a dam across a canyon and the river there immediately gets busy at washing it away. Somewhere humans must find a ready source of energy to keep that river blocked, to force it out of its bed and over tablelands and floodplains, or to lift it across mountain ranges to run in city pipes. Exhaust or lose that external source of energy to apply against the river and humans lose the ability to overcome the natural laws of watershed energetics. They must then let the water flow where it finds the going easiest. That is the prospect we are now facing in our man-made water regime.

In the ancient Egyptian world, the energy for water manipulation came from corvées, immense legions of peasants drafted by the government to build and maintain works, impelled by the whip when they got tired. The modern approach has been to substitute fossil fuels for much of that sweat. We have celebrated the change with expansive rhetoric: "unlimited abundance" and "plenty of water and electricity at the throwing of a switch." But no one has yet told us precisely and comprehensively how much energy it has required to erect works like Hoover Dam, to keep them in repair, and to pump their stored water away, nor have we been told how that energy demand compares with the hydropower they generate.[11] James Bethal and Martin Massengale have calculated that irrigation pumping and distribution alone consume 13 percent of all energy used in American agriculture. In a state like Nebraska, where the center-pivot sprinklers spread underground water over round, checker-like cornfields, ten times as much fossil fuel goes into irrigation as goes into all nonfarm requirements.[12] The mounting cost of fuel today may put the farmer out of that enterprise long before his well runs dry. Water cannot run uphill unless there is enough money to push it. Only the foolhardy will state unequivocally that no new source of low-cost fuel will ever be found, but it will be a bigger fool who will tell us that such a breakthrough can come with no strings attached, no undesirable side effects, no need to confront ecological limits. So long as we do not think as rivers do, our irrigated agriculture will always be an exercise in the ultimate futility of trying to repeal the natural laws of flow.

The decreasing supplies of water and energy are only the most obvious threats to the American irrigation empire. Perhaps a more serious, long-range nemesis is the salt poisoning of arable land, which seems to be an inevitable consequence of desert irrigation.[13] This is the problem of soil and water quality degraded through overuse. In regions of scarce rainfall, the earth contains a large amount of unleached salts; pouring water onto fields there brings those salts to the surface and into the river system. Continual stream diversions lead inexorably to poisoning downstream, for as the irrigation water evaporates from reservoirs or transpires from rows of plants, it leaves a whitish residue of salt behind. This salinization put the Mesopotamian irrigators out of business thousands of years ago. Today more than one-third of the world's irrigated land has salt-pollution problems that diminish the productivity of the soil and, in extreme cases, ruin it forever. There is very serious salinization of farmland in California, Hawaii, along the Rio Grande, and throughout the Colorado River Basin. The Coachella Valley near Palm Springs must use much of its canal water not to water crops but to flush away salt left behind by earlier irrigation. The nearby Imperial Irrigation District has already spent millions to keep ahead of creeping salinity and now hopes that taxpayers will foot the bill to stave off this self-induced destruction. No matter who pays for the remedies, the only cure is more water consumption, more drains to get rid of excess water quickly, more energy and capital for desalting installations—a cure that becomes at some point even worse than the illness. Is it really worth the risk of irreversible poisoning of the land to keep agricultural exports high? To have lettuce in January?

The list of the environmental problems caused by western irrigation schemes has grown longer and longer in the science journals. Where a considerable amount of groundwater is pumped out, the land may subside and form a great concavity, destroying roads, houses, and bridges, and disrupting the surface life.[14] When a river ceases to bring fresh water to the ocean, disaster strikes the biologically rich estuaries along the coast. Wastes put into the diminished current upstream can no longer be adequately diluted; oxygen in the rivers consequently gets depleted. In streams that have been dammed, temperature changes occur, killing the native fish if oxygen depletion does not. And only recently we have begun to investigate the impact that widespread irrigation has on regional climate patters: irrigation water lost to evaporation, for example, may add significantly to the rainfall downwind.[15] In the face of such potentially destructive, always unpredictable possibilities, it has become clear that making "the desert blossom as the rose" is a far more complicated job than we once, in our juvenile innocence and self-assurance, believed.[16]

Now too we are beginning to admit what some critics have long claimed: that irrigation development in the American West has done much damage to a thriving agriculture and rural life in other regions. In congressional debate over the 1902 National Reclamation Act, eastern opponents protested that they were being taxed to create competition for themselves.[17] With a long sun-filled growing season, a national transportation network, and publicly subsidized water, irrigated farmers in the West did in fact come to enjoy a clear market advantage. Today the effects of the competition have been painstakingly studied and calculated; no longer can they be denied by western apologists. The Bureau of Reclamation's projects alone have replaced five to eighteen million cultivated acres elsewhere. The South, for instance, saw a sharp decline from 1944 to 1964 in cropland harvested—about one-third of its total. In the same period, western reclamation projects added more than 60 percent to their acreage, and much of it has been growing cotton the South once would have grown. Potatoes, wheat, feed grains, sugar beets, fruit, and vegetables have all shifted westward, too. If that were not enough, the federal government paid out in the same years as much as $179 million annually in crop-reduction payments to farmers on reclamation projects. What was added to cropland with one hand was taken away by the other, although in both cases eastern farmers did some of the paying, sending their tax money to the more arid region, then suffering from the low commodity prices brought about by the resulting overproduction, then shelling out reduction incentives.[18]

Even in the profit-maximizing terms of economists, there is little sense in American irrigation policy. It has made paupers of many living on the land, depleted farm communities, and sent the uprooted and defeated off to city unemployment offices. Those easterners leaving the farm have packed along in their suitcases a hard-acquired experience of working the earth. Someday when we need again a fund of practical experience to till eastern lands, much of it may have been lost. Instead of investing in the preservation of existing know-how at the eastern grassroots, we have poured billions of dollars into the conquest of desert rivers, into technological virtuosity, into powerful government bureaucracies and agribusinesses. The result is an agriculture seemingly immune to the vagaries of climate, but in reality highly fragile as all leviathan systems are.

The West provides the most glaring evidence of the economic confusion and ecological irrationality of American thinking about water. But in the rain-rich states, too, there is ample testimony that we have not learned to farm the hydrological flow with consistent insight and prudence. Why else are we losing more soil to erosion than ever before? With all of agronomic and biological science at our fingertips, with a collective wealth beyond anything previously experienced, we allow five tons of topsoil to wash away from an average acre on an average farm every year. In western Tennessee not far from the Mississippi River, where landowners have plowed up their hilly pastures to plant soybeans, the annual soil losses average 30 to 40 tons per acre, and some farms lose 150 tons. Tennessee farmers, in the words of the Des Moines farm journalist James Risser, "have been caught up in the runaway growth of an American food-production machine and an inflation spiral in prices and may be mortgaging the future for quick profits today."[19] Old Man River says to those men and women: Keep the earth covered or I will take it away. But they cannot hear that warning so long as the louder roaring in their ears says: Make money—pay for that new tractor—produce produce produce.

It is time we began to rethink our agricultural relation to water. The problems are so numerous and complex that a flurry of quick-fix solutions is no longer adequate. What is needed is a fundamentally new approach to the challenge of how to extract a farm living from the hydrological cycle, both in humid and in arid regions. That requires vision more than technique: a way of perceiving, a set of mental images, an ethic controlling agricultural policy and practice. It demands, as I have said before, learning to think like a river.

For a long while this country has been perfecting a strategy of comprehensive river planning. We have called this approach "conservation," though it has drastically remade rather than conserved what nature has given us. It has always been based on technological instead of ecological thinking; planners have defined their task as taking entire river systems apart, putting them back together in more "useful" arrangements, and delivering the goods wholesale to the farmer.[20] A more reasonable strategy would be to focus on the individual farm, asking what its particular needs are and how they can be met with the least possible interference with the water cycle. Start with the local and specific rather than the general and grand. Develop a well-considered set of ends for public water policy. Seek then to meet those ends with the most elegantly simple means of water use possible, means that are economical, appropriately scaled to place and need, and capable of enduring indefinitely.

No farmer needs to grow corn in the desert or to use the Colorado River to do so. He may be inclined to choose to raise corn because he grew up in Indiana where corn was the traditional crop and then took his habits west, or because a county agent has told him that the world price of corn will be soaring after harvest. But that is not an analysis of need; it is a selection of methods. What the farmer really needs is a comfortable living for himself and his family, along with a chance to use intelligence and initiative to gain a measure of satisfaction from his work. The American consumer needs something to eat—nutrition and taste on the table at a not outlandish price. Can those genuine needs be met without turning the Colorado or Snake River into an elaborate artificial plumbing system, plagued by mounting costs and environmental destruction at every joint and faucet? Of course they can, if we are willing to put our ingenuity to work inventing, disciplining, and adapting; they can be met, that is, if we will undertake a radical reconstruction of methods.

The first specific step toward a new water consciousness is to end all federal subsidies of irrigation projects in the West.[21] The subsidies should not be halted abruptly, but gradually, reversing with care and sensitivity the existing policy that has been in effect nearly a century now. Americans have no reason to fear such a change. The greatest portion of artificially watered acreage in the West raises crops that can be grown more cheaply elsewhere: 37 percent of all federal reclamation land, for example, is used for hay and forage; 21 percent for corn, barley, and wheat; 10 percent for cotton.[22] The United States will hardly starve if we do not subsidize those crops, for farmers in the East will raise them instead, and they can do so in ways far less disturbing ecologically. But since western farmers have long been induced by government incentives to move west and set up their irrigation plans, they should not be made to suffer by this policy reversal. What is needed is a new "homestead program," equivalent to the one devised in the mid-nineteenth century, that will encourage many western farmers to relocate in the more humid areas and learn the best practices for those places. For most of our national history we have assumed that to go forward was to go west. Now a sustainable agriculture requires a redirection of progress: Go east, young man or woman, and grow up with the country.

The West is now overpopulated, grossly exceeding its natural river capacity, and a new sense of water limits should stimulate the region's city residents as well as farmers to resettle eastward where they can be supported more easily. Those who remain, who constitute a permanent population in equilibrium with the environment, must have new water technologies that will enable them to survive, enjoy a modest prosperity, and grow some of their food close at hand. Unfortunately, almost no official thought has been devoted to alternative technologies that can provide for that population, although we know that at some point the great reservoirs will be filled with silt. It is time, perhaps past time, to begin the process of reinventing the West. The farsighted desert or plains farmer will start now to work out his own salvation, not wait for the planners, although he can use the advice of hydrologists, geneticists, and engineers. He will study the art of adaptive dry farming. He will demand some new crop varieties that can survive in places of little rain, and perhaps he will convince legislators to grant some aid to ease that changeover, much as they have subsidized home solar-energy conversions. With his neighbors, he will devise ways of diverting floodwaters without appropriating the entire river, ways of guaranteeing a minimum flow in the channel to support its ecology while making use of the river for crops. Where local markets require fresh fruits, vegetables, and milk, he will install drip irrigation, which uses far less water than furrow methods. Confronting the decline of fossil fuels, he will let the sun and gravity do most of the work of lifting and circulating water through his farm. These are a few of the ways in which agriculture can begin to adjust to an arid setting. Rather than insisting that drylands be made over into a version of Missouri, producing crops for which they are ill suited, we should begin imagining a future West that is finely tuned to its unique environment.

In more humid areas, farmers face the challenge of not letting a wealth of rain wash away their common sense and with it their soil. The first principle of good water management, it still bears repeating, is the maintenance of soil cover. In many places this means restoring the natural forest vegetation or planting the strong defense of a tree crop. In other places a thick sponge of grass will be enough to absorb the impact of falling water, slow its race to the sea, and keep the rivers clean and sweet. New perennial crops that make plowing unnecessary can cut erosion losses to natural replacement levels. Diminished use of pesticides and chemicals can reduce groundwater contamination. These familiar therapies are all parts of a larger vision: an agriculture in which every farm fits harmoniously within the dynamics of its own local watershed, rather than an agriculture in which every farm seeks to maximize its share of the money economy.

By now it should be evident that no market will ever pay farmers for accommodating themselves to their watershed. To be sure, the marketplace will reward long-range calculation more handsomely than many farmers are aware. But finally the marketplace is an institution that teaches self-advancement, private acquisition, and the domination of nature. Its way of thinking is incompatible with the round river. Ecological harmony is a nonmarket value that takes a collective will to achieve. It requires that farmers living along a stream cooperate to preserve it and to pass a fertile world down to another generation. It requires that urban consumers be willing to pay farmers to use good conservation techniques as well as to produce food. Without a public willingness to bid against market pressures, there will not be a radical reconstruction of farming methods or a rapprochement between agriculture and nature.

Americans, like people in other places and times, have a history of considerable violence toward the land and its life-giving rivers. Perhaps we have done more violence than most nations—certainly we have done more damage in a shorter period than most. Violence is typically a sporadic act, ill considered and destructive to the perpetrator as well as the victim; it is never the basis for permanence. What is now required in our agriculture, if it is to be secure, is a rejection of violence. Fortunately, we still can find in this country a broad enough margin of resources that we are not forced to violent land and water use; we can make other choices and avoid frantic, draconian measures.[23] We are in a position to think not only about self-preservation but also about generosity and peace—about ethics.

Almost forty years ago, Aldo Leopold wrote that we will never get along well with nature until we learn to regard it morally. We must develop, he maintained, a sense of belonging to the larger community of nature, a community that has many interests and claims besides our own. We must cultivate a moral sensitivity to that community's integrity and beauty. He spoke of the need for a "land ethic," including in it a moral responsiveness to all parts of the ecological whole.[24] But given the centrality of water in our lives, and given the magnitude of the problems we confront in farming our watersheds, it also makes sense to talk about a "water ethic." Water, after all, covers most of this planet's surface. Even more than land, water is the essence and the context of life, the sphere of our being and that of other creatures. It has a value that extends beyond the economic use we make of it on our farms. Preserving that value of water through a new American agriculture is an extension of ethics as well as of wisdom.

11

An End to Ecstasy

◆

BACK in the halcyon days of 1951, when the United States was entering its golden years of wealth and power and proclaiming that this was the American Century, there seemed no limit to what we could do with nature. Were some climates too hot? We could air-condition them. Were some too cold? We could thaw them out or raise tomatoes under glass. Were some too dry? We could, through hydraulic engineering, make them over into a veritable Eden of delights. In that year a *Time* magazine reporter traveled to the arid West to write about "the endless frontier" being won there by the engineers of the Bureau of Reclamation. They promised to develop enough water to redeem fifty million acres from aridity, enough acres to feed the equivalent of a whole new nation the size of France or Germany. And the engineers were not in the least reluctant to say what pleasure they got out of the work: "We enjoy pushing rivers around," they told the reporter. Whether the pushing had any real direction, any clear sense of ends, was secondary; they (and by extension, we Americans) were a people who enjoyed dominating nature and we would look for rationales later.[1]

In a spirit of what the magazine called "engineering ecstasy," almost every river in the western part of the country came under control and was made to raise alfalfa, fruit, and cotton. Our agricultural base shifted abruptly westward into the desert, and eastern and midwestern farmers suffered substantial damage to their fortunes. By the last agricultural census, the West counted over 45 million irrigated acres, producing one-fourth of the nation's annual farm market sales. Though it irrigated only a small percentage of that acreage, the Bureau of Reclamation was unexcelled among water pushers for ambition and scale. It was the Bureau that had erected some of the biggest dams ever: Hoover, Grand Coulee, Shasta, Glen Canyon, Teton, Navajo, Flaming Gorge, etc., the clearest, brightest expressions we had of our national drive to conquer the land. But the big dams were more than that. They were also part of our larger drive to conquer, not merely the surface of North America, but of the earth. To friends and foes alike, they said that we were a people who had risen, through destiny and virtue, to pre-eminent leadership over the entire planet, that we were now ready to push the world around.

There are still many Americans who believe in that dream of endless conquest, but they may no longer be the majority. Today, we are a people who often seem more confused, uncertain, and anxious than aggressive or designing. To be sure, our military budgets are larger than ever, our old hunger for higher and higher levels of affluence is still there, and, like people in every nation, we are still woefully ignorant about the ecological consequences of what we do. But as a society we are more uneasy than we once were about the desirability of pushing anything around, rivers included. Will it really pay, we wonder. Is there any site left that we can profitably dam? If so, what will be its true, as opposed to its officially announced, benefits and costs? Will I or my community get hurt in the pushing? In fact, we are reaching the point where we are embarrassed by any talk of domination, whether it be of nature or other peoples. In this respect the United States has changed dramatically since 1951.

Our new way of thinking is strongly manifested in the fate of water projects over the last decade or so. From 1976 to 1986 not a single major new one got past Congress. The reasons for that long hiatus are many. The liberals, who supported big dams since the days of Theodore Roosevelt and at no point more so than in the heyday of the New Deal, have become disillusioned with technology as a means of spreading the blessings of democracy. Radicals have successfully demonstrated that the projects have mainly benefited a small, privileged elite, allowing them to drink very cheaply at the public faucet. And now some of the neo-conservatives, in contrast to their predecessors who always voted for "development" while assailing "welfare," have discovered what has been true since early in the twentieth century: federal dams seldom meet the economic test of efficient return on capital invested. Then, adding to the clamor, there have been the environmentalists, newly risen to a measure of power, fighting each and every new dam proposal in courts, hearing rooms, and the media, fighting to preserve some remnant of what our wild rivers looked like before they were ravaged. Of late they have been winning more often than losing. For instance, in spring 1986, when the Garrison Diversion Unit in North Dakota was finally given the go-ahead after a protracted legal struggle, it had to be scaled back from 250,000 to 130,000 acres, and its backers had to accept a number of environmental safeguards that would have been unthinkable compromises in the old days. Similarly, in November 1986, when Congress at last broke its impasse and moved to fund 296 water projects, none of them was on the scale of Glen Canyon or Grand Coulee and all of them henceforth had to find matching funds from local sources, a requirement that likely will force many to be cancelled and others to be reduced considerably in size. These days, anyone seeking to build a new dam anywhere in the United States (or for that matter in most other nations) must anticipate a long, discouraging battle, rather like that involved in constructing a new nuclear power plant; he must be prepared for immense cost overruns and, when finished, must fend off potential saboteurs.

This change in the national culture has left employees in the Bureau of Reclamation feeling dispirited and frustrated. Once they had a mission—now it is gone. Their mission had been to "build the West," and when the building was done, when every river in the region had been dammed, and dammed several times over, the Bureau's main reason for existence disappeared. Unlike the other great federal agencies that have their roots in the West—the Forest Service, the Park Service, and the Bureau of Land Management—BuRec has never been a *stewardship* agency. It has never been given a piece of real estate to hold and nurture in perpetuity in the name of the American people. Undoubtedly, the stewardship agencies have at times done a poor job of fulfilling their responsibilities, but it is always possible to bring them back to their original purpose. The Bureau, on the other hand, has been essentially a *construction* agency, and from this point on it can only dwindle away. For a few more decades, it may have some useful work to do operating and maintaining its apparatus, distributing water into the ditches of local irrigation districts and selling power to urban consumers; but that job will require fewer staff and a much smaller budget than traditionally the Bureau has enjoyed. More dispiriting still, it faces the long-term prospect of fighting a losing war against the endemic weaknesses that plague any

and all large-scale irrigation infrastructures: namely, an irreversible salinization of soil and a buildup of silt deposits behind the dams, lowering
their capacity to store water and generate electricity.

A natural ecosystem like a forest has considerable regenerative
strength encoded in its genes. Though it can be destroyed by changes in
climate or by human abuse, it has a more reliable future than any man-
made technological achievement. It can evolve, adapt, and come back
from its degradation. So also can an agency like the Forest Service, which
depends on it. Reclamation, on the other hand, is only a temporary
achievement. It is a technological stunt that, as the experience of other
irrigation societies shows, cannot be indefinitely sustained. As the irrigation system approaches maximum efficiency, as rivers get moved
around with more and more thorough, consummate skill, the system
begins to grow increasingly vulnerable, subject to a thousand ills that
eventually bring about its decline. Despite all efforts to save the system,
it breaks down here, then there, then everywhere. Agents of that technology, like the Bureau of Reclamation, must endure a parallel fate.

Can the leopard change its spots? Can the Bureau transform itself
from an agency of construction into one of stewardship, whose function is
to safeguard in the public interest the long-term health, beauty, and
integrity of western watersheds? Surely, somebody ought to be put in that
role, and put there for the sake of eastern as well as western rivers. These
great national treasures are the most neglected, misused resources we
have; everybody wants a piece of them, wants to siphon them off, dump
wastes in them, drink from them, or move barges along them, but no one
has ever been given overall charge of protecting their renewability. Unfortunately, BuRec is not the ideal candidate for that mission. In order to
serve well in that new role, it would have to develop an entirely new mentality, learning to think (so to speak) as rivers do, learning the language
of nature rather than that of irrigators, and be willing to sacrifice some
economic uses in the interests of ecological well-being. That is surely too
great a transformation to expect of this agency.

A few years ago Arthur Morgan, in his book *Dams and Other Disasters,*
made much the same argument against the Army Corps of Engineers,
which was likewise facing, as it is now, a changed culture, a diminished
justification for its work, and mounting public criticism.[2] The Corps,
Morgan noted, was deeply and hopelessly embued with the West Point
Academy spirit of gearing up for war and no questions allowed. In an
actual wartime emergency it might be an indispensable tool for building
forts and landing fields quickly, but in peacetime it does not respond sen-
sitively to democratic processes. It was, and is, the wrong institution for

the work of developing and protecting America's riverways, coastlines, and estuaries. Similarly, the Bureau of Reclamation is an agency that cannot escape its origins. Restoring the Corps to the strictly military realm where it belongs, and phasing out the Bureau's presence in the West now that it has finished its mission, is the only practical strategy. Though neither goal will be politically easy to accomplish, they have behind them the movement of the country. Both agencies were formed for domination, and that purpose, we may hope and have reason to believe, belongs to the American past, not its future.

Reorganizing the nation's water agencies is a far more momentous issue than it may appear. More than we want to admit, our lives are lived within the framework of institutions and bureaucracies, tables of organization and assignments of responsibility. Like it or not, the state of the earth these days depends largely on those bureaucracies—depends on tens of thousands of government employees toiling away in anonymity; depends on their ethos, carefulness, and sense of purpose; depends on how those are determined for them by institutional history. Agencies may be created to pursue the ends of peace or those of war; they may help us accommodate ourselves to the land or conquer it. But they cannot do or be all things at once. When President Jimmy Carter and his Secretary of the Interior Cecil Andrus sought to replace the BuRec with a new agency called Water and Power Services, they were acknowledging the inertia of old identities and the need to transcend them. When in 1981 Secretary James Watt remanded their order and restored the Bureau's name, he too was acknowledging the strong legacy of the past, the legacy of domination, but trying to keep it alive. Though Watt's restoration has turned out to have been a Pyrrhic victory for the Bureau—its budget has continued to be cut severely—the old name endures. Until it disappears from Washington and Denver and Sacramento, the Bureau will continue to stand irremediably for a certain attitude toward the land and its surface waters.

In the past this nation created impressive instruments like the Bureau and the Corps to satisfy its drive for domination. Now it is faced with the task of creating altogether new instruments of government that can help harmonize its life with rivers.

But there is another significant issue that is emerging from the new political setting: What is to be the future of the American West as it enters a post-reclamation era? Can it learn to be content with the amount of water it has already developed? Can it adjust, farther down the road, to a shrinking supply? More fundamentally, can this region, so lately won from its wild state and still full of the spirit of conquest, learn the habits of negotiation and restraint?

There is enough water in the West for its future urban consumers, provided they act sensibly; and new technologies such as desalinization of the sea may in time modestly augment their supply. What the region cannot continue to do is support agriculture on so ambitious a scale. Presently, agriculture takes as much as 85 to 90 percent of the water supply in states west of the hundredth meridian, with most of that water going to raise supplementary feed for cattle and to irrigate staple grain and fiber crops, all of which are or could be grown elsewhere in the nation. Only a very little water is used to grow the specialty crops that have made the western farmer famous; according to the Bureau's statistics, a mere 17 percent of its water flows to vegetables, fruits, and nuts, and the portion flowing to winter-season lettuce or citrus fruits is only a minuscule part of that. Clearly, any opportunities for conserving water depend mainly on taking some land out of agricultural production.

Any such rollback is, of course, not a pleasant prospect in a society where farmers are widely regarded as God's chosen people and their territorial conquests are designated as "redeemed" ground. They are not by any means uniquely virtuous people, but they are a vulnerable group and therefore worthy of the nation's concern. In the coming days of water scarcity many western farmers will have heaped on them new burdens, and it will be the smaller operators among them who will be hardest hit. They will simply be unable to afford much water, while their larger agribusiness competitors stay on in the business, hiring their wetbacks as usual, poisoning them and the soil with lots of chemicals, wielding considerable power in the legislative chambers; and they will be joined by city industrialists who will be able to afford the high water prices too. Such a tragic outcome will be unavoidable when water comes to be treated as a commodity for sale to the highest bidder in the marketplace, which is precisely what is already happening in the region. To be sure, a more competitive market for water will bring some undeniable gains; it will enforce a degree of conservation, ending some waste and marginal uses; it may even save our last wild rivers from extinction. But all the same competition in the market will work to intensify existing hierarchies of wealth and influence, and the losers in that situation will be whatever genuine rural folk we have left in the West. Environmentalists may want to cheer some of those outcomes, but they should not cheer them all. Again and again in American experience, from the South and New England to the Dust Bowl of the Great Plains all the way to the Pacific coast, we have often won conservation and restoration victories through a strategy that has meant displacing from the land the weakest, and even the least harmful, among us. The West is poised today to repeat the old tragic story.

This talk of scaling back on water use should not be misunderstood: The arid part of the country, like the humid, is, for better or worse, going to have dams on its rivers for a long time to come, perhaps as long as people want to live on this continent. Dams will be maintained for purposes of flood protection, water supply, and agricultural production, at least until we can figure out some alternative form of technology. All that can be said at this time is that, having conquered most of our rivers, we are now beginning to wonder what comes next. We are aware, on the one hand, of the enormous damage that has been visited on them, the scenic and ecological losses that have occurred. An increasing number of Americans would like to see some rivers flowing wild and clean and free as they once did before the coming of the white man. On the other hand, we are aware that there are a quarter-billion of us residing in the country, all driven by great and growing thirsts both biological and cultural in origin, and that our rivers are expected to satisfy those thirsts without stint. We are aware of the contradictions, and we don't know how to resolve them easily.

12

The Shaky Ground of
Sustainable Development

◆

THE FIRST thing to know when starting to climb a hill is where the summit lies. The second is that there are no completely painless ways to get there. Failing to know those things may lead one up a deceptively easy path that never reaches the top but meanders off into a dead-end, frustrating the climber and wasting energy.

The currently popular slogan of "sustainable development" threatens to become such a road. Though appealing at first view, it appeals particularly to people who are disheartened by the long, arduous hike they see ahead of them or who don't really have a clear notion of what the principal goal of environmental politics ought to be. After much milling about in a confused, contentious mood, they have discovered what looks like a broad easy path where all kinds of people can walk along together, and they hurry toward it, unaware that it may be going in the wrong direction.

When contemporary environmentalism first emerged in the 1960s and '70s, and before its goals became obscured by political compromising and diffusion, the destination was more obvious and the route more clear. The goal was to save the living world around us, millions of species of plants and animals, including humans, from destruction by our technology, population, and appetites. The only way to do that, it was easy enough to see, was to think the radical thought that there must be limits to growth in three areas—limits to population, limits to technology, and limits to appetite and greed. Underlying that insight was a growing awareness that the progressive, secular, and materialist philosophy on which modern life rests, indeed on which Western civilization has rested for the past three hundred years, is deeply flawed and ultimately destructive to ourselves and the whole fabric of life on the planet. The only true, certain way to the environmental goal, therefore, was to challenge that philosophy at its foundation and find a new one based on material simplicity and spiritual richness—to find other ends to life than production and consumption.

I do not claim this conclusion was shared by everyone in those years who wore the label environmentalist, but it was obvious to the most thoughtful leaders of the movement that this was the road we had to take. But since it was so painfully difficult to make that turn, to go in a diametrically opposite direction from the way we had been going, many began looking for a less strenuous way. By the mid-1980s such an alternative had emerged, called "sustainable development." First it appeared in the *World Conservation Strategy* of the International Union for the Conservation of Nature (1980), then in the book *Building a Sustainable Society,* by Lester R. Brown of Worldwatch Institute (1981), then in another book *Gaia: An Atlas of Planet Management,* edited by Norman Meyers (1984), and then most influentially in the so-called Brundtland Report, *Our Common Future* (1987), directed by Gro Harlem Brundtland, Norwegian Prime Minister and chairwoman of the World Commission on Environment and Development. The appeal of this alternative lay in its international political acceptability among the rich and poor nations alike, in its potential for broad coalition among many contending parties. As Richard Sandbrook, executive vice-president of the International Institute for Environment and Development, explained: "It has not been too difficult to push the environment lobby of the North and the development lobby of the South together. And there is now in fact a blurring of the distinction between the two, so they are coming to have a common consensus around the theme of sustainable development."[1]

So: lots of lobbyists coming together, lots of blurring going on—inevitably, lots of shallow thinking resulting. The North and the South, we were told, could now make common cause on a new, more progressive environmentalism without much difficulty. The capitalist and the socialist, the scientist and the economist, the impoverished masses and the urban elites could now all happily march together on a straight and easy path, if they did not ask any potentially divisive questions about where they were going.

Like most popular slogans, sustainable development wears thin after a while, revealing a lack of any new core idea. Although it seems to have gained a wide acceptance, it has done so by sacrificing real substance. Worse yet, the slogan may turn out to be irredeemable for environmentalist use because it may inescapably lead us back to using a narrow economic language, to relying on production as the standard of judgment, and to following the progressive materialist world-view in approaching and utilizing the earth, all of which was precisely what environmentalism once sought to overthrow.

My own preference is for an environmentalism that talks about ethics and aesthetics rather than about resources and economics, that places priority on the survival of the living world of plants and animals regardless of their productive value, that cherishes what nature's priceless beauty can add to our deeper-than-economic well-being. I will return to that alternative later on, but first want to expose more fully the shaky ground of sustainable development. So far we have not had a probing analysis of this slogan, despite all those books and reports mentioned above. Although I myself cannot offer any full analysis of it here, I do want to draw attention to the important subject of language, the words we cobble together to capture our ideals, and particularly to ask what is implied in that magic word of consensus, "sustainability."

We have no full history of the word, but its origins appear to lie in the concept of "sustained-yield" that appeared in Germany during the late eighteenth and early nineteenth century. Germany depended in a most essential way on its forests for the wood needed to support its economy, and those forests were in a state of decline—shrinking with overuse, disappearing as the population increased. Fear of impending resource depletion, poverty, and social chaos prompted some citizens to find a solution based on the authority of science. They began talking (the exact date is still not clear) about *managing* the forests so that periodic harvests matched the rate of biological growth. Science could reveal that rate, they believed, thus indicating precisely how many trees could be taken without diminishing the forests themselves or undermining their long-term biological continuity. It was a hope based on a view of the natural world as a stable, enduring order, a view Newtonian in its roots, in which even the growth of a complex entity like a forest followed a steady, predictable cycle on a chart.

Science, according to this ideal of sustained-yield, could become the basis for a steady prosperity, a tool of economic growth, and could thereby lay the foundations for a lasting social order. Laws and regulations of harvest could be made scientific, and experts in the science of biological growth could become the architects of a more secure nation. Robert Lee has argued that Germany of the period was not yet the "stable, hierarchical, stratified and highly structured society" it later became but rather was still divided into competing religious persuasions, Protestant and Catholic, and had been devastated by a long era of war, rebellion, and many antisocial, private usurpations of resources. "Sustained-yield," he writes, "appears to have been a response to uncertainty and instability ... [It] was an instrument for ordering social and economic conditions."[2]

Americans like Bernhard Fernow (1851-1923), an immigrant from Germany, and Gifford Pinchot (1865-1946), the first Chief Forester in the Department of Agriculture, imported the sustained-yield theory of environmental management into the United States in the last two decades of the nineteenth century. Fernow was of Prussian extraction, trained in sustained-yield techniques in the Prussian Forest Academy at Munden, and a critic of the laissez-faire economy of his adopted home. The forest resource, he explained,

> is one which, under the active competition of private enterprise, is apt to deteriorate, and in its deterioration to affect other conditions of material existence unfavorably; ... the maintenance of continued supplies as well as of favorable conditions is possible only under the supervision of permanent institutions with whom present profit is not the only motive. It calls preeminently for the exercise of the providential functions of the state to counteract the destructive tendencies of private exploitation.[3]

German notions of the state as a necessary counterweight to the anarchic, short-term thinking of laissez-faire capitalism were a key part of the sustained-yield idea. Pinchot, who studied at the French Forest School in Nancy and examined model forests in France, Germany, and Switzerland, likewise believed the state, guided by technically trained professionals like himself, must take an active role in managing the nation's natural resources in order to secure a sustainable future. For both men, nature was little more than a utilitarian commodity to be managed and harvested for the common good. They had absorbed completely the dominant world-view of their era, which taught that the primary goal of social life is economic progress—steadily increasing production over the long term— adding only the corollary that such production must be directed by the state and its experts to avoid destroying the organic social order.

"Sustained development" is therefore not a new concept but has been around for at least two centuries; it is a product of the European Enlightenment, is at once progressive and conservative in its impulses, and reflects uncritically the modern faith in human intelligence's ability to manage nature. All that is new in the Brundtland Report and the other recent documents is that they have extended the idea *to the entire globe.* Now it is Planet Earth, not merely a beech forest, that is to be managed by trained minds, an eco-technocratic elite. Though never explicitly, the contemporary advocates of sustained development are pushing a political ideal as well as an environmental policy: one of more centralized authority that can manage disinterestedly the whole global ecosystem. Neither capitalistic corporations nor traditional folk communities can be trusted, they hint, to find unaided the sustainable path to the summit of universal affluence.

I cannot disagree that a world of aggressive nations and individuals grabbing resources for their own selfish enrichment, regardless of how others are faring, is bound to end in violence. And it will cause an ecological degradation that will finally bring everybody down. The multinational corporations are taking us that way fast, while the little folk villages of the past are dwindling away and seem powerless to stop the outcome. But can we really trust the state and its scientific experts to save us from this situation and show us how to manage successfully the global ecosystem, 8,000 miles in diameter, 500 million square miles in extent— show us how to make it yield greater and greater production, until everyone on earth enjoys a princely life, and all that without destroying its capacity for renewability? The ground on which this hope rests is suspicious terrain.

Sustainability, to begin with, is an idea that has never been really defined. Until we have a clearer consensus on it, we cannot know what is being promised or sought. Consider the matter of a time frame. Is a sustainable society one that endures for a decade, a human lifetime, or a thousand years? It is not enough merely to say "sustainable for a long time," or even "for the next generation," if we want to hand over more authority to the development experts. On the other hand, no one really expects sustainable to mean "forever"; that would be a utopian expectation that no society has ever achieved. If we cannot expect to achieve a *perfect* sustainability that lasts forever, what then can we hope for and work toward? What *degree* of sustainability should we settle on? No one, to my knowledge, has yet made a definitive answer.

Besides giving us no clear time frame, the ideal of sustainability presents us with a bewildering multiplicity of criteria, and we have to sort out which ones we want to emphasize before we can develop any specific program of action. Among the dozens of possible sets of criteria, three or four have dominated public discussion of late, each based on a separate body of expertise, and they share little common ground.[4]

The field of economics, for example, has its own peculiar notion of what sustainability means. Economists focus on the point where societies achieve a critical take-off into long-term, continuous growth, investment, and profit in a market economy. The United States, for instance, reached that point around 1850, and ever since has been growing endlessly, despite a few recessions and depressions. By that standard any and all of the industrial societies are already sustainable, while the backward agrarian ones are not.[5]

Students of medicine and public health, on the other hand, have a different notion of the word; sustainability for them is a condition of individual physiological wellness, a condition to be measured by physicians and nutritionists. Thus, they focus on threats of water and air pollution or on food and water availability, or they talk about the threat of diminished genetic stock to the practice of medicine and the supply of pharmaceuticals. Despite the existence of many such threats today, most health experts would admit that human health has made great strides over the past few centuries in every part of the earth. By their criteria, therefore, the human condition is far more sustainable today than it was in the past—a fact that explosive population growth and longer lifespans for most societies demonstrate. By the standard of physiological fitness people living in industrial societies are doing far better than our ancestors or our contemporaries in the nonindustrial societies.

Still another group of experts, the political and social scientists, speak of "sustainable institutions" and "sustainable societies," which apparently refer to the ability of institutions or ruling groups to generate enough public support to renew themselves and hold onto power.[6] Sustainable societies are then simply those that are able to reproduce their political or social institutions; whether the institutions are benign or evil, compassionate or unjust, does not enter into the discussion. By this reasoning, the communist regimes of eastern Europe and the Soviet Union have not proved to be sustainable and are being swept onto the ashheaps of history.

These are all leading, important uses of the word found among various fields of expertise, and undoubtedly they all can be given very sophisticated (and far more precise than I have indicated) measurements. In contrast to them, we also have some simpler, more popular notions of the word. One of the clearest, most pithy, and least arcane definitions comes

from Wendell Berry, the American writer and trenchant critic of all expertise. He called specifically for a more sustainable agriculture than we have
today, by which he meant an agriculture that "does not deplete soils or
people."[7] That phrase expresses, as so much of Berry's work does, an old-
fashioned agrarian way of thinking, steeped in the folk history and local
knowledge of his rural Kentucky neighbors. Like everything Berry writes,
it has a concise, elemental ring, and the great virtue of recalling to our
attention that people and the earth are interdependent, a fact that those
specialized academic approaches by economists and the rest generally
ignore.

In Berry's view the only truly sustainable societies have been small-
scale agrarian ones; no modern industrial society could qualify. His own
model, which is based on the livelihood and culture of the Jeffersonian
yeoman farmer, must be seen as part of the economic past; it has virtually
disappeared from modern American life. One might ask, as Berry's critics
regularly do, whether he is offering us more of a myth than a reality: Did
such non-depleting rural communities ever really exist in the United
States, or are they only idealizations or indulgences in a false nostalgia?
But even if we accept Berry's distinction between "sustainable agrarian"
and "unsustainable industrial," it is still not clear what the precondi-
tions for sustainability, or the measurement of its success, would be.
What meaning can we give to the idea of "people depletion"? Is it a demographic or a cultural idea? How much self-reliance or local community
production does it require, and how much market exchange does it allow?
For that matter, what is referred to in Berry's notion of soil depletion? Soil
scientists point out that the United States has lost, on average, half of its
topsoil since white European settlement began; but then many of them
go on to argue that such depletion is not a problem so long as we can substitute chemical fertilizers. Once more we are back in the muddle of whose
expertise, language, and values are to define sustainability. Berry would
answer, I suppose, that we should leave the definition to local people, but
national and international policy makers will want something more
objective than that.

All those definitions and criteria are floating around in the air today,
confusing our language and thinking, demanding far more of a consensus
of meaning before we can achieve any concerted program of environmental action. To be sure, there is a widespread implication in the literature
I have cited that sustainability is at bottom *an ecological concept:* the goal
of environmentalism should be to achieve "ecological sustainability."
What that means is it that the science of ecology is expected to cut
through all the confusion and define sustainability for us; it should point

out what practices are ecologically sustainable and which are not. Once again we are back in the business of looking for a set of expert, objective answers to guide policy. But how helpful really are those experts in ecology? Do they have a clear definition or set of criteria to offer? Do they even have a clear, coherent perception of nature to provide as a basis for international action?

Ecologists traditionally have approached nature as a series of overlapping but integrated biological systems, or ecosystems. In contrast to most economists, for whom nature is not a relevant category of analysis, they have insisted that those systems are not disorganized or useless but are self-organizing and productive of many material benefits that we need. The role of ecologists then, as we have generally come to understand it, is one of revealing to laymen how those ecosystems, or their modifications into agroecosystems, undergo stress from human demands and of helping us determine the critical point when that stress is so severe that they collapse.

If we accept that expert tutoring, the ecological idea of sustainability becomes, quite simply, another measure of production, rivaling that of the economists: a measure of productivity in the economy of nature where we find such commodities as soils, forests, and fisheries, and a measure of the capacity of that economy to rebound from stresses, avoid collapse, and maintain output. Unfortunately, compared with economists, the ecologists have lately become very uncertain about their own advice. Their indices of stress and collapse are in dispute, and their expertise is in disarray.

A few decades ago ecologists commonly believed that nature, when left free of human interference, eventually reaches a balance or equilibrium state where production is at a steady rate. The origins of this idea go back deep into the recesses of human memory, deep into the past of every civilization before the modern. For westerners in particular the idea of nature as a balanced order has ancient Greek, medieval Christian, and eighteenth-century rationalist antecedents, and it survived even the profound intellectual revolution wrought by Charles Darwin and the theory of evolution through natural selection. From the time of its emergence in the late nineteenth century the science of ecology echoed that long-standing faith in the essential orderliness of nature, and until recently almost all ecologists would have agreed that sustainability is a matter of accommodating the human economy to that constancy and orderliness. Now that is no longer the case.[8]

Beginning around 1970, ecology went off in search of new ways to describe forests, grasslands, oceans, and all the other biomes of the planet, and the outcome is the emergence today of a more permissive set of ideas that rejects virtually all notions of stability, equilibrium, balance, and order, new or ancient, and instead portrays a nature that is far more lenient toward human activity. We live in midst of a nature that has been undergoing profound and constant change for as far back as we can look, scientists now argue with the aid of new scientific techniques; we confront a nature populated by rugged individualists, eager opportunists, and self-seekers. There is no integrated community in that nature, no enduring system of relationships; no deep interdependence. To be sure, the sun seems to come up regularly every day and in predictable spots; the four seasons come and go with a great deal of regularity. But pay no attention to all that, they say; look at the populations of plants and animals that live in any given area that we might call wild, pristine, or natural, and you will find no regularity, no constancy, no order there at all.

Many of these ideas appear in a recent book entitled *Discordant Harmonies* (1990), which is self-described as "a new ecology for the 21st century." Here is how its author, Daniel Botkin, a leading California ecologist, sees the current situation in his science:

> Until the past few years, the predominant theories in ecology either presumed or had as a necessary consequence a very strict concept of a highly structured, ordered, and regulated, steady-state ecological system. Scientists know now that this view is wrong at local and regional levels ... that is, at the levels of population and ecosystems. Change now appears to be intrinsic and natural at many scales of time and space in the biosphere.

"Wherever we seek to find constancy" in nature, Botkin writes, "we discover change."[9]

The basis for this new ecology is a body of evidence that is essentially historical, including pollen samples, tree rings, and animal population cycles, all of which show the world of nature to be in a constant flux, as unstable as the human scene where wars, assassinations, invasions, depressions, and social turmoil of every sort constitute the only normal condition we know.

For example, one can observe the history of a small, old-growth forest in New Jersey that was preserved from real-estate development in the 1950s under the assumption that it was a surviving remnant of the mature climax forest, dominated by oaks and hickories, that once grew in the area. Scientists suppressed fire in the forest to keep it pristine and undisturbed. By the 1960s, however, they began to discover that maple trees were invading their preserve from the outside. If they suppressed all fires, if they tried to keep their forest "natural," they were bound to fail. What then, they had to ask themselves, was the state of equilibrium in this habitat? What could be called natural? What was the true order of nature?

Other evidence comes from pollen taken from pond and lake sediments all over North America, and indeed from all the major continents. They show that every area of the earth has experienced a wide variation in vegetation cover from year to year, from century to century, and from the glacial to the interglacial period. When the great ice sheets flowed over the North American continent, all the plants retreated south or into the lowlands—and it was not the orderly retreat of an organized, superorganismic community but a chaotic rout. Then when the glaciers retreated, leaving the land bare, the same plants made a ragged, chaotic invasion of their old ground. There was no organized return of whole communities.

Here is Botkin again:

> Nature undisturbed by human influence seems more like a symphony whose harmonies arise from variation and change over every interval of time. We see a landscape that is always in flux, changing over many scales of time and space, changing with individual births and deaths, local disruptions and recoveries, larger scale responses to climate from one glacial age to another, and to the slower alterations of soils, and yet larger variations between glacial ages.[10]

But Botkin later makes a very telling amendment to that statement when he adds that "nature's symphony" is more like several compositions being played at once in same hall, "each with its own pace and rhythm." And then he comes to what is really the practical upshot of his ecology for policy makers, environmentalists, and developers: "We are forced to choose among these [compositions], which we have barely begun to hear and understand." Or one might say that after learning to hear all those discordances of nature, we humans must also assume the role of conducting the music. If there is to be any order in nature, it is our responsibility to achieve it. If there is to be any harmony, we must overcome the apparent discord. "Nature in the 21st century," this scientist concludes, "will be a nature that we make." Such a conclusion is where Botkin's science has been leading him all along: to a rejection of nature as a norm or standard for human civilization and to an assertion of a human right and need to give order and shape to nature. We are arriving, he proclaims, at a new view of Earth "in which we are a part of a living and changing system whose changes we can accept, use, and control, to make the Earth a comfortable home, for each of us individually and for all of us collectively in our civilizations." I believe that this new turn toward revisionism and relativism in ecological science is motivated, in part, by a desire to be less disapproving of economic development than environmentalists were in the 1960s and '70s. Botkin criticizes that era for its radical, sometimes hostile, rejection of modern technology and progress. We need a science of ecology, he believes, that approaches development in a more "constructive and positive manner."[11]

Those conclusions constitute what I would call a new permissiveness in ecology—more permissive toward human desires than the the traditional, pre-1970 ecology was and emphatically more permissive than the ecological imagination found among environmentalists of the 1960s and '70s was. This new ecology makes human wants and desires the primary test of what should be done with the earth. It denies that there is to be found in nature, past or present, any standard for, or even much of a limitation on, those desires. Botkin hints at this denial in the beginning of his book when he criticizes the environmentalism of the sixties and seventies as "essentially a disapproving, and in this sense, negative movement, exposing the bad aspects of our civilization for our environment . . . ." What we must do, he argues, is move away from that critical environmentalism toward a stance "that combine[s] technology with our concern about our environment in a constructive and positive manner."

This new turn in ecology presents several difficulties that I do not think the sustainable development advocates have really acknowledged. In the first place, the whole idea of a normal "yield" or "output" from the natural economy becomes, if we follow Botkin's reasoning, far more ambiguous. Scientists once thought they could determine with relative ease the maximum sustained-yield that a forest or fishery could achieve. They had only to determine the steady-state population in the ecosystem and then calculate how many fish could be caught each year without affecting the stock. They could take off the interest without touching the fixed capital. Botkin argues that it was just such assurance that led to overfishing in the California sardine industry—and to the total collapse of that industry in the 1950s.[12]

But if the natural populations of fish and other organisms are in such continual flux that we cannot set maximum sustained-yield targets, could we instead set up a more flexible standard of "optimum yield," one that would allow a more generous margin for error and fluctuations? That is where most ecological sustainability thinking rests today. Harvest commodities from nature, but do so at a slightly reduced level to avoid overstressing a system in stochastic change. Call it the safe optimum notion. But that formula does not really address the more basic challenge implicit in recent ecological thinking. What can sustainable use, let alone sustainable development, mean in a natural world subject to so much disturbance and chaotic turbulence? Our powers of prediction, say ecologists, are far more limited than we imagined. Our understanding of what is normal in nature now seems to many to be arbitrary and partial.

The only real guidance Botkin gives us, and this is likewise true of most ecologists today, is that slow rates of change in ecosystems are "more natural," and therefore more desirable, than fast rates. "We must be wary," Botkin says, "when we engineer nature at an unnatural rate and in novel ways."[13] And that is all he really offers. But when we have to have more specific advice to manage this or that acre of land successfully, the ecologist is embarrassingly silent; he or she can hardly say anymore what is "unnatural" or what is "novel" in light of the incredibly changeable record of the earth's past.

In the much acclaimed partnership between the advocates of ecological sustainability and of development, who is going to lead whom? This is the all-important question to ask about the new path that so many want us to take. I fear that in that partnership it will be "development" that makes most of the decisions, and "sustainable" will come trotting along, smiling and genial, unable to assert any firm leadership, complaining only about the pace of travel. "You must slow down, my friend, you are going too fast for me. This is a nice road to progress, but we must go along at a more 'natural' speed."

In the absence of any clear idea of what a healthy nature is, or how threats to that collective biological whole might impinge on us, we will end up relying on utilitarian, economic, and anthropocentric definitions of sustainability. That's where, it seems to me, the discussion is right now. Sustainability is, by and large, an economic concept on which economists are clear and ecologists are muddled. If you find that outcome unacceptable, as I do, then you must try to change the elementary terms of the discussion.

I find the following deep flaws in the sustainable development ideal:

First, it is based on the view that the natural world exists primarily to serve the material demands of the human species. Nature is nothing more than a pool of "resources" to be exploited; it has no intrinsic meaning or value apart from the goods and services it furnishes people, rich or poor. The Bruntland Report makes this point clear on every page: the "our" in its title refers to people exclusively, and the only moral issue its raises is the need to share natural resources more equitably among our kind, among the present world population and among the generations to come. That is not by any means an unworthy goal, but it is not adequate to the challenge.

② Second, sustainable development, though it acknowledges some kind of limit on those material demands, depends on the assumption that we can easily determine the carrying capacity of local and regional ecosystems. Our knowledge is supposedly adequate to reveal the limits of nature and to exploit resources safely up to that level. In the face of new arguments suggesting how turbulent, complex, and unpredictable nature really is, that assumption seems highly optimistic. Furthermore, in light of the tendency of some leading ecologists to use such arguments to justify a more accommodating stance toward development, any heavy reliance on their ecological expertise seems doubly dangerous; they are experts who lack any agreement on what the limits are.

③ Third, the sustainability ideal rests on an uncritical, unexamined acceptance of the traditional world-view of progressive, secular materialism. It regards that world-view as completely benign so long as it can be made sustainable. The institutions associated with that world-view, including those of capitalism, socialism, and industrialism, also escape all criticism, all close scrutiny. We are led to believe that sustainability can be achieved with those institutions and their values intact.

Perhaps my objections can be fully answered by the advocates of the sustainable development idea. I suspect, however, that their response will, in the end, rest on the argument that the idea is the only politically acceptable kind of environmentalism we can expect at this point. It is desirable simply because it represents the politics of compromise.

Having been so critical toward this easy, sloganeering alternative, I feel obliged to conclude with a few ideas of my own about what a real solution for the global crisis will require. I grant that it will be more difficult to achieve, but would argue that it is more revolutionary in impact and more morally advanced.

We must make our first priority in dealing with the earth the careful and strict preservation of the billion-year-old heritage achieved by the evolution of plant and animal life. We must preserve all species, subspecies, varieties, communities, and ecosystems that we possibly can. We must not, through our actions, cause any more species to go extinct. To be sure, we cannot stop every death or extinction, since the death of living things is part of the inevitable workings of nature, but we can avoid adding to that fateful outcome. We can stop reversing the processes of evolution, as we are doing today. We can work to preserve as much genetic variety as possible. We can save endangered habitats and restore those needed to support that evolutionary heritage. We can and must do all this primarily because the living heritage of evolution has an intrinsic value that we have not created but only inherited and enjoyed. That heritage demands our respect, our sympathy, and our love.

Unquestionably, we have a right to use that heritage to improve our material condition, but only after taking, in every community, every nation, and every family, the strictest measures to preserve it from extinction and diminution.

To conserve that evolutionary heritage is to focus our attention on the long history of the struggle of life on this planet. In recent centuries we have had our eyes fixed almost exclusively on the future and the potential affluence it can offer our aspiring species. Now it is time to learn to look backward more of the time and, from an appreciation of that past, learn humility in the presence of an achievement that overshadows all our technology, all our wealth, all our ingenuity, and all our human aspirations.

To conserve that heritage is to put other values than economic ones first in our priorities: the value of natural beauty, the value of respectfulness in the presence of what we have not created, and above all the value of life itself, a phenomenon that even now, with all our intelligence, we cannot really explain.

To learn truly to cherish and conserve that heritage is the hardest road the human species can take. I don't even know, though I have plenty of doubts about, whether it is realistic at this point, given the state of affairs in global politics, to expect most nations to be ready or willing to take it. But I do know that it is the right path, while following the ambiguities, compromises, and smooth words of sustainable development may lead us into quicksand.

13

The Ecology of Order and Chaos

◆

THE SCIENCE of ecology has had a popular impact unlike that of any other academic field of research. Consider the extraordinary ubiquity of the word itself: it has appeared in the most everyday places and the most astonishing, on day-glo T-shirts, in corporate advertising, and on bridge abutments. It has changed the language of politics and philosophy—springing up in a number of countries are political groups that are self-identified as "Ecology Parties." Yet who ever proposed forming a political party named after comparative linguistics or advanced paleontology? On several continents we have a philosophical movement termed "Deep Ecology," but nowhere has anyone announced a movement for "Deep Entomology" or "Deep Polish Literature." Why has this funny little word, *ecology*, coined by an obscure nineteenth-century German scientist, acquired so powerful a cultural resonance, so widespread a following?

Behind the persistent enthusiasm for ecology, I believe, lies the hope that this science can offer a great deal more than a pile of data. It is supposed to offer a pathway to a kind of moral enlightenment that we can call, for the purposes of simplicity, "conservation." The expectation did not originate with the public but first appeared among eminent scientists within the field. For instance, in his 1935 book *Deserts on the March,* the noted University of Oklahoma, and later Yale, botanist Paul Sears urged Americans to take ecology seriously, promoting it in their universities and making it part of their governing process. "In Great Britain," he pointed out,

> the ecologists are being consulted at every step in planning the proper utilization of those parts of the Empire not yet settled, thus . . . ending the era of haphazard exploitation. There are hopeful, but all too few signs that our own national government realizes the part which ecology must play in a permanent program.[1]

Sears recommended that the United States hire a few thousand ecologists at the county level to advise citizens on questions of land use and thereby bring an end to environmental degradation; such a brigade, he thought, would put the whole nation on a biologically and economically sustainable basis.

In a 1947 addendum to his text, Sears added that ecologists, acting in the public interest, would instill in the American mind that "body of knowledge," that "point of view, which peculiarly implies all that is meant by conservation."[2] In other words, by the time of the 1930s and 40s, ecology was being hailed as a much needed guide to a future motivated by an ethic of conservation. And conservation for Sears meant restoring the biological order, maintaining the health of the land and thereby the well-being of the nation, pursuing by both moral and technical means a lasting equilibrium with nature.

While we have not taken to heart all of Sears's suggestions—have not yet put any ecologists on county payrolls, with an office next door to the tax collector and sheriff—we have taken a surprisingly long step in his direction. Every day in some part of the nation, an ecologist is at work writing an environmental impact report or monitoring a human disturbance of the landscape or testifying at a hearing.

Twelve years ago I published a history, going back to the eighteenth century, of this scientific discipline and its ideas about nature.[3] The conclusions in that book still strike me as being, on the whole, sensible and valid: that this science has come to be a major influence on our perception of nature in modern times; that its ideas, on the other hand, have been reflections of ourselves as much as objective apprehensions of nature; that scientific analysis cannot take the place of moral reasoning; that science, including the science of ecology, promotes, at least in some of its manifestations, a few of our darker ambitions toward nature and therefore itself needs to be morally examined and critiqued from time to time. Ecology, I argued, should never be taken as an all-wise, always trustworthy guide. We must be willing to challenge this authority, and indeed challenge the authority of science in general; not be quick to scorn or vilify or behead, but simply, now and then, to question.

During the period since my book was published, there has accumulated a considerable body of new thinking and new research in ecology. I mean to survey some of that recent thinking, contrasting it with its predecessors, and to raise a few of the same questions I did before. Part of my argument will be that Paul Sears would be astonished, and perhaps dismayed, to hear the kind of advice that ecological experts have got to give these days. Less and less do they offer, or even promise to offer, what he would consider to be a program of moral enlightenment: of "conservation" in the sense of a restored equilibrium between humans and nature.

There is a clear reason for that outcome, I will argue, and it has to do with drastic changes in the ideas that ecologists hold about the structure and function of the natural world. In Sears's day ecology was basically a study of equilibrium, harmony, and order; it had been so from its beginnings. Today, however, in many circles of scientific research, it has become a study of disturbance, disharmony, and chaos, and coincidentally or not, conservation is often not even a remote concern.

At the time *Deserts on the March* appeared in print, and through the time of its second and even third edition, the dominant name in the field of American ecology was that of Frederic L. Clements, who more than any other individual introduced scientific ecology into our national academic life. He called his approach "dynamic ecology," meaning it was concerned with change and evolution in the landscape. At its heart Clements's ecology dealt with the process of vegetational succession—the sequence of plant communities that appear on a piece of soil, newly made or disturbed, beginning with the first pioneer communities that invade and get a foothold.[4] Here is how I have defined the essence of the Clementsian paradigm:

> Change upon change became the inescapable principle of Clements's science. Yet he also insisted stubbornly and vigorously on the notion that the natural landscape must eventually reach a vaguely final climax stage. Nature's course, he contended, is not an aimless wandering to and fro but a steady flow toward stability that can be exactly plotted by the scientist.[5]

Most interestingly, Clements referred to that final climax stage as a "superorganism," implying that the assemblage of plants had achieved the close integration of parts, the self-organizing capability, of a single animal or plant. In some unique sense, it had become a live, coherent thing, not a mere collection of atomistic individuals, and exercised some control over the non-living world around it, as organisms do.

Until well after World War II Clements's climax theory dominated ecological thought in this country.[6] Pick up almost any textbook in the field written forty, or even thirty, years ago, and you will likely find mention of the climax. It was this theory that Paul Sears had studied and took to be the core lesson of ecology that his county ecologists should teach their fellow citizens: that nature tends toward a climax state and that, as far as practicable, they should learn to respect and preserve it. Sears wrote that the chief work of the scientist ought to be to show "the unbalance which man has produced on this continent" and to lead people back to some approximation of nature's original health and stability.[7]

But then, beginning in the 1940s, while Clements and his ideas were still in the ascendant, a few scientists began trying to speak a new vocabulary. Words like "energy flow" and "trophic levels" and "ecosystem" appeared in the leading journals, and they indicated a view of nature shaped more by physics than botany. Within another decade or two nature came to be widely seen as a flow of energy and nutrients through a physical or thermodynamic system. The early figures prominent in shaping this new view included C. Juday, Raymond Lindeman, and G. Evelyn Hutchinson. But perhaps its most influential exponent was Eugene P. Odum, hailing from North Carolina and Georgia, discovering in his southern saltwater marshes, tidal estuaries, and abandoned cotton fields the animating, pulsating force of the sun, the global flux of energy. In 1953 Odum published the first edition of his famous textbook, *The Fundamentals of Ecology*.[8] In 1966 he became president of the Ecological Society of America.

By now anyone in the United States who regularly reads a newspaper or magazine has come to know at least a few of Odum's ideas, for they furnish the main themes in our popular understanding of ecology, beginning with the sovereign idea of the ecosystem. Odum defined the ecosystem as "any unit that includes all of the organisms (i.e., the 'community') in a given area interacting with the physical environment so that a flow of energy leads to clearly defined trophic structure, biotic diversity, and material cycles (i.e., exchange of materials between living and nonliving parts) within the system."[9] The whole earth, he argued, is organized into an interlocking series of such "ecosystems," ranging in size from a small pond to so vast an expanse as the Brazilian rainforest.

What all those ecosystems have in common is a "strategy of development," a kind of game plan that gives nature an overall direction. That strategy is, in Odum's words, "directed toward achieving as large and diverse an organic structure as is possible within the limits set by the available energy input and the prevailing physical conditions of existence."[10] Every single ecosystem, he believed, is either moving toward or has already achieved that goal. It is a clear, coherent, and easily observable strategy; and it ends in the happy state of order.

Nature's strategy, Odum added, leads finally to a world of mutualism and cooperation among the organisms inhabiting an area. From an early stage of competing against one another, they evolve toward a more symbiotic relationship. They learn, as it were, to work together to control their surrounding environment, making it more and more suitable as a habitat, until at last they have the power to protect themselves from its stressful cycles of drought and flood, winter and summer, cold and heat. Odum called that point "homeostasis." To achieve it, the living components of an ecosystem must evolve a structure of interrelatedness and cooperation that can, to some extent, manage the physical world—manage it for maximum efficiency and mutual benefit.

homeostasis

I have described this set of ideas as a break from the past, but that is misleading. Odum may have used different terms than Clements, may even have had a radically different vision of nature at times; but he did not repudiate Clements's notion that nature moves toward order and harmony. In the place of the theory of the "climax" stage he put the theory of the "mature ecosystem." His nature may have appeared more as an automated factory than as a Clementsian super-organism, but like its predecessor it tends toward order.

The theory of the ecosystem presented a very clear set of standards as to what constituted order and disorder, which Odum set forth in the form of a "tabular model of ecological succession." When the ecosystem reaches its end point of homeostasis, his table shows, it expends less energy on increasing production and more on furnishing protection from external vicissitudes: that is, the biomass in an area reaches a steady level, neither increasing nor decreasing, and the emphasis in the system is on keeping it that way—on maintaining a kind of no-growth economy. Then the little, aggressive, weedy organisms common at an early stage in development (the r-selected species) give way to larger, steadier creatures (K-selected species), who may have less potential for fast growth and explosive reproduction but also better talents at surviving in dense settlements and keeping the place on an even keel.[11] At that point there is supposed to be more diversity in the community—i.e., a greater array of species. And there is less loss of nutrients to the outside; nitrogen, phosphorous, and calcium all stay in circulation within the ecosystem rather than leaking out. Those are some of the key indicators of ecological order, all of them susceptible to precise measurement. The suggestion was implicit but clear that if one interfered too much with nature's strategy of development, the effects might be costly: a serious loss of nutrients, a decline in species diversity, an end to biomass stability. In short, the ecosystem would be damaged.

The most likely source of that damage was no mystery to Odum: it was human beings trying to force up the production of useful commodities and stupidly risking the destruction of their life support system.

> Man has generally been preoccupied with obtaining as much "production" from the landscape as possible, by developing and maintaining early successional types of ecosystems, usually monocultures. But, of course, man does not live by food and fiber alone; he also needs a balanced CO_2-O_2 atmosphere, the climatic buffer provided by oceans and masses of vegetation, and clean (that is, unproductive) water for cultural and industrial uses. Many essential life-cycle resources, not to mention recreational and esthetic needs, are best provided man by the less "productive" landscapes. In other words, the landscape is not just a supply depot but is also the *oikos*—the home—in which we must live.[12]

Odum's view of nature as a series of balanced ecosystems, achieved or in the making, led him to take a strong stand in favor of preserving the landscape in as nearly natural a condition as possible. He suggested the need for substantial restraint on human activity—for environmental planning "on a rational and scientific basis." For him as for Paul Sears, ecology must be taught to the public and made the foundation of education, economics, and politics; America and other countries must be "ecologized."

Of course not every one who adopted the ecosystem approach to ecology ended up where Odum did. Quite the contrary, many found the ecosystem idea a wonderful instrument for promoting global technocracy. Experts familiar with the ecosystem and skilled in its manipulation, it was hoped in some quarters, could manage the entire planet for improved efficiency. "Governing" all of nature with the aid of rational science was the dream of these ecosystem technocrats.[13] But technocratic management was not the chief lesson, I believe, the public learned in Professor Odum's classroom; most came away devoted, as he was, to preserving large parts of nature in an unmanaged state and sure that they had been given a strong scientific rationale, as well as knowledge base, to do it. We must defend the world's endangered ecosystems, they insisted. We must safeguard the integrity of the Greater Yellowstone ecosystem, the Chesapeake Bay ecosystem, the Serengeti ecosystem. We must protect species diversity, biomass stability, and calcium recycling. We must make the world safe for K-species.[14]

That was the rallying cry of environmentalists and ecologists alike in the 1960s and early 1970s, when it seemed that the great coming struggle would be between what was left of pristine nature, delicately balanced in Odum's beautifully rational ecosystems, and a human race bent on mindless, greedy destruction. A decade or two later the situation has changed considerably. There are still environmental threats around, to be sure, and they are more dangerous than ever. The newspapers inform of us of continuing disasters like the massive 1989 oil spill in Alaska's Prince William Sound, and reporters persist in using words like "ecosystem" and "balance" and "fragility" in describing such disasters. So do many scientists, who continue to acknowledge their theoretical indebtedness to Odum. For instance, in a recent British poll, 447 ecologists out of 645 questioned ranked the "ecosystem" as one of the most important concepts their discipline has contributed to our understanding of the natural world; indeed, "ecosystem" ranked first on their list, drawing more votes than nineteen other leading concepts.[15] But all the same, and despite the persistence of environmental problems, Odum's ecosystem is no longer the main theme in research or teaching in the science. A survey of recent ecology textbooks shows that the concept is not even mentioned in one leading work and has a much diminished place in the others.[16]

Ecology is not the same as it was. A rather drastic change has been going on in this science of late: a radical shifting away from the thinking of Eugene Odum's generation, away from its assumptions of order and predictability, a shifting toward what we might call a new *ecology of chaos*.

In July 1973 the *Journal of the Arnold Arboretum* published an article by two scientists associated with the Massachusetts Audubon Society, William Drury and Ian Nisbet, and it challenged Odum's ecology fundamentally. The title of the article was simply "Succession," indicating that old subject of observed sequences in plant and animal associations. With both Frederic Clements and Eugene Odum, succession had been taken to be the straight and narrow road to equilibrium. Drury and Nisbet disagreed completely with that assumption. Their observations, drawn particularly from northeastern temperate forests, strongly suggested that the process of ecological succession does not lead anywhere. Change is without any determinable direction and goes on forever, never reaching a point of stability. They found no evidence of any progressive development in nature: no progressive increase over time in biomass stabilization, no progressive diversification of species, no progressive movement toward a greater cohesiveness in plant and animal communities, nor toward a greater success in regulating the environment. Indeed, they found none of the criteria Odum had posited for mature ecosystems. The forest, they insisted, no matter what its age, is nothing but an erratic, shifting mosaic of trees and other plants. In their words, "most of the phenomena of succession should be understood as resulting from the differential growth, differential survival, and perhaps differential dispersal of species adapted to grow at different points on stress gradients."[17] In other words, they could see lots of individual species, each doing its thing, but they could locate no emergent collectivity, nor any strategy to achieve one.

Prominent among their authorities supporting this view was the nearly forgotten name of Henry A. Gleason, a taxonomist who, in 1926, had challenged Frederic Clements and his organismic theory of the climax in an article entitled "The Individualistic Concept of the Plant Association." Gleason had argued that we live in a world of constant flux and impermanence, not one tending toward Clements's climaxes. There is no such thing, he argued, as balance or equilibrium or steady-state. Each and every plant association is nothing but a temporary gathering of strangers, a clustering of species unrelated to one another, here for a brief while today, on their way somewhere else tomorrow. "Each . . . species of plant is a law unto itself," he wrote.[18] We look for cooperation in nature and we find only competition. We look for organized wholes, and we can discover only loose atoms and fragments. We hope for order and discern only a mishmash of conjoining species, all seeking their own advantage in utter disregard of others.

Thanks in part to Drury and Nisbet, this "individualistic" view was reborn in the mid-1970s and, by the present decade, it had become the core idea of what some scientists hailed as a new, revolutionary paradigm in ecology. To promote it, they attacked the traditional notion of succession; for to reject that notion was to reject the larger idea that organic nature tends toward order. In 1977 two more biologists, Joseph Connell and Ralph Slatyer, continued the attack, denying the old claim that an invading community of pioneering species, the first stage in Clements's sequence, works to prepare the ground for its successors, like a group of Daniel Boones blazing the trail for civilization. The first comers, Connell and Slatyer maintained, manage in most cases to stake out their claims and successfully defend them; they do not give way to a later, superior group of colonists. Only when the pioneers die or are damaged by natural disturbances, thus releasing the resources they have monopolized, can latecomers find a foothold and get established.[19]

As this assault on the old thinking gathered momentum, the word "disturbance" began to appear more frequently in the scientific literature and be taken far more seriously. "Disturbance" was not a common subject in Odum's heyday, and it almost never appeared in combination with the adjective "natural." Now, however, it was as though scientists were out looking strenuously for signs of disturbance in nature—especially signs of disturbance that were not caused by humans—and they were finding them everywhere. By the present decade these new ecologists have succeeded in leaving little tranquility in primitive nature. Fire is one of the most common disturbances they have noted. So is wind, especially in the form of violent hurricanes and tornadoes. So are invading populations of microorganisms and pests and predators. And volcanic eruptions. And invading ice sheets of the Quaternary Period. And devastating droughts like that of the 1930s in the American West. Above all, it is these last sorts of disturbances, caused by the restlessness of climate, that the new generation of ecologists has emphasized. As one of the most influential of them, Professor Margaret Davis of the University of Minnesota, has written: "For the last 50 years or 500 or 1,000—as long as anyone would claim for 'ecological time'—there has never been an interval when temperature was in a steady state with symmetrical fluctuations about a mean. . . . Only on the longest time scale, 100,000 years, is there a tendency toward cyclical variation, and the cycles are asymmetrical, with a mean much different from today."[20]

One of the most provocative and impressive expressions of the new post-Odum ecology is a book of essays edited by S. T. A. Pickett and P. S. White, *The Ecology of Natural Disturbance and Patch Dynamics* (published in 1985). I submit it as symptomatic of much of the thinking going on today in the field. Though the final section of the book does deal with ecosystems, the word has lost much of its former meaning and implications. Two of the authors in fact open their contribution with a complaint that many scientists assume that "homogeneous ecosystems are a reality," when in truth "virtually all naturally occurring and man-disturbed ecosystems are mosaics of environmental conditions." "Historically," they write, "ecologists have been slow to recognize the importance of disturbances and the heterogeneity they generate." The reason for this slowness? "The majority of both theoretical and empirical work has been dominated by an equilibrium perspective."[21] Repudiating that perspective, these authors take us to the tropical forests of South and Central America and to the Everglades of Florida, showing us instability on every hand: a wet, green world of continual disturbance—or as they prefer to say, "of perturbations." Even the grasslands of North America, which inspired Frederic Clements's theory of the climax, appear in this collection as regularly disturbed environments. One paper describes them as a "dynamic, fine-textured mosaic" that is constantly kept in upheaval by the workings of badgers, pocket gophers, and mound-building ants, along with fire, drought, and eroding wind and water.[22] The message in all these papers is consistent: the climax notion is dead, the ecosystem has receded in usefulness, and in their place we have the idea of the lowly "patch." Nature should be regarded as a landscape of patches, big and little, patches of all textures and colors, a patchwork quilt of living things, changing continually through time and space, responding to an unceasing barrage of perturbations. The stitches in that quilt never hold for long.

Now, of course, scientists have known about gophers and winds and the Ice Age and droughts for a considerable time. Yet heretofore they have not let those disruptions spoil their theories of balanced plant and animal associations, and we must ask why that was so. Why did Clements and Odum tend to dismiss such forces as climatic change, at least of the less catastrophic sort, as threats to the order of nature? Why have their successors, on the other hand, tended to put so much emphasis on those same changes, to the point that they often see nothing but instability in the landscape?

One clue comes from the fact that many of these disturbance boosters are not and have never been ecosystem scientists; they received their training in the subfield of population biology and reflect the growing confidence, methodical maturity, and influence of that subfield.[23] When they look at a forest, the population ecologists see only the trees: see them and count them—so many white pines, so many hemlocks, so many maples and birches. They insist that if we know all there is to know about the individual species that constitute a forest, and can measure their lives in precise, quantitative terms, we will know all there is to know about that forest. It has no "emergent" or organismic properties. It is not some whole greater than the sum of its parts, requiring "holistic" understanding. Outfitted with computers that can track the life histories of individual species, chart the rise and fall of populations, they have brought a degree of mathematical precision to ecology that is awesome to contemplate. And what they see when they look at population histories for any patch of land is wildly swinging oscillations. Populations rise and populations fall, like stock market prices, auto sales, and hemlines. We live, they insist, in a non-equilibrium world.[24]

There is another reason for the paradigmatic shift I have been describing, though I suggest it quite tentatively and can offer only sketchy evidence for it. For some scientists, a nature characterized by highly individualistic associations, constant disturbance, and incessant change may be more ideologically satisfying than Odum's ecosystem, with its stress on cooperation, social organization, and environmentalism. A case in point is the very successful popularizer of contemporary ecology, Paul Colinvaux, author of *Why Big Fierce Animals Are Rare* (1978). His chapter on succession begins with these lines: "If the planners really get hold of us so that they can stamp out all individual liberty and do what they like with our land, they might decide that whole counties full of inferior farms should be put back into forest." Clearly, he is not enthusiastic about land-use planning or forest restoration. And he ends that same chapter with these remarkably revealing and self-assured words:

> We can now . . . explain all the intriguing, predictable events of plant successions in simple, matter of fact, Darwinian ways. Everything that happens in successions comes about because all the different species go about earning their livings as best they may, each in its own individual manner. What look like community properties are in fact the summed results of all these bits of private enterprise.[25]

Apparently, if this example is any indication, the Social Darwinists are back on the scene, and at least some of them are ecologists, and at least some of their opposition to Odum's science may have to do with a revulsion toward what they perceive are its political implications, including its attractiveness for environmentalists. Colinvaux is very clear about the need to get some distance between himself and groups like the Sierra Club.

I am not alone in wondering whether there might be a deeper, half-articulated ideological motive generating the new direction in ecology. The Swedish historian of science Thomas Söderqvist, in his recent study of ecology's development in his country, concludes that the present generation of evolutionary ecologists

> seem to do ecology for fun only, indifferent to practical problems, including the salvation of the nation. They are mathematically and theoretically sophisticated, sitting indoors calculating on computers, rather than traveling out in the wilds. They are individualists, abhorring the idea of large-scale ecosystem projects. Indeed, the transition from ecosystem ecology to evolutionary ecology seems to reflect the generational transition from the politically consciousness generation of the 1960s to the "yuppie" generation of the 1980s.[26]

That may be an exaggerated characterization, and I would not want to apply it to every scientist who has published on patch dynamics or disturbance regimes. But it does draw our attention to an unmistakable attempt by many ecologists to disassociate themselves from reform environmentalism and its criticisms of human impact on nature.

I wish, however, that the emergence of the new post-Odum ecology could be explained so simply in those two ways: as a triumph of reductive population dynamics over holistic consciousness, or as a triumph of Social Darwinist or entrepreneurial ideology over a commitment to environmental preservation. There is, it seems, more going on than that, and it is going on all through the natural sciences—biology, astronomy, physics—perhaps going on through all modern technological societies. It is nothing less than the discovery of chaos. Nature, many have begun to believe, is *fundamentally* erratic, discontinuous, and unpredictable. It is full of seemingly random events that elude our models of how things are supposed to work. As a result, the unexpected keeps hitting us in the face. Clouds collect and disperse, rain falls or doesn't fall, disregarding our careful weather predictions, and we cannot explain why. Cars suddenly bunch up on the freeway, and the traffic controllers fly into a frenzy. A man's heart beats regularly year after year, then abruptly begins to skip a beat now and then. A ping pong ball bounces off the table in an unexpected direction. Each little snowflake falling out of the sky turns out to be completely unlike any other. These are ways in which nature seems, by all our previous theories and methods, to be chaotic. If the ultimate test of any body of scientific knowledge is its ability to predict events, then all the sciences and pseudo-sciences—physics, chemistry, climatology, economics, ecology—fail the test regularly. They all have been announcing laws, designing models, predicting what an individual atom or person is supposed to do; and now, increasingly, they are beginning to confess that the world never quite behaves the way it is supposed to do.

Making sense of this situation is the task of an altogether new kind of inquiry calling itself the science of chaos. Some say it portends a revolution in thinking equivalent to quantum mechanics or relativity. Like those other twentieth-century revolutions, the science of chaos rejects tenets going back as far as the days of Sir Isaac Newton. In fact, what is occurring may be not two or three separate revolutions but a single revolution against all the principles, laws, models, and applications of classical science, the science ushered in by the great Scientific Revolution of the seventeenth century.[27] For centuries we have assumed that nature, despite a few appearances to the contrary, is a perfectly predictable system of linear, rational order. Give us an adequate number of facts, scientists have said, and we can describe that order in complete detail—can plot the lines along which everything moves and the speed of that movement and the collisions that will occur. Even Darwin's theory of evolution, which in the last century challenged much of the Newtonian worldview, left intact many people's confidence that order would prevail at last in the evolution of life; that out of the tangled history of competitive struggle would come progress, harmony, and stability. Now that traditional assumption may have broken down irretrievably. For whatever reason, whether because empirical data suggest it or because extrascientific cultural trends do, the experience of so much rapid social change in our daily lives, scientists are beginning to focus on what they had long managed to avoid seeing. The world is more complex than we ever imagined, they say, and indeed, some would add, ever can imagine.[28]

Despite the obvious complexity of their subject matter, ecologists have been among the slowest to join the cross-disciplinary science of chaos. I suspect that the influence of Clements and Odum, lingering well into the 1970s, worked against the new perspective, encouraging faith in linear regularities and equilibrium in the interaction of species. Nonetheless, eventually there arrived a day of conversion. In 1974 the Princeton mathematical ecologist Robert May published a paper with the title "Biological Populations with Nonoverlapping Generations: Stable Points, Stable Cycles, and Chaos."[29] In it he admitted that the mathematical models he and others had constructed were inadequate approximations of the ragged life histories of organisms. They did not fully explain, for example, the aperiodic outbreaks of gypsy moths in eastern hardwood forests or the Canadian lynx cycles in the subarctic. Wildlife populations do not follow some simple Malthusian pattern of increase, saturation, and crash.

More and more ecologists have followed May and begun to try to bring their subject into line with chaotic theory. William Schaefer is one of them; though a student of Robert MacArthur, a leader of the old equilibrium school, he has been lately struck by the same anomaly of unpredictable fluctuations in populations as May and others. Though taught to believe in "the so-called 'Balance of Nature'," he writes, ". . . the idea that populations are at or close to equilibrium," things now are beginning to look very different.[30] He describes himself has having to reach far across the disciplines, to make connections with concepts of chaos in the other natural sciences, in order to free himself from his field's restrictive past.

The entire study of chaos began in 1961, with efforts to simulate weather and climate patterns on a computer at MIT. There, meteorologist Edward Lorenz came up with his now famous "Butterfly Effect," the notion that a butterfly stirring the air today in a Beijing park can transform storm systems next month in New York City. Scientists call this phenomenon "sensitive dependence on initial conditions." What it means is that tiny differences in input can quickly become substantial differences in output. A corollary is that we cannot know, even with all our artificial intelligence apparatus, every one of the tiny differences that have occurred or are occurring at any place or point in time; nor can we know which tiny differences will produce which substantial differences in output. Beyond a short range, say, of two or three days from now, our predictions are not worth the paper they are written on.

The implications of this "Butterfly Effect" for ecology are profound. If a single flap of an insect's wings in China can lead to a torrential downpour in New York, then what might it do to the Greater Yellowstone Ecosystem? What can ecologists possibly know about all the forces impinging on, or about to impinge on, any piece of land? What can they safely ignore and what must they pay attention to? What distant, invisible, minuscule events may even now be happening that will change the organization of plant and animal life in our back yards? This is the predicament, and the challenge, presented by the science of chaos, and it is altering the imagination of ecologists dramatically.

John Muir once declared, "When we try to pick out anything by itself, we find it hitched to everything else in the universe."[31] For him, that was a manifestation of an infinitely wise plan in which everything functioned with perfect harmony. The new ecology of chaos, though impressed like Muir with interdependency, does not share his view of "an infinitely wise plan" that controls and shapes everything into order. There is no plan, today's scientists say, no harmony apparent in the events of nature. If there is order in the universe—and there will no longer be any science at all if all faith in order vanishes—it is going to be much more difficult to locate and describe than we thought.

For Muir, the clear lesson of cosmic complexity was that humans ought to love and preserve nature just as it is. The lessons of the new ecology, in contrast, are not at all clear. Does it promote, in Ilya Prigogine and Isabelle Stenger's words, "a renewal of nature," a less hierarchical view of life, and a set of "new relations between man and nature and between man and man"?[32] Or does it increase our alienation from the world, our withdrawal into post-modernist doubt and self-consciousness? What is there to love or preserve in a universe of chaos? How are people supposed to behave in such a universe? If that is the kind of place we inhabit, why not go ahead with all our private ambitions, free of any fear that we may be doing special damage? What, after all, does the phrase "environmental damage" mean in a world of so much natural chaos? Does the tradition of environmentalism to which Muir belonged, along with so many other nature writers and ecologists of the past, people like Paul Sears, Eugene Odum, Aldo Leopold, and Rachel Carson, make sense any longer? I have no space here to attempt to answer those questions, or to make predictions, but only a warning that they are too important to be left for scientists alone to answer. Ecology cannot today, no more than in the past, be assumed to be all-knowing or all-wise or eternally true.

Whether they are true or false, permanent or passingly fashionable, it does seem entirely possible that these changes in scientific thinking toward an emphasis on chaos will not produce any easing of the environmentalist's concern. Though words like ecosystem or climax may fade away, and some new vocabulary take their place, the fear of risk and danger will likely become greater than ever. Most of us are intuitively aware, whether we can put our fears into mathematical formulae or not, that the technological power we have accumulated is *destructively* chaotic; not irrationally, we fear it and fear what it can do to us as well as the rest of nature.[33] It may be that we moderns, after absorbing the lessons of today's science, find we cannot love nature quite so easily as Muir did; but it may also be that we have discovered more reason than ever to respect it—to respect its baffling complexity, its inherent unpredictability, its daily turbulence. And to flap our own wings in it a little more gently.

14

Restoring a
Natural Order

◆

A FEW years ago I came down a backcountry road in Wisconsin looking for a place where a man had given his life. The road had once been the route of pioneers moving west, then a farm road running through dry, sandy, marginal fields. In the days of Prohibition it had carried illegal whiskey distilled hereabouts, some of the last trees having been cut down to cook the bootlegger's brew. Then in 1935 another sort of settler came along. It was the time of the Great Depression, and he could buy a lot of land, 120 acres in all, land abandoned by its owners, for a little money in back taxes. The land had no economic value left in it. The man, whose name was Aldo Leopold, knew that but did not mind; he was not after gain or even subsistence. He began coming out regularly from the city of Madison, where he taught at the university, to plant trees. For thirteen years he planted and nurtured. Then, in 1948, he died fighting a forest fire on a neighbor's land. Knowing those few details, I came wanting to know what manner of man he was and what he had died for.

There was no publicity, no tour guide provided, but the dense forest of pines was a sufficient announcement that here was Leopold's place, now all grown up again to natural splendor. I walked through an open field rich in wild grasses and forbs to a small, gray, weathered shack where he had stayed on those weekends, regaled by the smell of his new pines coming up and the sound of birdsong and wind in their branches. From the shack, I found my way down a short path to the Wisconsin River, rolling silently between its pungent banks, the warm summer sun glinting on its ripples. One August years ago Leopold, as recalled in a sketch he wrote and collected in *A Sand County Almanac,* found the river "in a painting mood," laying down a brief carpet of moss on its silty edges, spangling it with blue and white and pink flowers, attracting deer and meadow mice, then abruptly scouring its palette down to austere sand. For me, that painting had long disappeared but not the memory of it, which had been lastingly captured in the words of the man who had seen it, and who, in its presence, must have stood for a breathless moment or two, intensely sure that he had nature on his side. The land, he realized, could come back from its degradation. It had an inexhaustible capacity to create harmony and grace out of the most ordinary, valueless materials, even out of silt, minute spores, and the trackings of herons along a bar. And no matter how abused its history had been, it could regenerate itself. In the thirties, a time of national despair brought on by severe economic and ecological collapse, that must have been a reassuring fact to discover. Today, it is still a needed fact. And Leopold's homeplace is where the world can come to see demonstrated those processes of natural regeneration, aided by human commitment and intelligence. There is, after all, a way back to the Garden.

I am increasingly an admirer of Leopold's wisdom and, though aware of the need for collective effort, find the most hopeful message in his intensely private, unaffected dedication to a humble dream. He did not turn the job of restoration over to someone who had more money or authority or free time. Though a busy professional, active in research and teaching, with another home and a family in the city to care for, he put his own shovel and his own back to work rehabilitating his piece of land.

Leopold does not appear at any point to have had the notion that what he was doing on those cutover, depleted acres was building an investment for himself or others, that one day the property would again be worth something on the market for lumber or recreation. Though trained in the modern school of natural resource management—he was a game specialist in his other life—he was not here to "manage" the wildlife or forests or water, at least not as profitable commodities that we manipulate for our own instrumental ends. What brought him out on weekends was, first, a desire to know the place intimately and, then, to apply his knowledge and love toward its healing. He came as a kind of doctor, a "country doctor"

[handwritten margin note top: moral commitment toward nature]

we might say, who had found an ailing, neglected patient who could use his care. In accepting moral responsibility for the patient, he disregarded all chance of remuneration except for whatever satisfaction he could get simply in watching the recovery progress.

Alternatively, though it comes to the same thing, we could say that he came as an artist and, finding damage done to a thing of beauty, he felt an urge to bring back its glory. Health for him was beauty, and beauty was health. Leopold had the kind of aesthetic temperament that seeks not to find an outlet for its own subjective impulses, but to learn what there is of wonder in the world, latent or achieved, and to become its appreciator, its caretaker, accepting that beauty has an objective existence outside oneself, that beauty is a quality that can be discovered as well as invented. No one who had settled Leopold's place before him had paid much attention to its aesthetic qualities; perhaps, given the pressures of survival, they could not. They saw only the surface of things. "The incredible intricacies of the plant and animal community," he wrote, "the intrinsic beauty of the organism called America," had disappeared under the heavy tread of settlement without much thought or perception.

What draws visitors like myself to Leopold's wild, blooming garden today is a shared belief that the world of nature constitutes a pattern of order which we are bound to respect and care for, perhaps even risk our lives to save.

I don't know where the idea of such an order originates. Probably it has been there in the human mind all along, like the ability to count and make things and raise children. Certainly the earliest cultures, pagan and animistic, had a strong, lively view of it. So too, though with varying degrees of commitment, have such modern religious traditions as Judaism, Christianity, Taoism, and Hinduism. Christians, for example, sometimes speak rapturously of the "Creation," having in mind some ordered arrangement of natural things that is at once rational and beyond comprehension. Its harmony is functional but not narrowly utilitarian for them. It demands that they admire as well as use it. Christians along with Jews go on to insist that there must be someone who contrives that beauty out of the void and constantly holds it intact in time and space. The heavens declare the glory of God, they say with the Psalmist, and the earth shows His handiwork. But surely the power conjured up as explanation came later, the awareness of beauty in the world was there first. The Taoists of China, in contrast, believe that the order of nature has not been contrived by any outside force but inheres in nature itself—that there is a Way, and all things move together harmoniously in it and under their own power. Whatever these differences in concept, every religionist can

[handwritten margin note right: Wonder believe in natural order — but we have moral obligation toward it]

agree that, because there is luminous beauty in the world, there is some obligation on the part of humans to respect it, Although we did not design or organize that order, we are capable of being, and therefore are obliged to be, its stewards and guardians. That is one of the fundamental truths that men and women of many faiths have held to be self-evident.

I grew up believing that religion had a permanent enemy in science, that the victory of one must mean the defeat of the other. It still seems clear that religion has lost considerable ground in modern times to science as a source of authority. But how astonishing to realize that science, whatever its competitive effect on any particular creed, itself emerged originally out of an awareness of natural beauty that was very like that in religion. Take away the assumption that the world is an orderly whole whose parts all work together toward a self-regulated stability, that there is an arrangement and coherence to things that can be understood, and science would cease to exist. I now see that science, and every branch of it, had to begin with some holistic ideal. It is a bedrock assumption. And quite possibly, like its religious analogue, it cannot be proven once and for all by appealing to facts or texts, but instead is derived from some deeper process of insight—from an intuition that comes to almost everyone living in close, observing relationship with nature. Scientists commonly do so; it is not surprising, therefore, to find that many of them have spoken with awe and delight about the exquisite order they find in the world.

Beginning with Charles Darwin and his theory of evolution, ecologists have insisted that nature is not to be understood as a fixed or permanent order but is constantly undergoing change, much of it violent and destructive. Did that understanding destroy the age-old confidence in natural coherence? For a long while it did not. Darwin, for example, did not let the new way of seeing shake his conviction that nature manages to contrive a remarkable degree of order, that despite all the ragged opportunism of individual organisms striving for success, all the catastrophic upheavals of geology and climate, all the evidences of imperfect adaptation, there is still a pattern to be found in the sum of things. Wherever he looked, even in the most tumultuous settings, he discerned a condition of beauty, though it was more the beauty of process than of fixed relationships. Nature in his view remained a system tending toward balance and, as such, offered something of a model for humanity—not a model frozen in time but one that was through and through historical, dynamic, and innovative.

Such was the understanding that the scientist Leopold had too, and his work on the land was meant to restore that process of growth and movement to its former vigor. The beauty of the organic world for him lay in its continuous creativity rather than in any rigidly prescribed table of organization.

At the time Leopold wrote, the ideas scientists held about the ecological order were undergoing a major transition. An older notion, dominant in America since early in the twentieth century and associated with the Nebraska ecologist Frederick Clements, had maintained that organic nature in the composite resembles a kind of organism—a "superorganism" as Clements called it—and that entity was supposed to grow up on the land until it reached a mature or climax state of development. By the 1930s and 40s that notion was losing support, though traces of it may be found in Leopold's writings and have even lingered down to the present.

The notion that replaced the superorganism was the ecosystem, first introduced in 1935 by the Oxford ecologist A. G. Tansley. His source of inspiration was not biology but physics. Nature is organized into inflows and outflows of energy, and the whole is an amalgamation of both living and nonliving components. Ecosystems, wrote Tansley,

> are of the most various kinds and sizes. They form one category of the multitudinous physical systems of the universe, which range from the universe as a whole down to the atom. The whole method of science . . . is to isolate systems mentally for the purposes of study. . . . The systems we isolate mentally are not only included as parts of larger ones, but they also overlap, interlock and interact with one another. The isolation is partly artificial, but is the only possible way in which we can proceed.

In other words, the notion of the ecosystem was founded on the assumption that the entire universe is firmly structured into complex physical interactions and that science can make sense of that structuring only by selecting small ordered pieces of it to study and describe.

Undoubtedly the discipline of environmental restoration owes much to these ideas, especially the concept of the ecosystem. Restoration, as I understand it, takes as its mission the repair of damaged ecosystems.

But now we enter the era of agnosticism. Within the past couple of decades many scientists have lost faith in either the superorganism or the ecosystem idea. A few of them, pushing Tansley's ideas farther than he meant them to go, have declared that the entire idea of the ecosystem is nothing more than a fiction, impossible to verify and therefore worthless. In fact the assumption that there is some comprehensive order in organic nature, or in any subset of it, has become increasingly suspect as a scientific proposition. *chaos?*

One key source of this skepticism has been the radical historicizing that has been going on in the science of ecology. These days ecologists are far more likely to be interested in describing changes that have been taken place in the environment over thousands, even millions, of years rather than in analyzing the structures and functions that exist at any one time. Stand on any acre of land, they say, and look backward into the past; the further back you look, the more flux you find. The whole continent of North America has been migrating through vast oceans, and on this none too solid earth the plants and animals also come and go with incredible mobility. Nature is no longer order; it is a process of endless change.

We historians of human communities have known for a long time that the historical imagination is intensely relativistic. Nothing lasts for long, we say, nothing is true forever. To a point this is a valuable discovery. It frees us from the parochialism of the present. But it can also be a dangerous habit of thought, leaving people bewildered and uncertain to the point of paralysis, demolishing all the cherished myths of tradition but leaving nothing in their place. Now that it has become so thoroughly embued with historical consciousness, ecology runs the risk of total relativism. A cutover land can be seen as good ecologically as a forested one. A landscape riddled with opencast coal mines, bleeding acid into streams, is as "natural" as any other. Only human subjectivity can decide which state of the earth is preferable to another.

To be sure, it is still possible today for a scientist to find an unchanging normative forest in all those changing trees. I offer as an illustration an essay by the University of Wisconsin botanist Orie Loucks, entitled "New Light on the Changing Forest," published in the 1983 book *The Great Lakes Forest*. Loucks reviews carefully all the recent evidence on forest disturbance. He discusses windstorms that have leveled as much as 40,000 wooded acres in a blow. He examines records of tree rings, pollen sediments, the impact of fire and ice. Seen in short intervals, the forests of Wisconsin appear to be extremely restless and unstable. But looked at in the longer run, over the last thirty million years or so, he points out, these forests are remarkably resilient. Despite repeated interventions and a few extinctions in them, "the principal characteristics of the forest or the primary adaptations evolved during the Tertiary era" have not changed.

Loucks is certainly no exception, but in much current revisionist ecology the changing (or even disappearing) trees have become far more emphasized than the enduring forest. Some scientists have carried the idea of continuous change in nature so far that they have begun to lose sight completely of the long-range order and pattern that is also there.

Perpetual anarchy is all that many find present. There is no discernible direction in nature, they say, no coherent community over time, no point of "climax" or "balance" or "mature state" that nature ever reaches, no reliable standard by which we can evaluate the effect of our own interventions. There is in fact no whole, they insist, there are only fragments. Nature appears in this skeptical light as a multitude of limited, specific processes going on, all of them grinding against one another and never merging into some unified flow or outcome. It would seem that these ecologists, having completely discredited older integrative concepts like "the balance of nature" as being too riddled with exceptions to be true or meaningful, too imprecise to test mathematically, are now unable to find a new holistic idea to put in their place. Some have even gone so far as to insist that all order exists only in the human mind, that nature is nothing but disorganized raw material on which we are free to impose both our ideas and desires.

Clearly, more than a debate over scientific evidence is going on in today's ecology. Some scientists are predisposed to find one thing in nature, others to find something very different. What one sees or does not see is partly the result of where one stands, or more precisely, where one chooses to stand. The significant question thus becomes, why do many scientists today *choose* to stand where all they can see is disorder?

The answer to that question must come from outside the realm of science, strictly defined. Scientists are people embedded in their societies and cultures. Consequently, the degree of order they find in nature, along with the degree of disorder, is inevitably influenced by their social and historical circumstances. To some extent they must see what their times allow them to see. From the mid-nineteenth century on, and especially over the past half-century or so, the times have become more and more disorderly. And that social condition has come to be reflected in the notions many scientists have developed about the natural world.

Science is, after all, basically one of the many ways we humans go about socially constructing what we mean by reality. Put another way, the scientist's models of nature, because they are the product of broader social processes, often tell us as much about what kind of people we are or think we are as they reveal about nature. In the eighteenth century the world of nature looked permanently stable and fixed in place because the human community looked stable and fixed in place. Over the last two hundred years, however, the rate of social change has been accelerating faster and faster, to the point that now we have all become historical-minded, even to the point that the past, any past, appears radically different from our own time. And some of us, who have been most acutely affected by this present social milieu, have become agnostics or even unbelievers about the very order of nature.

The most powerful forces impelling that change in cultural conscious-ness and the skepticism it has produced among scientists have been eco-nomic and technological ones. More precisely, they are the forces of mod-ern industrialism. By industrialism I mean the extensive mechanization of productive processes in clothing, food, transportation, and the like, typified by the large, centralized factory. Goods in this economy are pro-vided to consumers, not directly by their own effort, but through elabo-rately organized commercial markets. But that is only the external aspect. It has also an inner dimension, vast, complex, and effective: the habits of thought and perception that are needed to make the system and its demands appear reasonable. All economic systems are, after all, first mental systems. The revolution in modern production started in the mind. Or more accurately, it started in a few people's minds, and from there it spread to others, until eventually a fullblown culture of industri-alism could be said to exist, more or less unified in the pursuit of certain goals.

It is hard to exaggerate how far industrialism has gone in breaking down all the old notions of stability, community, and order. Our entire world-view has been transformed profoundly by this force. It has, among other consequences, led us to think that it is necessary and acceptable to ravage the landscape in the pursuit of maximum economic production. There can be no doubt about this outcome; it is clearly written in the his-torical record of England, the United States, and every nation that has been brought under the industrial system.

Modern industrial culture first sprang from the minds of a rising class of entrepreneurial capitalists during the seventeenth and eighteenth cen-turies. Even now, it is that group who dominate overwhelmingly the insti-tutions, politics, media, and thinking patterns of industrial life. We might as well say then that we live within the culture of industrial capi-talism. There are, to be sure, some important variations on that culture—industrial socialism, for example—but all preach much the same notion of what has worth and what does not. Where they diverge is in their degree of concern for a just distribution of the products of manufacturing, their skill in the efficient management of industrial systems, and their willing-ness or reluctance to use the power of the state to impress their ideas on people. Globally, however, it has been the industrial capitalists who have been the most decisive voice in modern times; almost all the world is now their factory, and the fate of the earth is largely in their hands.

economic and technological forces

industrial capitalists — the world is their factory

Any suggestion that nature has an intrinsic order that must be preserved has been viewed by many industrial leaders as a serious threat. They have had another, rival order to create—an economic one. Industrialism has sought not the preservation but the total domination of the natural order and its radical transformation into consumer goods. The environment has been seen to exist mainly for the purpose of supplying an endless line of those goods and absorbing the byproducts of waste and pollution. Whatever has not been produced by some industry and placed on the market for sale has had little value. It has been viewed, in the most negative word that industrial culture knows, as "useless." Since the only way industrialists can use nature is to disorganize it, in order to extract the specific commodities they value, typically they have regarded as most useless of all those very qualities of stability, harmony, symbiosis, and integration that characterize the living world in the composite. They have tended to devalue both the services that natural systems provide people, like a forest regulating stream flow, and the aesthetic satisfaction that contemplating such order affords.

Constant innovation, constant change, constant adjustment have become the normal experience in this culture. We have so far forgotten that life can be otherwise that we have come to accept as natural much of the chaos, uncertainty, and disintegration we find in our institutions and communities. We find it difficult nowadays to believe in any form of stability.

One of the greatest critics of industrial capitalism, Karl Marx, made this penetrating observation on its destructive effects on all ideas of order and lasting relationship:

> Constant revolutionizing of production, uninterrupted disturbance of all social conditions, everlasting uncertainty and agitation distinguish [this] epoch from all earlier ones. All fixed, fast-frozen relations, with their train of ancient and venerable prejudices and opinions, are swept away. All new-formed ones become antiquated before they can ossify. All that is solid melts into air, all that is holy is profaned.

Marx was thinking only about the effects of industrial capitalism on our ideas of social community, but we can see how readily his words apply to our understanding of the natural order. The sense of the ecological whole that once seemed so solid and unshakeable has tended, along with other ideas, to melt into air.

Marx believed that such destruction of traditional ideas was necessary in order to free people from the prejudices of the past. You cannot therefore find in him or his disciples much concern about preserving some holistic understanding of nature. But the socialists did believe that eventually the economic revolution must come to an end and society must reach some steady state of established relations, from which it would follow that nature must also arrive at some point of equilibrium, though it be one firmly under human control. Industrial capitalism, on the other hand, holds out no such promise of a steady state. Its social and ecological vision is one of infinite change.

What is *truth,* what is *fact,* what is *health,* what is *beauty* in such a world? What can these words possibly mean? Total skepticism, total cynicism is the intellectual future offered by this industrial culture and its institutions.

I think it is accurate to describe modern industrial societies as, on the whole, actively seeking disequilibrium. We have so learned to associate that condition with the possibilities of personal satisfaction, with full self-realization, with the more abundant life, even with justice and liberation, that we have even felt threatened by any talk of maintaining or restoring the natural order. We have been afraid of "stagnating" or "falling behind" or being kept "in our place" by repressive forces. By that way of thinking the notion of preserving nature, or trying to restore some semblance of its order, has been known to evoke fear and hostility. Many among us demand a disorderly, which is to say a less restrictive, world in which to operate.

This may be the greatest revolution in outlook that has ever taken place. Traditional societies tended to see and value the order in nature; we of the modern industrial era have tended to deny it. And therein lies the deepest source of our contemporary environmental destructiveness.

Restoration must confront this social and mental condition. More, it must in some measure be engaged in changing it—changing the economy, changing the social relationships it has spawned, changing the ideas that have grown out of those relationships, changing some of the directions in which science has been moving. It is not enough these days to buy 120 acres (even if one could afford them) and put one's shovel to work. In his own day Aldo Leopold understood, though I think too vaguely and abstractly, this predicament. Despite the devotion he gave to his private work on the land, he acknowledged the need to confront more systematically this industrial civilization if restoration is to succeed on a broader scale. In a letter to the American conservationist William Vogt, he pointed out that the idea of a restorative relationship with the land is incompatible with the drives of industrial civilization; one insists that we discover and respect the order of nature, the other urges us to triumph over it. The clear implication in that letter is that individual acts of restoration are only the beginning. The end must be the creation of an alternative society.

How can such a massive cultural change take place? It is too much to expect that the richest among us, who have profited most from industrial expansion, will furnish many leaders in this larger act of digging and planting and restoring. Once they were the vanguard of change, rising out of obscurity to challenge established authority; now, with notable exceptions, they have too much invested in the present system to welcome its demise. Nor ought we look for much leadership from the army of industrial workers, for they will tend to follow out of a sense of desperation and necessity whoever is presently giving them jobs. When the post-industrial future comes into being, it will be the achievement primarily of those who have been the least dependent on the old productive processes and who have had the freest minds, the greatest discontent, and the most compelling alternative vision.

Some of the leaders in forming a new post-industrial future of stability and order may well be scientists. We will certainly need their talents and research. Ecology, I predict, will eventually come back with renewed confidence to some model of the whole, some consensus about the organization of nature, as it must if it is to continue as a scientific enterprise. But it follows from all that I have said that the main counterforce to industrial instability is not going to be science acting alone, as some primal, independent authority.

The philosopher Alfred North Whitehead once argued that, if we are to find our way forward, we will need to rely less on the scientific way of thinking, which he argued is inevitably reductive, and rely more on what he called "the habit of aesthetic apprehension." He meant an ability to see wholes instead of pieces. The accumulation of mere facts does not in itself correct that blindness Whitehead thought was most consequential. In fact, it sometimes seems that the more facts we gather, the more knowledge we disseminate, the less able we are to see into the heart of things. He complained of "the stone-blind eye with which even the best men of [the past] regarded the importance of aesthetics in a nation's life." Often, he indicated, it has been people of considerable intellect and ability who have been the most indifferent to the natural order and who have been in greatest need of learning to see it whole again.

Of course we can use more scientific facts to improve our relationship with nature; they have been known to open a few minds. But the cultural blindness from which we suffer most grievously is one that only something like Whitehead's aesthetic apprehension can remedy.

Most likely therefore, the chief source of cultural change will be those men and women who exemplify the most fully developed "habits of aesthetic apprehension." Call them artists if you like, but they will not be a brigade of specialists in some fine arts discipline. Instead, they will be in the tradition of all those who, from the early years of the industrial revolution onward, shocked and outraged by the ugly, ruthless new ways, have constituted "the opposition." I think of them as the party of Henry David Thoreau and William Morris, John Muir and Richard Jeffries, H. M. Tomlinson and Rachel Carson, and Leopold of course—a party of writers, painters, and scientists. But many in the party have left no novels, paintings, poems, or naturalist essays, have left no record of their thinking except for the mountains, forests, and marshlands they have saved or restored. Famous or obscure, these are the people who are likely to lead us to transcend the present industrial culture.

Aesthetic apprehension develops through exercising that faculty in our minds that we associate with the arts, like landscape painting or music or poetry, though it is broader than any such specialized activity. Different people may exercise their faculty in different ways: through science or religion, as I have said, or through bird-watching, photography, or simply walking through nature with senses all alert. Whatever the activity, the essential ingredient in aesthetic apprehension is the ability to look beyond the level of isolated details and perceive their underlying cohesion. The details remain important, but the habit of looking at them too closely for too long can atrophy the aesthetic faculty. One loses the awareness of how things are joined together, how they form patterns with one another, how fitness is achieved. Nature then ceases to please the eye, and in the saddest cases the eye does not even know it should be pleased. When the aesthetic awareness is well developed, on the other hand, one sees easily and surely the deeper harmony within, and the pleasure it affords is intense. Words like "beauty" and "integrity" come readily to mind. Indeed, such qualities become the most significant realities that exist, and their perception and enjoyment is the highest form of living.

The beauty discovered in nature through aesthetic apprehension has inspired people repeatedly to try to construct harmonies of their own, in the landscape as well as in song and picture. All human art, I am sure, has its primal impulse in the deep observation of nature. We see its close relation of parts, its adaptation of means to ends, its wonderful suitability, and, impressed by what we have seen or heard, we set out to express it in our own limited way. In every period of history and every corner of the earth people have done so, from the gardens of Japan to the hedgerows of rural England, from the aquarium in a child's bedroom to the miniature rain forest re-created in the foyer of a modern office building. None of these creations is "nature" in some final or complete sense of the term, but all are efforts by the human mind to find some part of the whole they can grasp, imitate, and make their own.

But these days we feel more and more compelled, as Aldo Leopold was, to try to repair the earth's beauty rather than merely select and copy from it. Before, it did not seem to need our help; it was our shining exemplar. Now, however, for those whose aesthetic faculty is vigorous and searching for inspiration, much of that larger glory of nature has departed, not to be encountered again in our lifetime.

This degradation of natural beauty was what Leopold lamented on his abandoned farm. It was not merely a stupid or unfortunate misuse of a resource, he felt; it was morally wrong. Every person or nation has a right to derive a living from the earth and to participate in the processes of natural creativity; but no one, no matter how desperate his condition or elevated his ambition, has any right to diminish the complexity, diversity, stability, fruitfulness, wholeness, beauty—in short, the order of the natural world. Everyone has the responsibility, whether acknowledged or not, to get his living in such a way as to preserve that order. In so many words, that was what Leopold called the idea of a "land ethic."

I submit that this idea, one of the most important anyone has put forward in the twentieth century, must be the basis of the field of restoration ecology. If observed consistently, at least as consistently as we have ever observed any principle, not one of our institutions, philosophies, systems of knowledge, or modes of life would remain the same. Something bigger than pines would come up out of the Wisconsin sand.

In the industrial era we have made the mistake of disregarding beauty altogether or of assuming it is something that we humans must impose on the chaotic realm of nature. A more complete and humble view would be to see that nature constitutes a different and greater kind of order than anything that we, acting as one species alone, can create. It is not a kind of order that gets finished at a certain hour in the afternoon, is wrapped up and sold, and later hung on a wall or put in a bookcase. Nature is a creative work that has been going on for billions of years, was going on before there was any mind to translate it into human understanding. It is a ceaseless and infinitely inventive process of creating, the work of anonymous, even invisible, multitudes. It has no purpose behind it that we have been able to find and agree on, but it does display at every moment an order far more complicated and marvelous than any substitute we have been able to devise. It is the most complete order we discover. In the work that lies ahead of restoring some of that creativity to a diminished earth, we may again, with Aldo Leopold, see how much we have forgotten.

15

John Muir and the Roots of American Environmentalism

◆

IN the wild garden of an early America there coiled and crawled the devil's own plenty of poisonous vipers—cottonmouths, copperheads, coral snakes, the whole nasty family of rattlers and sidewinders. A naturalist roaming far from the settlements regularly ran the risk of a fatal snake bite. Fortunately, he was reassured by the field experts of the day, the deadly reptile always furnishes its own antidote. It conceals itself in the very plants whose roots can counteract its poison, plants like the so-called "Indian snakeroot." As the viper sank its sharp fangs into your leg, you simply pulled up the roots of that plant, quickly chewed them down, and laughed in the viper's face. You were instantly immune. How many backwoods naturalists and hunters died from believing that bit of advice is not known. Science, ever improving its hypotheses, now suggests carrying a snakebite kit in your pack or calling in a helicopter.

But before we dismiss the old advice as completely foolish, we might ask whether it might not have had some useful, genuine logic in it. Sometimes the remedy for wounds does indeed lie near at hand among the shrubs and weeds in which the reptile lives; and sometimes dangerous forces do indeed suggest, or even contain, their own antidote. Take, for

instance, the case of North America's continuing environmental degradation. What we humans have done over the past five hundred years to
maim this continent and tear apart its fabric of life is in large degree the
consequence of the Judeo-Christian religious ethos and its modern secular offspring—science, industrial capitalism, and technology. I would
put almost all the blame on the modern secular offspring, but I have to
agree that religion too has been a deadly viper that has left its marks on
the body of nature. Paradoxically, I would add what no one else seems to
have noticed: an Indian snakeroot for this venom has appeared in the reptile's own nest. The antidote for environmental destruction has been a
movement called environmentalism and that movement has, in the
United States, owed much of its program, temperament, and drive to the
influence of Protestantism.

This connection was strongly suggested to me a few years ago by an
incident in a Japanese fishing village. Over a thousand dolphins had been
captured in a bay at Iki island off Kyushu and were fated to be slaughtered by a group of irate fishermen who charged that the dolphins were
"gangsters of the sea" because they were eating the fish the men wanted
to catch. (Actually, the decline in their fishing was probably due more to
industrial pollution than dolphin predation, but they had found an
enemy they could defeat and were preparing to grind up the dolphins'
bones for fertilizer.) In the dead of night, an American young man—a
long-haired schoolteacher, antiwar protester, animal lover and radical
environmentalist, son of Protestant parents in Arizona—paddled his
kayak out to the restraining nets and released many of the dolphins. Sub-
sequently, he was arrested, tried and convicted, and deported as an undesirable alien; his moral zeal, it was said, was "interfering with the legitimate business" of Iki fishermen. Then the captured dolphins were killed
and put through a grinder.[1]

Earlier the young criminal from America had sailed out of Honolulu as
a member of the Greenpeace organization, intent on interfering with the
factory whaling business in the Pacific. He was eager to practice the
Greenpeace creed, which according to their publications, runs as follows:

Ecology teaches us that humankind is not the center of life on the planet.
Ecology has taught us that the whole earth is part of our "body" and that
we must learn to respect it as we respect ourselves. As we feel for ourselves,
we must feel for all forms of life—the whales, the seals, the forests, the
sea. . . . Life must be saved by non-violent confrontations and by what the
Quakers call "bearing witness." A person bearing witness must accept
responsibility for being aware of an injustice. That person may then chose
to do something or stand by, but he may not turn away in ignorance. The

Greenpeace ethic is not only to personally bear witness to atrocities against life; it is to take direct action to prevent them.[2]

For all their emphasis on modern ecology, those words include some astonishing echoes from the early religious history of Protestantism in America. Practice Quaker non-violence. Bear witness to injustice. Act according to your inner light. Like Boston in the 1650s, Iki island was invaded by a determined, self-confident missionary for whom the threat of jail was no deterrent. The Boston authorities hanged four Quakers for interfering with established order. So far the Japanese government has been decidedly more humane in reacting to American environmentalists on the whale and dolphin issue.

It is unexpected confrontations like these that force us to reconsider the old, oft-repeated East-West cultural stereotypes. Japan, an admirable nation in so many respects, was for a long time idealized by many Americans who were disturbed by their own country's exploitative treatment of nature. They began to argue that the Japanese, and people in Asian cultures generally, do not see themselves as separate from and superior to nature; their Shinto, Buddhist, or Hindu roots encourage a reverence for all forms of life. They value nature in and of itself in contrast to the domineering, instrumental thinking of Westerners. Japanese writers have often made the same claim (and the same criticism of the West). "For the Japanese and for other Oriental peoples," argues Masao Watanabe, a Tokyo historian of science, "man was considered a part of nature, and the art of living in harmony with nature was their wisdom of life."[3] And Kenzo Tage claims: "The essence of Japanese culture as compared to Western culture . . . [is] the contrast between an animistic attitude of willing adaptation to and absorption in nature and a heroic attitude of seeking to breast and conquer it."[4] Undoubtedly some truth lies in these characterizations, but in light of recent experience they are obviously incomplete; for example, they do not explain how it was possible for the Iki fishermen, backed by their national government, to carry out such a bloody slaughter of dolphins, or why it was an American who felt compelled to make them stop.[5]

The fact that Japan is a country filled with cultural contradictions was pointed out more than two decades ago by the sociologist Robert Bellah. The contemplative devotion to nature found in Zen Buddhism, he indicated, has been counter-balanced by the idea that productive labor is sacred, that people must work hard to improve the world around them. Following the latter idea, Zen monasteries of the Tokugawa period became the country's busiest centers of trade and industry. An even more important source of the idea of turning nature to account was Confucianism, imported from China, teaching the economic virtues of obedience, diligence, and thrift, all of which helped create a merchant class strikingly similar to that in the West.[6] In other words, Japan has had its own cultural drives leading to commerce, profit-making, technological innovation, and, inevitably, environmental destruction. Thus its current domestic pollution, some of the worst in the world, its overseas assault on the tropical rain forests, and its other anti-ecological behaviors must be explained as a homegrown product as much as a cultural import from the West.

But if Japan has shown more than one relationship with nature, then is it possible that America too might defy our stereotypes? If non-Western religions like Buddhism and Confucianism have led in more than one direction, could Protestantism likewise have more than a single set of ecological tendencies, and could some of those tendencies be positive as well as negative? I think they could and they have.

For many years now the role of Western religious traditions in creating environmental problems has been fiercely debated. The dispute began in 1967 with a brilliant essay by the historian Lynn White, Jr., who threw all the blame onto Judeo-Christian "anthropocentrism." Essentially White had two arguments to make: first, that the environmentally destructive forces of science, capitalism, technology, and democracy had a religious origin (they were all derivations from medieval Christianity); and second, that the Bible—in particular the words in Genesis 1:28— teaches that man must subdue and dominate nature, thereby sanctioning an arrogant, abusive attitude.[7] However simplistic those arguments were or became in the process of debate, and I suppose everyone would now agree they were a little too facile, the White thesis performed the immense service of forcing many in the Christian community to re-examine their view of humankind's role in nature and to look more deeply for the roots of environmental problems. That reappraisal led Pope John Paul II to designate St. Francis of Assisi as the Church's official patron saint of ecology.[8] For their part Protestants began to hold symposia and publish books defining a religious response to the environmental crisis.

The most common reaction among Protestants to Lynn White's arguments has involved resurrecting the long-neglected biblical ideal of the good steward. Nature, according to this teaching, is to be understood as God's valued property, and humans are not called to be absolute lord and master but only a temporary steward or viceroy, who must at a later date make a full accounting of their caretaking. Many Christians have argued that this notion of stewardship shows that their religion has not been completely insensitive or arrogant toward nature but in fact has taught, and can still teach today, an ethic of caring for the earth.[9] In support of this claim, historians can agree that there have been a few Christian societies that have practiced a more careful use of resources than White acknowledges; for instance, the seventeenth-century New England Puritans may not have been the ruthless, unrestrained exploiters that their descendants often were. On the contrary, they passed the first laws in North America to protect forests and game from over-harvesting.[10]

On the other hand, many recent environmentalists have come to see in nature something more than a piece of property to be managed and want to locate a more radical ideal than Christian stewardship. For them, the core obstacle in the Judeo-Christian tradition, not really overcome by stewardship ethics, is the inescapably anthropocentric doctrine of human redemption. Uniquely among the world's religions, Judaism and Christianity have aimed at elevating human beings above nature—at making humans, and humans only, worthy to be the sons and daughters of God. That dream of transcending nature has led to a spiritual devaluation of the earth and an alienation of *Homo sapiens* from other forms of life. Out of such aspirations to rise above the rest of nature, one should add, has also come the Western drive for justice, equality, compassion, and material improvement; give credit for that outcome too. But it has always seemed to be nature that must provide the raw resources for human redemption and progress. That God's property must be used, and used intensely, if the drive toward redemption is to be successful, is one possible conclusion from the teaching of stewardship. Erase the moral line between humans and the rest of this groaning, toiling creation, and the unique Judeo-Christian sense of mission must falter. That is precisely what many contemporary environmentalists insist we must now try to do—elevate nature to a more equal footing with ourselves. That is also why there remains an unresolved antagonism between environmentalism and Western religion and why Lynn White still has a useful point to make.

Many modern environmentalists, in short, demand a stronger set of restraints on the use of nature than mainstream Western religion so far has been willing to provide. Consequently, they have often felt compelled to repudiate completely their cultural roots and search among the Buddhists, Navajos, Gnostics, and pagans of the world for alternative ideas.

Yet all the same there is that American dolphin liberator, "bearing witness" against Shinto-Buddhist-Confucian fishermen and judges. Where does he come from? Evidently neither Lynn White nor his critics have fully exhausted the possible relations between Western religious and environmental behavior. If we look beyond overt biblical doctrine, mainstream theology, and commonly accepted notions of Christian ethics, including stewardship, if we explore the fringes and byways of Protestantism, if we focus especially on the dissident tradition in American and northern European Protestantism, I think we may find some surprising connections with modern environmentalism.

My argument will be that Protestantism has in fact provided an important spawning ground for environmental reform movements. I have in mind mainly the Reformed churches—Presbyterian, Congregational, Quaker, Baptists, Disciples of Christ—along with evangelical Methodism. For a long period they exercised a decisive influence over the American moral imagination. True, they were often part of the established order and defended it vigorously against all challenge; and yes, they often became a conservative cover for power and authority. But we know also that at other times and places Protestantism has had a radically different effect, that it has frequently been an important source of resistance to power, that it has often disagreed with the established way of life and the voice of authority; that it has played a key role in the formation of such social movements as abolitionism and suffrage. We might call this reformist side the "left-wing" of Protestantism.[11] Not the least of its legacy, I believe, has been the conservation or environmental movement. My chief, indeed my pivotal example, of this legacy will be the spiritual father of American environmentalism, John Muir, a man who, I believe, was clearly a product of left-wing Protestantism.

The histories of environmentalism in the United States have so far been preoccupied with politics and careers, with public ideas and debates. Nowhere near enough attention has been given to the inward drives of reformers, to the elusive and hidden patterns of temperament and motive, to the shaping forces of religion, family, and class. Take, for instance, the case of John Wesley Powell (1834–1902), who is well known for having been the first American to penetrate the Colorado River country, for devising a plan of western settlement to meet the conditions of aridity, and for helping form the federal conservation bureaucracy. All those public achievements we know in detail, but of the deeper emotions of the man we know comparatively little. What, for example, should we make of the fact that he was raised by intensely evangelical parents? His father, Joseph Powell (oddly enough, his mother was named Mary), came to the United States in 1830 from Shrewsbury, England—a licensed Methodist exhorter who, from all accounts, was a restless, dogmatic man, intent on carrying the gospel to the uttermost parts of the earth. The son, John

Wesley, was intended by his parents for the ministry too and by the age of five had committed all the New Testament gospels to memory. Although eventually he turned to a career in natural science against his father's wishes, young Powell grew up to become no mean evangelist himself, as he proved through several decades in Washington dedicated to saving the American West from ill-conceived, destructive land policies. Was there, after all, more of Joseph Powell and a Methodist nurturing in the son's make-up than we have yet understood?[12]

Elsewhere the same correlation of personal Protestant roots and environmental reformism appears repeatedly. There was, for example, Stephen Mather (1867-1930), a direct descendant of the famous branch of the New England Puritan family, who became the first director, and one of the most dedicated, of the National Park Service.[13] There was the novelist and essayist Mary Austin (1868-1937), who as an adult abandoned her childhood Methodism but put in in its place the southwestern deserts, which she helped other Americans see through a mystic's eyes.[14] And more recently there was William O. Douglas (1898-1980) of the Supreme Court bench, one of the most influential environmentalists in the twentieth century as well as a controversial defender of civil liberties and an advocate of social justice. Douglas's father was a Presbyterian minister in the state of Washington; his mother, the widowed Julia Bickford Douglas, daughter of Vermont Yankees, raised her children on poverty and five church meetings a week. Although William grew up to reject institutional Protestantism (too often for him it was the defender of the status quo), he did not repudiate the family's religiosity. In one of his last books, *The Three Hundred Year War,* Douglas made clear just how much he remained his parents' son: "Whether we can make a religion out of conservation," he wrote, "or give that cause a messianic mission is the critical issue of this day."[15]

But easily the best case study in how a Protestant-oriented family background could provide a nursery for environmentalism is the strenuous mountain zealot John Muir (1838-1914). In Muir, Stephen Fox suggests, modern American environmentalism found its first great national leader, and his influence has grown steadily from decade to decade, until today he is the Siddharta, the Gandhi, the Luther, and the Muhammad of the movement.[16] To the practical resource conservationism of such social reformers as John Wesley Powell and Gifford Pinchot, he added an aesthetic and ethical responsiveness to wild nature, seeing it as the tangible presence of God. When in 1892 he and a group of college professors met in Warren Olney's law offices in San Francisco to form the Sierra

Club, that responsiveness to nature acquired an organizational base—became the church, as it were, that Muir built.[17]

Muir was born and lived the first eleven years of his childhood in the town of Dunbar on the coastal fringe of Scotland's Midlothian province. (This was also the home of Sir Walter Scott's ardent puritan Jeanie Deans, in the novel *The Heart of Midlothian,* published in 1818). Easily the most powerful, if sometimes resisted, force in his early life was his father Daniel, a Scott character out of time, a relic of that fierce Scottish enthusiasm that took so readily to Calvinism and Protestant piety. At first a conventional Presbyterian, Daniel Muir came under the influence of two missionary brothers named Gray, who brought to the little town of Dunbar the New World gospel of Campbellism. Father Daniel thereupon determined to emigrate to America where he could exercise his piety and acquire land at the same time. Settling in Wisconsin, the father raised his children, not with the indulgence of the prosperous, but with regular jeremiahs and severe overwork. If he was not an easy man to satisfy, if he seemed ever to be looking for an even more difficult world than that of a pioneer farm, Daniel Muir did leave his imprint on his son's approach to life.

Father Daniel's new religion, the gospel of Campbellism, was the creation of two other Scots, father Thomas and son Alexander, and if we are to understand son John's own inner development, we need to pay more attention to that other father-son pair. Thomas Campbell was born in County Down, Ireland, in 1763 and emigrated to the southwestern corner of Pennsylvania in 1807; Alexander was also born in northern Ireland, in 1788, and followed his father to America in 1809. In the old country the pair had been embroiled in a religious controversy that could find no end. Everyone they knew, it appears, was, like them, trying to secede from everyone else, but especially from the National Church, which was, in the eyes of the Campbells, corrupted by theological and moral abuses. What the Campbells wanted, and what they sought in the mountain valleys of West Virginia, Pennsylvania, and Ohio, was a new religion based strictly on the primitive New Testament model, eschewing all man-made ideas and modern innovations. They wanted too a faith that would be lodged in the heart as much as in the head: a piety that burned with intense heat, unquenched by academic disputations over text or tradition, free of all schisms. During the antebellum years they spread their ideas over the entire American frontier, all the way westward to California, as well as overseas to Ireland and Scotland. By 1860 their movement had acquired a permanent form, the Disciples of Christ church, and it counted about

200,000 members. By the end of the Civil War both father and son were dead; but those members continued to thump their Bibles vigorously—all we need to know about the essentials, they insisted, is written down in scripture—and to defend their autonomy against every form of higher ecclesiastical authority.[18]

The peculiar, distinguishing quality of the Campbellites was their amalgamation of two quite contrary tendencies: Enlightenment rationalism, which denounced all tyranny over the individual human mind, and evangelical piety, or what we would now call fundamentalism. The Campbells had heeded the words of Voltaire, John Locke, David Hume, and other rationalists when they denounced the established church along with monarchy; they took from such rationalists the idea that all human beings have an inalienable right to be free of such arbitrary power. Natural rights, independent reason, and political dissent were themes the Campbells preached on regularly. On the other hand, they were appalled by the Enlightenment tendency to set up science or reason as a substitute for divine revelation. They wanted a revival of faith, not a modern road to skepticism, a recommitment to the ancient truths, not a discovery of new modes of thought. Were they revolutionaries or reactionaries? In some tangled way, they were both. Vehemently they ridiculed organized Christianity as superstitious and rotten. They asserted their liberty of conscience in terms Tom Paine could have admired. Yet they sought to return humanity to a more pure and unspoiled past when the way was perfectly clear to every person, the truth unequivocal. Alexander once explained, "We became skeptics in everything sectarian—in everything in religion—but the Bible."[19]

Such were the temperament and ideas that so deeply touched Daniel Muir that he felt compelled to leave his ancestral homeland for Wisconsin and eventually to leave his own family for an itinerant life as a Campbellite preacher. Growing up in the household of such a father, young Johnny must have been drenched in the same gospel (literally drenched, for the Campbellites believed in total immersion in water as the culmination of redemption, and it is unlikely that Daniel would have neglected his child's salvation by omitting this ritual). The future founder of the Sierra Club grew up on intimate terms with the Bible—in fact learned by heart the entire New Testament and three-fourths of the Old—and must have fed almost daily on that whole composite diet of Scottish Enlightenment thinking and Protestant evangelical piety.

That fact, and its profound significance for American environmentalism, has pretty much eluded Muir's biographers. Two of the most recent of them, Michael Cohen and Stephen Fox, do not even mention the Campbellite religion or its role in the Muir household, and the only one who does, Frederick Turner, treats it only in passing to explain the father's decision to emigrate, not as a powerful shaping force within the family.[20] John Muir is supposed by all of them never to have been touched by that Scottish ethnic and frontier religious background, though for more than a decade it surrounded him in his native land, was in the air as much as the smell of heather and salt sea, and for another decade in the New World looked down at him steadily in the form of his father at the head of the pioneer table.

The biographers neglect this religious background because Muir himself never quite acknowledged its hold on him. On the contrary, he insisted that he had broken free from it at an early age, that he had been a total subversive lurking resentfully in his father's house, waiting for his moment to rebel and escape. "Wildness was ever sounding in our ears," he wrote about his days in Scotland, "and Nature saw to it that besides school lessons and church lessons some of her own lessons should be learned, perhaps with a view to the time when we should be called to wander in wildness to our heart's continent."[21] Later, indeed, he left the family homestead for the university in Madison and eventually made his way to the Yosemite Valley of California; and the valley, the mountains, the pine forests became all the church and all the school he needed or wanted. He steadfastly rejected his father's impassioned plea to give up the idolatrous worship of nature that kept him rambling around the Sierra Nevada, climbing trees and leaping over streams. "You cannot warm the heart of the saint of God with your cold icy-tipped mountains," old Daniel wrote. "O, my dear son, come away from them to the spirit of God and His holy word, and He will show our lovely Jesus to you."[22] But John would not be called back to the faith. At age 28, in the prime of his rebellion, he wrote to a friend, "I take more intense delight from reading the power and goodness of God from 'the things which are made' than from the Bible."[23]

Moreover, John criticized sharply the common views Christians held of man's proper relations with other living things. "The world, we are told, was made especially for man"—a presumption, he pointed out, that was not supported by the facts. Nature had its own intrinsic value and meaning for him; it existed before humans did and could still exist without them. Resisting that truth, Christianity was filled, he thought, with self-conceit; it was incapable of seeing that animals "are our earth-born companions and fellow mortals."[24] Muir's strategy of rebellion was to celebrate in his life and writings "all God's people"—a category that included whales, squirrels, gnats, microbes, even the "plant people." Given such defiance it would appear that Muir did indeed leave completely behind all the Campbellite teaching, all the schisms and wranglings of Scottish Calvinists, the entire Protestant reformation, indeed the whole Judeo-Christian tradition. Some have even decided, based on his passionate celebration of nature, that he became in all but name a Chinese Taoist or a Buddhist. Supposedly, he walked out of frontier Wisconsin and ended up in Asia, or at least in a California approximation of it.

But such a reading of Muir defies all our understanding of how people form their minds and characters. It ignores the well-demonstrated fact that the early years are the most decisive in human development.[25] It refuses to look for any continuing legacy of Protestantism because it cannot see, in theological terms, how there could be any. In contrast, I want to suggest that though Muir's challenge to traditional religion was quite radical, he did not express a completely alien set of ideas. His life became a process not only of rebelling against the mainstream but also of working out some of the tendencies in his father's logic and emotion. In short, John Muir became a kind of frontier evangelist himself, following in his father's footsteps with remarkable faithfulness, more or less as Alexander followed in father Thomas's steps.

Several times in his mature life John came very close to endorsing his father's evangelical temperament. For example, as an old man Daniel heard once more a call in the night, sold the Wisconsin farm, and prepared to move to England to help save Bristol orphans. John managed to divert his energies to a less disruptive campaign of preaching in Hamilton, Ontario—and it proved to be a most ecstatic experience in the old man's life. But opposed though he was to this "morbid and semi-fanatical outbreak," John admired all the same the intense spirit in his father: "His moral disease is by no means contemptible, for it is only those who are endowed with poetic and enthusiastic brains that are subject to it." Near the end of his own life John proudly compared his father to that New England Puritan sort who from "youth to death" never abated one jot their "glorious foundational religious enthusiasm."[26]

More than this, John followed his father in the very pattern of his life. Like Muir *père,* he acquired a farm—this one near Martinez, California—and raised a family there. But farming soon grew tiresome and boring; he kept wandering off to answer a higher calling of preaching and converting the world. A spiritual rapture similar to his father's, demanding and uncompromising in its intensity, drove him to the mountains. With a scanty supply of tea bags and bread he ranged the high country from California to Alaska, pushing himself with classic evangelical discipline as many as fifty miles a day, sleeping nights on a bed of granite. Increasingly, he cast his life into the revivalistic mode, not only seeking his own spiritual joy but also trying to awaken his fellow citizens to the possibilities of regeneration. To save humans from their depravity, indifference, and destructiveness became his chief reason for being. In fits of righteous indignation he denounced the "barbarous wickedness" of buffalo hunters, the "abomination" of sheepmen and prospectors, and the "temple destroyers, devotees of ravaging commercialism," who were trying to dam and flood the Hetch Hetchy Valley in Yosemite National Park to provide a water supply for San Francisco.[27] Go stand on a cold blue glacier, he urged his followers, and recover your innocence. Cleanse your soul of worldly evil by hanging precipitously, as he had done, from a narrow rock ledge into the thunderous spray of a waterfall. "Heaven knows," he declared in one of his early journals, "that John the Baptist was not more eager to get all his fellow sinners into the Jordan than I to baptize all of mine in the beauty of God's mountains." In short, Muir invented a new kind of frontier religion: one based on going to the wilderness to experience the loving presence of God. Only corrupt, ignorant, arrogant human beings stood outside that divine beauty, spoiling and abusing it. Separating himself from human corruption, Muir found redemption in the wild and he called the rest of the nation to join him. The Sierras became his Cane Ridge revival camp.[28]

As with many other frontier evangelists, this one had strongly democratic tendencies. Muir, as I have said, accepted all the wild plants, rocks, and animals as his fellow citizens, as good as himself or better. He asserted the rights of nature to be free of the arrogant rule of "Lord Man." Recently, Roderick Nash has written that though Muir was an early advocate of the rights of nature, he downplayed the idea as he got into politics and was forced to become more pragmatic; he found that his moral views were too radical for the times.[29] I think Nash is right, but an interesting question remains: Where did that early idea of the rights of nature originate? My answer is that it must have come out of the mingling of Scottish and Campbellite mentality, out of left-wing Protestantism, out of Enlightenment rationalism, and out of frontier evangelism. Where his father had rebelled against the social hierarchy of the established Scottish church and of English rule, so John revolted against the conventional distinction people made between the "higher" and "lower" forms of life, holding as he did that all things are "sparks of the Divine Soul variously clothed upon with flesh, leaves, or that harder tissue called rock, water, etc."[30] Later on he may have learned to suppress some of his egalitarian impulses in public, but the most distinctive, astonishing thing about him was that he never could see any valid moral distinction to be made between a human and a worm.

John Muir has become a hero for many Americans who have made a similar transition from Judeo-Christianity to modern environmentalism. Their new faith grew up within the shell of the old. It remains to be said what specific qualities of thought and feeling in American Protestantism shaped that emerging environmentalist temperament. I think there were four such qualities, each holding the potential for subversive challenge: moral activism, ascetic discipline, egalitarian individualism, and aesthetic spirituality. When they flashed together, as they did in the case of Muir, a new radical variant to conventional Judeo-Christian beliefs was born. The environmental reformer had come onto the world's stage.

The first of those formative Protestant qualities I have identified as *moral activism.* So accustomed are we to seeing Protestantism defend its privileged position that we persistently forget that Protestant began as a movement of critics. The early legendary figures—John Calvin, Ulrich Zwingli, John Knox—were all energetic radicals hacking away at obstacles to social change.[31] From their time forward, Protestantism was a religion for activists. It emerged from the expectation that the world and its institutions could be better organized, that people could behave in new and better ways. In America that impulse to act—to express faith in deeds—produced legions of disapproving missionaries and zealous crusaders against Indians and wilderness: produced a self-righteous "redeemer nation" that made God's work its own.[32] In the more tolerant person of Benjamin Franklin it gave the city of Philadelphia cleaner streets, better lighting, and more efficient stoves; the good citizen was, in Franklin's words, "a Great Promoter of Useful Projects."[33] There was no common goal in all that busyness, but there was a shared moralizing energy, an ambition to herd one's fellows down this path or that.

Conservation, I want to suggest, has been an important expression of that urge to reform the world. When the nation's forests were threatened by fraudulent and short-sighted greed, Theodore Roosevelt (of Dutch Reformed stock) and Gifford Pinchot (his family was out of New England Puritans and Picardian Huguenots) took as their "project" the creation of a system of publicly owned forest reserves. As Pinchot put it in 1910, "the conservation questions is a question of right and wrong."

[It] is a moral issue because it involves the rights and duties of our people—their rights to prosperity and happiness, and their duties to themselves, to their descendants, and to the whole future progress and welfare of this Nation.[34]

Although Pinchot called his forest project "utilitarian," it owed more to that useful-minded son of New England, Ben Franklin, than it did to Jeremy Bentham.

Today, environmentalism defines its reform mission in less strictly utilitarian terms than Pinchot or Roosevelt did, but the urgency to act energetically on moral principles is still there. The small but effective group calling itself the Friends of the Earth, founded in 1969 by David Brower, reminds one of such eighteenth-century groups as the Society for the Propagation of the Gospel in Foreign Parts or the antebellum American Board of Commissioners for Foreign Missions. Like its predecessors, FOE is determined to convert the rest of the world to its ideals; and it now claims branches in thirty-eight countries, ranging from Argentina to Japan and Tanzania, a record of moral activism that would have impressed even the likes of Lyman Beecher or Brigham Young.[35] To be sure, such zealousness is not itself sufficient to create environmentalism; however, it is an essential ingredient and it has deeply affected the direction of the movement, turning a private response to nature into a crusading cause.

The second legacy from Protestantism is *ascetic discipline.* In large measure Protestantism began as a reaction against a European culture that seemed to be given over, outside the monastic orders, to sensuous, gratification-seeking behavior. As Sebastian Franck has noted, Protestantism aimed to make every Christian a monk all his life.[36] Never mind that the ideal was repeatedly forgotten, as in the uninhibited fervor of many frontier camp meetings; there was from the beginning, and it reappeared with vigor from time to time, a deep suspicion in the Protestant mind of unrestrained play, extravagant consumption, and self-indulgence, a suspicion that tended to be very skeptical of human nature, to fear that humans were born depraved and were in need of strict management.[37] During the early years of Protestantism that suspicion was an indispensable aid to the rise of capitalism, enforcing hard work and careful, systematic savings. More recently, capitalism, in its push to expand profits, has chipped away with great success at the Protestant dams of asceticism. Now it is apparently only one's workers who must be taught self-denial; one's customers, on the other hand, are encouraged to let their hedonistic impulses be their guide.

Increasingly betrayed in its alliance with business, the Protestant ascetic tradition may someday survive only among the nation's environmentalists, who tend to drive older rusting cars and compulsively turn off the lights. By today's scale of values on Madison Avenue, environmentalists seem to be killjoys who would ban cigarettes, force people to walk more often, and force us back to the cold, damp deprivations of the Stone Age.[38] They are a drag on a nation that wants to have more fun. Too often for the public they sound like gloomy echoes of Gilbert Burnet's ringing jeremiad of 1679: "The whole Nation is corrupted . . . and we may justly look for unheard of Calamities."[39] Nonetheless, the environmental jeremiahs persist in warning that a return to the disciplined, self-denying life may be the only way out for a world heading towards environmental catastrophe.

A third characteristic handed down from the Protestant reformation to modern environmentalists is what we might call *egalitarian individualism*. It originates in the conviction that God's promise is to the individual, freed from the bonds of tradition and hierarchy; and in that promise every person, regardless of learning or social rank, stands equal to every other. Among the more rigorous American disciples of this thinking were the Quakers, the Antinomians, and Henry David Thoreau ("any man more right than his neighbors constitutes a majority of one already").[40] Moreover, the very core of our public political life has been committed to this social philosophy: the sovereignty of the individual, the natural right of self-determination.[41] In contrast to the more de-egotized ideal taught by Zen Buddhism, Protestantism has promoted an unusually assertive, individualistic stance toward life, along with the capacity to sympathize with others' needs for similar assertiveness.

Once set in motion, this teaching can prove exceedingly difficult to control. It may lead not only to elevating the poor and despised in society but also to investing whales, forests, and even rivers with new dignity—to the discovery of the concept of the rights of nature. This tendency was apparent at least as early as the 1830s, when the French Catholic traveler Alexis de Tocqueville, though otherwise intrigued by the rising democratic spirit of the United States, warned against its drift toward what he called a "pantheistic" tendency, an inclusive embrace of the world in which every proper distinction was lost. "All those who still appreciate the true nature of man's greatness," he urged, "should combine in the struggle" to overcome this pantheism and to restrain the democratic spirit in more sensible channels.[42] Whether pantheism was something to fear or not, Tocqueville was certainly right on one matter: egalitarianism produced a strange combination of holistic inclusiveness toward nature and radical individualism. But he was wrong if he thought that in a Protestant-based society a firm, convincing line could be drawn for very long between human aspirations, human dignity, and the needs and rights of other living things.

Nothing has been more unsettling to traditional Judeo-Christian assumptions than this internally generated challenge to deference, extending at last even to humankind's place in nature. By the 1970s it was possible for a Presbyterian minister in Virginia, ironically a state where religion once supported chattel slavery, to write:

> Human and social rights must be limited by an explicit recognition of the rights of the natural environment itself. . . . It is bizarre that we should imagine that this God wants us to maintain tyranny over the natural world rather than to tend it lovingly, even sacrificially.[43]

Recent echoes of such thinking can be heard again and again in many liberal Protestant circles and even among conservative groups. So far, however, rather little support for this position has come from Catholic bishops, Jewish rabbis, or Hindu holy men. Why is that? Is it because it is not so clear a possibility in their religious and ethical logic?

My final connecting link between Protestantism and environmentalism, and probably the most important of all, is the idea of *aesthetic spirituality*. The phrase is historian William Clebsch's, who defines its meaning thus: "Not so much the appreciation of beauty attributed to or inhering in objects of artistic creation but rather a consciousness of the beauty of living in harmony with divine things—in a word, being at home in the universe."[44] Or, we can call it the capacity to see beyond instrumental values, to find beauty in the unaltered Creation, and to identify that beauty with goodness and truth. Was the Protestant capable of such nature-appreciating spirituality? The answer seems to be yes, though the capability was not always exercised. In early America the outstanding example of that spirituality was the eighteenth-century theologian Jonathan Edwards, who, seeking to reformulate the faith of his fathers, turned to nature. In nature's beauty he discovered that one could find the glory of the Creator and by contemplating that beauty one could be delivered from evil. Describing his own spiritual rebirth (it occurred "in a solitary place in my father's pasture"), Edwards rhapsodized:

> God's excellency, his wisdom, his purity and love, seemed to appear in everything, in the sun, moon, and stars; in the clouds and blue sky; in the grass, flowers, trees; in the water, and all nature.[45]

This was the same man who, in an earlier, more conventional moment, wrote that "this world is all over dirty" and warned his congregation in Northampton, Massachusetts, that too much contact with nature tends "to pollute us."[46] But his sudden awakening to the loveliness of the natural world, to its order and harmony and virtue, changed that view. It was unregenerate, unredeemed humans who were the real polluters. Through that spiritual awakening, he came to believe that God made it possible for humans to participate deeply and inwardly in the loveliness of nature.

From Jonathan Edwards one can trace this aesthetic spirituality to the Transcendentalists of the nineteenth century and on to their more recent intellectual descendants, including John Muir in the Sierra Nevada and a hundred thousand backpackers trekking along the Appalachian Trail or camping in Yellowstone National Park, eager to lose themselves in the mountain haze and then return home, spiritually refreshed. A key historical link in this chain of influences were the New England Transcendentalists, Emerson and Thoreau in particular. For all their reading of Spinoza, Coleridge, and the Bhagavad-Gita, Perry Miller told us some years ago, they were unmistakably the children of the mystical Protestant minister Jonathan Edwards in Northampton, Massachusetts. We might therefore extend Miller's famous title, "From Edwards to Emerson," to read: "From Edwards to Emerson to Thoreau, and then on to John Muir, Rachel Carson, William Douglas, and David Brower."[47] Once learned in New England pastures or Wisconsin oak openings, this Protestant tendency to go back to nature in search of divine beauty could be exercised in an infinite number of landscapes: at the edge of the sea, in a sandstone canyon, or on the forested slopes of the Cascades. And what people came to invest with divinity, with intrinsic value and meaning, they found difficult to exploit thoughtlessly and necessary to protect.[48]

To suggest these possible connections between Protestantism and environmentalism is not to say that the connection was always made by individuals; of course it was not. The recently departed, and notorious anti-environmentalist, Secretary of the Interior James Watt never made it. He could kneel beside his desk each morning, praying the prayers of an evangelical Christian, and never achieve Edwards's or Muir's breakthrough to nature; apparently, the only beauty Watt could ever see was in a bank account or an oil well. Nor do I mean to argue that other religions did not have any connections of their own to make with environmentalism; of course they have. My aim has been merely to suggest that Protestantism, like any religion, lays its hold on people's imaginations in diverse, contradictory ways and that hold can be tenacious long after the explicit theology or doctrine has gone dead. Surely it cannot be surprising that in a culture deeply rooted in Protestantism, we should find ourselves speaking its language, expressing its temperament, even when we thought we were free of all that.

But having explored the connection with the religious past, I find that it now creates for American environmentalism a predicament for the future. As America has become more pluralistic in its religious and ethnic makeup, as Jews, Catholics, and others have come to play an increasingly prominent role in the nation's moral discourse and Protestantism has weakened as a cultural force, environmentalism has had to face the challenge of change. What kind of environmentalist movement can win support in a morally pluralistic society? And what direction will that movement have to take in the future if it wants to reach more people than to date it has? Will the John Muir type, the enraptured individual going out into the wilderness, some day be a diminished force in American environmental politics? Will there be less emphasis placed on preserving sanctuaries for wildlife and more on the social effects of pollution? Or will environmentalism swing more and more to Barry Commoner's strategy, a socialist critique of corporate power, a strategy that may owe a great deal to the fact that Commoner was reared in a New York Jewish family instead of a Campbellite pioneer one.[49] Commoner seems radically different in temperament and approach from John Muir, and one wonders what contrasting religious traditions may have had to do with the difference. In any case, American environmentalism has increasingly had to become a pluralistic movement, united in some respects but deeply divided in others, and I suspect those divisions reflect the religious and moral diversity of the modern nation.

Finally, an even bigger question confronting American environmentalism is what its future prospects may be in a *world* made up of so many conflicting moral traditions. The confrontation of Greenpeace protesters with Japanese dolphin and whale killers may be only the first of a endless series of angry misunderstandings. In places where Protestantism is an alien tradition, what kind of language must environmentalism learn to speak? Wholesale conversion of the rest of the world to the gospel of John Muir may be a hopeless project, and American environmentalists may have to realize that their best strategy is to turn toward a more ecumenical message. In addition to Muir and Thoreau they may have learn to read, as some are already trying to do, the Chinese sage Lao-tzu or the German-Jewish social critic Karl Marx. In that more ecumenical future they may gain a new perception of humankind's relations with nature, based on exposure to other moral traditions, and come to appreciate more fully other notions of what should be done and can be done.[50] Such an ecumenical openness to global diversity might in turn make American environmentalism a rather different movement than it has been so far. And one day it might be that, instead of American protesters going to Japan,

Japanese fishermen would come to America, singing an ancient Shinto song to soothe the troubled spirits of Lake Erie.

John Muir's movement has now entered a very different world than the one he knew, one that is pluralistic and global. The Protestant past he knew so intimately may still profoundly condition the present, but it does not control the future.

16

The Wealth of Nature

◆

WHOEVER made the dollar bill green had a right instinct. There is a connection, profound and yet so easy to ignore, between the money in our pocket and the green earth, though the connection is more than color. The dollar bill needs paper, which is to say it needs trees, just as our wealth in general derives from nature, from the forest, the earth and waters, the soil. That these are all limited and finite is easy to see, and so also must be wealth; it can never be unlimited, though it can be expanded and multiplied by human ingenuity. Somewhere on the dollar bill that message might be printed, a warning that you hold in your hand a piece of the limited earth that should be handled with respect: "In God we trust; on nature we must depend."

The public is beginning to understand that connection in at least a rudimentary way and to realize that taking better care of the earth will cost money, will lower the standard of living as it is conventionally defined, and will interfere with freedom of enterprise. By the evidence of opinion polls, something like three out of four Americans say they are ready to accept those costs, a remarkable development in our history. The same can be said for almost every other nation on earth, even the poorest, who are learning that, in their own long-term self-interest, the preservation of nature is a cost they ought to pay, though they may demand that

203

the rich nations assume some of the cost. Having money in one's pocket, no matter how green its color, is no longer the unexamined good it once was. Many have come to realize that wealth might be a kind of poverty.

The human species, according to a team of Stanford biologists, is now consuming or destroying 40 percent of the net primary terrestrial production of the planet: that is nearly one half of all the energy fixed by photosynthesis on the land. We are harvesting it, drastically reorganizing it, or losing it through urbanization and desertification in order to support our growing numbers and even faster growing demands. In addition, much of the remaining 60 percent is profoundly affected by the pumping and burning of fossil fuels, the spreading about of so many chemicals new to evolution, the accelerating interventions into the water cycle, the atmosphere, the climate.[1]

That impact is sure to increase, as more than ever we seek to turn the earth into wealth. The United Nations now projects that world population will grow to more than eight billion by 2025, then go on to ten billion before it stabilizes toward the end of the next century, so that the present heavy impact on ecosystems has only just begun. One-fourth of the world's total stock of plant and animal species are at risk of being eliminated in the next twenty years. About half of the rain forests in tropical areas have already been lost to deforestation, and an additional area the size of Kansas is being lost every year to clear-cutting for timber, cattle grazing, and other uses. The increased burning of fossil fuels is beginning to raise atmospheric carbon dioxide levels so rapidly that global shifts in climate appear imminent. Those are some of the costs forcing the public to re-evaluate the ends and means of wealth.[2]

Suddenly, we humans are waking up to the massive influence we are having on the planet in the pursuit of greater production and are beginning to wonder whether the wealth is excessive or how long it can last. We are beginning to fear that we cannot really manage this enormous productive apparatus that we have superimposed on nature. The earth has begun to look like a savings and loan office six months after bankruptcy: the furniture disappearing, the water cooler empty, the looks on the faces of the office staff blank or bewildered.

A recent big surprise has to do with deodorants and automobile air conditioning, two of the more essential material comforts of our time. For a number of years now some of our best minds have been at work figuring out ways to keep Americans from sweating so much. Perspiration, we know from our counselors on Madison Avenue, has ruined many good contracts in business and marriage, so this would seem to be an area worthy of our most intensive efforts at control. The answer that experts came up with involved the use of a group of chemicals called the chlorofluoro-carbons, or CFCs, which they manufactured and used as propellents in aerosol deodorants and as coolants in automobile air conditioners. By 1985 the United States was producing more than 900 tons of these chemicals, roughly one-third of the world total. I suppose that must be a lot of gas; I have trouble visualing what *one* ton of gas looks like, let alone 900 of them.

The surprise was not they didn't work. On the contrary, they proved pretty effective in keeping people cool and dry, and in keeping Big Macs warm (in the form of styrofoam containers), putting out fires (the CFC's are an important component in many fire extinguishers), fumigating grain, and dry-cleaning clothes. No, the surprise came from way up in the stratosphere, far removed from the places where the chemicals were normally used. CFCs eventually float free from their original purposes, drift into the upper levels of the air, and set off chemical reactions there that destroy ozone. Ozone is a form of oxygen that screens out, we have only recently learned, most of the solar ultraviolet-B radiation that is hazardous to humans and all other forms of life. Destroying that ozone is clearly not a smart thing to do. The surprise is not only that we have been destroying ozone far from any human eyes but also that the rate of destruction may have been happening at a much faster rate than anyone supposed. The National Cancer Institute estimates that every one percent depletion of the ozone layer will result in about 20,000 additional cases of non-melanoma skin cancer in the United States. And a Norwegian team of scientists estimates that by the end of this century 8 percent of the ozone layer lying over the fiftieth degree latitude will be gone, and by the year 2030 A.D. 4 percent of the ozone over the fortieth latitude (roughly the line from Philadelphia through Denver) will have disappeared, threatening a national epidemic of cancer. That seems a high price to pay for a few companies' profits, for wealth trickling down to the rest of us, even for an America that has achieved "underarm freshness."[3]

The more we think we have this planet under firm, rational control, turning empty wasteland into an endless supply of useful commodities, the more we are hit with such surprises. They are occurring with increasing frequency because the control that we thought we were achieving was, in fact, only partial, based as it was on a limited knowledge, a knowledge that was improving but not nearly so fast as the productive machinery, and, most important, because we did not understand how limited our knowledge was, is, and always will be. We may manage to control perspiration all right, but in the process unwittingly end up increasing our susceptibility to skin cancer.

The environmental crisis that has emerged over the last half century, though unprecedented in scope and complexity, is not the first in history. The human past reveals a long chain of crises stemming from a lack of knowledge or foresight, though typically before the modern era they were highly localized. The migrants from Asia, for instance, who entered North America some 30,000 to 40,000 years ago had no idea, as they stalked and slaughtered the hairy mammoths gathering around a waterhole, that they would one day run out of easy meat and then would have to make drastic changes in their weapons and hunting targets. I am sure too that the ancient Mesopotamians never imagined, as they dug their irrigation ditches to raise crops in the desert, that one day they would find those ditches filling with silt and their fields poisoned with salt. Much of human history appears as a succession of ecological surprises, many of them tragic, that communities have encountered on their way to dinner or a warm bed.

From our own vantage today it might seem that all those past people of history failed to achieve some enduring method of getting a living from the earth because they were ignorant of how the natural world works. Had the Pleistocene hunters had a few of our computer-armed population biologists advising them, had the Mesopotamians had the advantage of modern hydraulic engineering, no surprises would have happened. Those folks lived in illiterate, irrational times, in contrast to our state of enlightenment.

But if all that was lacking in the past was scientific understanding, then we men and women of the late twentieth century surely ought to be beyond almost all possibility of ecological surprise and failure. Somebody has calculated that one out of every ten scientists who ever lived is alive today. We ought, therefore, to have enough of them around, and enough laboratories and research programs, to manage our relations supremely well with the natural world, so well that we could leave all fear of failure behind us. This ought to be the age of absolutely reliable control, when human life runs along in a steady course, when the earth hums like a Japanese factory, when no one ever sweats and no one ever has to worry about their children getting skin cancer.

Perhaps the single most impressive lesson of history, however, is that, despite all our scientific expertise, all our investment in productive machinery, all the wealth we have acquired, we still have not escaped from the inadequacy of our knowledge. On the contrary, each year we encounter greater ecological steering problems than before, which we are unprepared to handle. And this managerial crisis threatens to go on increasing in seriousness well into the next century.

In 1967, when the phrase "environmental" or "ecological crisis" first began to appear widely in the press, the distinguished medievalist Lynn White, Jr., presented a historical analysis of our predicament that deserves to be read and reread regularly by the world's policy makers, though I will argue in a moment that it was ultimately an unpersuasive analysis. White doubted that we could resolve the crisis by "applying to our problems more science and more technology."[4] In fact, trying to resolve it without understanding its roots, as our technicians seemed to be doing, ran the risk of making it even worse. He was not advocating that we do nothing unless we can do something grandiose, nor was he unsympathetic toward the technicians pressured to find some immediate, pragmatic solutions. But as a historian he saw in the crisis some larger cultural challenges that too often scientists, engineers, economists, politicians, and others had not even studied, let alone understood, and he insisted that addressing those larger challenges must be part of any lasting resolution of the crisis.

"Human ecology," White pointed out, "is deeply conditioned by beliefs about our nature and destiny—that is, by religion." He argued that the environmental crisis emerged, not just yesterday, but over the long sweep of Western civilization. Specifically, it was the outgrowth of the Judeo-Christian religious heritage, going all the way back to the time of Moses but emerging most aggressively in the Middle Ages. "By destroying pagan animism," White wrote, which had taught humans a respect for the power and spirit dwelling in the natural world, "Christianity made it possible to exploit nature in a mood of indifference to the feelings of natural objects." The Western religious tradition saw humans as the only species of moral significance on the earth and thereby sanctioned the uninhibited use, the misuse, even the wholesale extermination of the rest of the living world for the sake of satisfying human needs. Modern science and technology inherited from that religious tradition an attitude of indifference toward the intrinsic value of other forms of life, an attitude of militant anthropocentrism. To focus all the blame on contemporary technology for the crisis was to miss that profound moral conditioning that determined how technology was developed and used. The modern crisis, in other words, could not be explained as a mere deficiency in managerial skill among the technicians. More and better job training for them would not be enough, nor more and better tools. Rather, all people needed to think in less anthropocentric terms about our place in nature. We had to confront the powerful moral influence of Christianity and find an alternative relationship with the earth if human ecology was to escape its mounting crisis.[5]

Historians like Lynn White never make things easier for others, for they tend to give big, abstract answers to questions that most people hope are concrete, uncomplicated, and quickly solvable. Couldn't we just recycle newspapers, we want to ask. Couldn't someone just give us a list of "fifty simple things we can do to save the earth"? No, White would have answered, we've got to do much more than that—do nothing less than reinvent our religion. We've got to think about the burdens of history, the deep, complex trap that traditional culture has left us in; we've got to question the ways we have learned to react to the world around us. It's a tough project.

As a fellow historian, I share White's ambition to dig deeply into the past to illuminate the present. But it seems to me that we don't have to look so far back as the Book of Genesis nor do we have to indict the entire Christian heritage for our situation. We have a much shorter and distinctly *modern* cultural history to understand and fix.

Take, for example, the matter of human population. Most of us would agree that a world population of five billion, going on ten billion, is an important cause of our ecological problems and that solving them would be far easier if local, national, and global populations were far smaller than they are. But how did we ever let ourselves rise to these incredible numbers? What is the historical explanation?

White's analysis would refer us back to the passage in the first chapter of Genesis where God told Adam and Eve to "multiply and replenish the earth" as part of their mission to exercise dominion over the other creatures. They did so—and here we are today, turning the Garden of Eden into the streets of Calcutta. Well, perhaps there is some truth in that analysis, but it is not a very large truth. Most men and women have thought of something other than Genesis 1:28 when they coupled. Even if they did take personally the commandment to "multiply and replenish" the earth, they could not have imagined they were called on to reproduce five billion of their kind, swarming and eating and defecating, could not have imagined a Mexico City approaching thirty million inhabitants. Only the Pope or Jimmy Swaggert could look at such a scene and say it is the will of God working wonderously through the human loins.

Genesis must be read in the context of its times, which was an altogether more static one than we know today. If God gave humans an explicit order to maintain dominion over the world of nature, what He had in mind was a fixed, orderly kind of nature, a permanent world of ecological relationships, a stable hierarchy organized in a predetermined chain of being. He did not sanction or license any *revolution* in the earth's ecosystems. Read correctly, Genesis does not give any real support to the modern runaway growth syndrome in world population, or for that matter in gross national product or personal affluence. The extraordinary increase in human numbers is unmistakably a modern phenomenon, responding to modern secular forces, and we must seek to understand it in distinctly modern terms.

Population growth began in dreadful earnest only after the year 1750. Whatever growth had occurred before then was much more gradual, and so tenuous that a single microorganism could nearly wipe out a country. From 1750 to 1845, however, the population in Europe increased by 80 percent, more than twice the previous record, a 36 percent increase achieved in the twelfth century. Such extraordinary growth has gone on ever since, becoming even ordinary and expected, but the big increases now are outside of Europe. Since 1900, the population of Africa has shot up from 110 million to 630 million. Maybe a small bit of that is due to the influence of Catholic missionaries railing against contraceptives, but I doubt if very much of it is. Families began to grow bigger in Europe, and then in Africa, Latin America, and Asia, because more of their children survived infancy, and more survived infancy because the economic conditions of the modern world allowed them to survive. It was wealth that allowed the numbers to explode. Even among the poorest nations of the world people acquired enough wealth to be able to afford better sanitation, better nutrition, and better medicine than they had had before.[6]

If we want to understand this significant aspect of the modern environmental crisis, therefore, we must understand the new condition of wealth—understand how and why it was generated. The book of Genesis does not say anything about it, nor do the teachings of Jesus (on the contrary; Jesus denounced wealth and held up the ideal of voluntary poverty), nor did Lynn White's medieval church. In fact, throughout most of their history Jews and Christians have not been notable for the size of their wealth or for their productivity or economic ambitions; compared with, say, the Egyptians or Chinese, they were a shabby lot. Perhaps they were more arrogant toward the rest of nature and toward their pagan neighbors, but they were not richer or more acquisitive. Instead of focusing on that ancient religious heritage to try to explain how so many people have been kept alive in the modern world, we must try to discover what it is that has created in recent centuries so much wealth and, despite a great deal of inequity, has spread it to so many people.

I believe the most important roots lie not in any particular technology of production or health care—the advent of medical inoculations, for example, or better plows and crops, or the steam engine, or the coal industry, all of which were outcomes more than causes—but rather in modern culture itself, in its world-view that has swept aside much of the older religious outlook. Let us call this modern culture by a simple name but think about it as a complex phenomenon: the world-view of *materialism*. It has two parts, economic and scientific, so intertwined and interdependent that even now historians have not fully probed their intellectual linkage. Together, the two parts forced a powerful cultural turn as important as what Karl Jaspers has called the "Axial Period" of human history, which occurred in the sixth and fifth centuries B.C., when so many of the world's great religious and philosophical systems took form—Confucianism, Buddhism, the pre-Socratics in Greece, the Old Testament prophets.[7] I see this new world-view—"post-Axial" we might call it—taking over western Europe in the seventeenth and especially the eighteenth century A.D., after a long spawning period, and manifesting itself in many so-called "revolutions," including the Scientific, the Industrial, the Capitalist, all of which were only surface manifestations of a more fundamental change of thought.

For the biophysical world the more immediately significant impact came from the materialism that was economic. I mean the view that improving one's physical condition—i.e., achieving more comfort, more bodily pleasure, and especially a higher level of affluence—is the greatest good in life, greater than securing the salvation of one's soul, greater than learning reverence for nature or God. It encompasses the view that any individual's or people's success is best judged in terms of the number of their worldly possessions and their economic productivity. In current parlance, I mean worshiping the god of GNP. All through earlier history there were individuals who lived by a materialistic standard, but we cannot find any whole culture where materialism defined the dominant system of values until we arrive at the modern age, which is emphatically, unabashedly materialist in its ultimate goals and daily strategies.

This materialist revolution was also notable, I have hinted, for its *secularism*. That is, it was not motivated primarily by religious motives or visions; in fact it undertook to free people from a fear of the supernatural and tried to direct attention away from the after-life to this-life and to elevate the profane over the sacred. This secularized culture came to supersede not only Judeo-Christianity but almost all the other traditional religious and ethical systems of the world—not entirely but enough to make them secondary, marginal influences. A growing secularism put religious feelings on the defensive, even invaded the very core of religious expression, subverting and distorting it into many strange new forms, so that today we can find unembarrassed Hindu gurus buying fleets of Rolls-Royces or Protestant television evangelists selling glitzy condos in a religious theme park.

Materialist culture was also *progressive*. It repudiated the attitude toward time in traditional mentality, where preserving ancient, well-established cycles of nature and culture was considered one of the highest duties. Now, duty meant moving oneself and one's society ahead, escaping the patterns of the past, throwing off the dead weight of tradition. We call this the idea of progress and, though it has a moral or spiritual aspect, we think of progress mainly as an endless economic or technological improvement on the present. Take the materialist core out of progressivism and it loses most of its appeal, its power over the imagination, its driving force. And that material improvement, moderns assume, is due wholly to the exertions of human will. As J. B. Bury pointed out in his classic study of the idea, "The process must be the necessary outcome of the psychical and social nature of man; it must not be at the mercy of any external will; otherwise there would be no guarantee of its continuance and its issue, and the idea of Progress would lapse into the idea of Providence."[8]

And then, appearing as a third charactistic, this new world-view of materialism armed itself with an all-sufficing, elegant, self-reliant mode of thought called *rationalism*, which was supposed to take the place of authority or spiritual revelation. Rationalism taught a new confidence in the ability of human reason to discover all the laws of nature and turn them to account. It emphasized the inherent capability of average men and women to discover the right principles of action, or at least to discover their own enlightened self-interest and act accordingly. This new rationalism urged people to overcome their self-doubt and humility and strike out on their own. Pride, lust, gluttony, envy, selfishness, and greed all vanished as sins or were redeemed from their sordid past by the alchemy of reason and thus—extraordinary transvaluation!—became acceptable as the very engines of progress.

I have said that there are two dimensions to materialism as a world-view: economic and scientific. The latter is absolutely essential to the former, and may even be the prerequiste for its existence. This other materialism is the philosophy that nature is nothing but physical matter organized under and obeying physical laws, matter rationally ordered but devoid of any spirit, soul, or in-dwelling, directing purpose. On this view of nature converge many of our modern university departments of learning along with our extra-academic institutions of research and development, governmental bureaucracies, and multinational corporations, all of which tend to approach nature as nothing more than dead matter.

Historians of ideas point to the French philosopher René Descartes as the chief prophet of scientific (or mechanistic) materialism, for it was he who laid the foundations for the modern mechanistic perspective in both physics and biology. One of Descartes's main assumptions was that animals and plants are mere machines, constructed from material particles and somehow arranged to conform with the mathematical laws of motion: mere clocklike apparatuses, capable of complex behavior but lacking souls. In a way that no truly traditional Christian, believing in the sanctity of God's creation, could share, Descartes looked on nature simply as raw material to be exploited by the human brain. The aim of modern science, he argued, is to "know the power and action of fire, water, air, the stars, the heavens and all the other bodies in our environment, as distinctly as we know the various crafts of our artisans; and we could use this knowledge—as the artisans use theirs—for all the purposes for which it is appropriate, and thus make ourselves, as it were, the lords and masters of nature."[9] It is a dream that resonates down through the centuries, promising an intellectual conquest of mind over matter that knows no bounds.

Descartes did his most influential work in the second quarter of the seventeenth century, but even before him, in the first quarter of that century, another philosopher of science, the Englishman Francis Bacon, made even more explicit the link between the two halves of modern materialism. Scientific materialism, Bacon promised, would provide the means for improving the human economic estate—harnessing ideas to practical ends, thereby making us all rich beyond counting. Through active science, he promised, we could do more than sit passively in a seat of honor over the rest of creation, as Genesis had allowed; we could become creators ourselves, turning the rest of creation into power and wealth, using our reason to enlarge "the bounds of Human Empire, to the effecting of all things possible." Bacon was a modern materialist through and through. The chief end of human existence for him was not the quietistic worship or contemplation of nature or of nature's God, nor mortifying the flesh, nor learning meekness and virtue; instead, we must seize the chance to expand our empire over the earth. "The world," he declared, is made for man, not man for the world."[10]

Thus this new world-view—a materialistic outlook that was secular, progressive, and rational—stole onto the European scene, fought against the declining power of the Church and feudal order, and eventually won over the leading minds of the era. This world-view was carried along in the minds of Europeans invading the New World, conquering and exploiting its riches. They had the vast treasure room of Africa in their sights too, and soon would open up India for the new empire of commerce and reason, founding trading posts at Bombay in 1661 and Calcutta in 1691.

Everywhere they came upon civilizations of stunning beauty, but always it was a beauty embedded in outworn religious and philosophical systems, which put the highest human value on the immaterial and spiritual. Those backward foreign peoples all seemed to be slogging along in ignorance of the great material possibilities that lay around them—the potential of their lands to produce inexhaustible wealth.

The natives of North America, for instance, seemed to the English and French invaders to be a very unenterprising people, lazy and indifferent to their poverty and discomfort. Even a Jesuit missionary, Chrétien Le Clercq, would emphasize mainly their astonishing ignorance of the materialist point of view:

> They are convinced [he wrote] that fifteen to twenty lumps of meat, or of fish dried or cured in the smoke, are more than enough to support them for the space of five to six months. Since, however, they are a people of good appetite, they consume their provisions very much sooner than they expect. This exposes them often to the danger of dying from hunger, through lack of the provision which they could easily possess in abundance if they would only take the trouble to gather it.[11]

The most revealing words in that indictment are the ones reading "to possess in abundance," which distill perfectly the new European cultural principle, one that even a priest, ostensibly seeking to convert souls to Christianity, would use to judge others by. During the seventeenth century such words served as a powerful justification for conquest, warning the invaded nations that they too must be in hot pursuit of abundance or they must lose their right to occupy the land. Eventually those words would echo back from the wildest, most remote parts of the earth, overrun by a people of enterprise, though only since World War Two have they become a nearly universal *global* creed, influencing the minds of all but the most inaccessible peasant communities. To "possess in abundance" is nothing less than the modern project.

All these ideas have been so often and so well studied that it seems a little trite to insist on them here, yet even today the profound environmental consequences in that shift to materialism, or even the very fact of the shift, are not understood widely enough, nor do many people, in reading about the disappearance of tropical rain forests or the disposal of toxic wastes, stop to realize that these current problems have their roots in a cultural turn that began centuries ago and often in a land far away.

Such cultural shifts do not, of course, come full-blown from the mind of a single man or woman, but rather indicate deep, nearly simultaneous shifts in the minds of thousands, even millions, of people—whole civilizations suddenly taking off in unison like a flock of geese migrating to the north country, wheeling and dipping in close formation as though wired together. A single great mind, however, can reveal the general direction in which the flock is flying and draw the map that others are following by instinct. The individual who more than any other served that function for the rising materialist world-view was an English-speaking philosopher and scientific economist, Adam Smith. I nominate him as the representative modern man, the most complete embodiment of that cultural shift; and recommend that it is he, not Moses, whom we must understand if we are to get down to the really important roots of the modern environmental crisis. Robert Heilbroner has spoken almost irreverently of "the wonderful world of Adam Smith," but in his time Smith was indeed a wonderful visionary, as he remains for many today who are just now discovering his logic and perspective.[12] So how did Adam Smith look on the world around him? Where did nature fit into his thinking? What were the long-term implications that his ideas had for the natural order of Planet Earth?

A large homely fellow with a bad twitch and an absent-minded air, Smith was a most unlikely looking leader for any intellectual revolution. He was born in 1723 in the seaside town of Kirkcaldy, directly across the Firth of Forth from Edinburgh, where he grew up among fishermen and smugglers with the smell of salt air in his nostrils. After university studies in Oxford, a teaching post in Glasgow, and travels as a gentleman's tutor in France, he returned home in his mid-forties to Kirkcaldy and, living unmarried with his mother, devoted himself to writing his great book, *The Wealth of Nations,* published in that revolutionary year 1776. Although he is described as one who liked to take long solitary walks along the seashore, he never actually expressed any love of the sea or admiration of its beauty, never seems to have watched with any interest a gull hovering in the air, a crab scurrying over the rocks, the tide moving in and out. And though he lived in a Scotland that had severe ecological problems caused by overgrazing, deforestation, and soil depletion, he never considered how the Scots might change their land-use practices and become better stewards of their patrimony. And though many of his contemporaries were enthusiastic naturalists—it was a fabulous age of natural history, including the remarkable Gilbert White of Selborne, Carolus Linnaeus of Sweden, comte Georges-Louis Leclerc du Buffon of France—Smith seems to have lived his entire life utterly oblivious of the nature around him. He set out to revolutionize the study of human economics in total disregard of the economy of nature.[13]

What Smith knew and thought about was the expanding life of commerce and industry, the rising class of businessmen, the mind of the entrepreneur, the factory system of production, most of which was found far from Kirkcaldy. Instead of moving to the very centers of commerce where he could make great bundles of money for himself, he chose to stand aside and observe, to see how it was done by others, and to help his nation, Great Britain, figure out how wealth had been and might be gained. Ironically, he was a humanitarian, a disinterested materialist who celebrated the amoral pursuit of self-interest.

The secret to increasing the wealth of nations turned out to be rather simple, though it took Smith an enormous body of text to reveal it. A nation that seeks wealth, he concluded, must establish a "system of natural liberty" in which "every man, as long as he does not violate the laws of justice, is left perfectly free to pursue his own interest in his own way, and to bring both his industry and capital into competition with those of any other man, or order of men."[14] Note that Smith called this system "natural," for he believed it was in harmony with the laws of human nature. It is natural, he believed, for humans to want, above all else, to increase their material comforts, to add to their sum of riches by "truck[ing], barter[ing], and exchang[ing] one thing for another." If that truly is the way all people naturally behave, then a society or culture would itself be most natural when it allowed, or even encouraged, people to enjoy as much freedom as possible in pursuit of their acquisitive natures. Smith did add what is overlooked by many of his later disciples that a society may also rightfully restrain those human natures in the interest of social justice, but such restraint should not interfere too much with private freedom. To attempt to legislate a general benevolence, he believed, would be to try to overturn the laws of nature.

So little did Adam Smith consider what most people, then and now, mean by nature—the flora and fauna, the soil and water—that we cannot really speak at length about his philosophy of the subject. This much can be said: he did not conceive that the non-human realm lays any obligations on humans. What Christians called the Creation, what their religion required them to respect as the handiwork of God, had become for the economist quite valueless in and of itself. Value, in his view, is a quality that humans create through their labor out of the raw materials afforded by nature. A thing has value only when and if it serves some direct human use ("value in use") or can be exchanged for something else that has value ("value in exchange"). One of Smith's most influential predecessors, John Locke, declared that "the intrinsic natural worth of anything consists in its fitness to supply the necessities or serve the conveniences of human life."[15] He meant that nothing in the unimproved natural world has any intrinsic worth—a worth in and of itself—but only an instru-

mental worth, measured by whatever human uses it can serve. Likewise
for Smith, nature is only instrumental and has worth or value only to the
extent it has been "improved" by human labor.

The wealth indicated in *The Wealth of Nations* does not include any of
the material benefits that humans derive from unimproved land: the air
and water that sustain life, the process of photosynthesis in plants, the
intricate food chains that we draw on for sustenance, the microorganisms
that decompose rotting carcasses and return them to the soil. In a passage
from the chapter "The Employment of Capitals," Smith does refer passingly to a "nature" that "labours along with man" in agriculture, adding
fertility to the soil just as servants and domestic animals add their labor
to improving the master's property. "Though her labour costs no ex-
pence," he writes, "its produce has its value, as well as that of the most
expensive workman." In another passage dealing with Columbus's discovery of the New World, he indicates that "the real riches of every country" are "the animal and vegetable products of the soil," but then adds
that Columbus found little wealth on his voyages but cotton and gold,
dismissing even the Indian corn, yams, potatoes, and bananas the Italian
brought back to Europe as unimportant economically. Smith mentions
among the fruits of the Americas "some reeds of an extraordinary size,
some birds of a very beautiful plumage, and some stuffed skins of the huge
alligator and manati [sic]," all of which he quickly dismisses as "objects
of vulgar wonder and curiosity." In these two isolated passages from the
book, nature does put in a brief appearance, but only as a kind of servant
adding to the stock of wealth: productive only in the sense of soil fertility
but otherwise almost contemptible. Unimproved nature was for Smith a
"vulgar" show, unworthy of a great man's interest. If he got anything out
of those seashore rambles in the way of spontaneous delight or spiritual
enlightenment, he kept it out of his text.[16]

The men who have followed Adam Smith's economic materialism
have, it is true, not always been as blind as the professor to the vulgar
wonders of nature. Many entrepreneurs, after gaining wealth by all the
rational greed that Smith wanted to encourage, have used their wealth to
buy a country estate where they could idle about in the presence of nature.
Often they have taken such places of retreat out of intensive production,
even turned them back into unimproved wasteland. Smith would have
strongly disapproved of the practice; those who don't want to use land to
make money, he would have said, should turn it over to those who do—to
the man-on-the-make who will sweat a profit out of every acre. But, ignoring Smith a bit, society has tolerated these lapses from the imperatives of
materialism and gone even farther to set aside large national and city

parks and wilderness areas where everyone, landowners and non-land-owners alike, can go to experience a nature that is devoted to something besides the pursuit of wealth.

With these exceptions, the worldly philosophy of Adam Smith has become the dominant one in all the industrial nations, from Great Britain and Germany to the United States and Japan (the bulk of Smith's library now resides in Tokyo). So also in the nations that have followed, however faithfully or not, the teachings of Karl Marx, including the late Soviet Union. Marx may have been a sharp critic of the Smithian model of promoting economic growth through market freedom, but like Smith he was emphatically a materialist: secular, progressive, and rationalistic to the core, a fierce critic of all the traditional religions, all forms of pagan animism or Christian superstition, all reverence toward the earth. Marx and the Marxists were radicals for social justice, but they had the goal of material abundance firmly in mind too and were devoted to the modern worldview.[17]

Now every economy in history, from that of the Bushman of Australia to that of global capitalism, has tried to extract resources from nature and turn them to human advantage. But no economy finds those resources in a void; they all must come out of a larger order or system. We can call that larger order "the economy of nature," following the lead of Smith's neglected contemporaries, the eighteenth-century naturalists.[18] In this light every economy that humans have devised must appear as only a dependent economy, deriving from that greater one. We have not invented nature's economy; we have inherited it through eons of evolution. We learn to take things out of it for our own use and circulate them for a while within our little economy, turning forests into houses and books before yielding them to rot and mildew. The human economy requires for its longterm success that its architects acknowledge their dependence on the greater economy of nature, preserving its health and respecting its benefits. By this standard every modern economy, whether built on the principles of Adam Smith or Karl Marx, is an unmitigated disaster.[19]

Once we acknowledge that the economy of nature is real and indispensable, then this entire modern way of thinking appears in a withering light as overweening pride in inadequate intelligence and skill. Living by overconfident materialism, people come to believe that they can create all the fertility they need by adding to the soil a bag of chemicals, that they can create any amount of wealth out of the most impoverished landscape, that they can even create life itself in a glass tube. To be sure, human artifice has improved our power over the elements, suggesting that nature's economy does not set rigid or fixed limits to our existence. But now we are learning that we cannot use that power as safely as we thought. We cannot anticipate all the consequences of our ingenuity, and greed, no matter how rationalized, remains the root of evil and self-destruction.

If my argument is right and the environmental crisis is really the long-preparing consequence of this modern world-view of materialism, economic and scientific, then it makes no sense to blame any of the traditional religions of the world. Religion, on the whole, acted to check that materialism, to question human arrogance, and to hold in fearful suspicion the dangerous powers of greed. Religion, including Christianity, stood firmly against a reductive, mechanistic view of the world. It pointed to a subordinate and restrained role for humans in the cosmos. And, most importantly for the sake of the biosphere, it taught people that there are higher purposes in life than consumption.

The ecological crisis we have begun to experience in recent years is fast becoming *the* crisis of modern culture, calling into question not only the ethos of the marketplace or industrialism but also the central story that we have been telling ourselves over the past two or three centuries: the story of man's triumph by reason over the rest of nature. But having presented that argument, I cannot now recommend that we slip backwards in time and solve the crisis by reading the Bible or Koran again. It is not possible, or even desirable, to try to go back to a pre-modern religious world-view. We cannot so simply undo what we have become. For this reason I must once more disagree with Lynn White, who proposed that the world convert to the religious teachings of St. Francis of Assisi, the famous thirteenth-century Italian monk who embraced the plants and animals as his equals and beloved kinfolk. The idea of making Franciscans of everyone in the world would be an ethnocentric and anachronistic solution to the modern dilemma.

So what can we do? What is the solution to the environmental crisis brought on by modernity and its materialism? The only deep solution open to us is to begin transcending our fundamental world-view—creating a post-materialist view of ourselves and the natural world, a view that summons back some of the lost wisdom of the past but does not depend on a return to old discarded creeds. I mean a view that acknowledges the superiority of science over superstitition but also acknowledges that all scientific description is only an imperfect representation of the cosmos, an acknowledgment that is the foundation of respect. I mean the view that all consumption beyond a level of modest sufficiency is pathological in both a personal and an ecological sense; like any kind of gluttony it deserves pity, not approval. I mean the view that greed is always a vice, not a virtue, that unlimited economic growth or "development" has become a fanatical drive against the earth. Whether such a viewpoint might first appear in the most advanced industrial societies, where so many people have begun to have doubts about the world they have made, or in the least advanced, where most people are still converting to the modern notions, though with many doubts of their own, I cannot say; only that such a post-materialist culture must appear somewhere in embryonic form and spread eventually, as the doctrines of Adam Smith have done, to the farthest corners of the earth. Historians make only indifferent prophets, and I will not try to predict when or how such a post-materialist culture will appear, though it seems inevitable that such a shift will occur at some point. No world-view has lasted forever.

A biologist at Cambridge University, Rupert Sheldrake, has recently written that traditional Cartesian science is already beginning to break down, mainly among biologists dissatisfied with that reductive approach to understanding the processes of life. He points to the continuing elusiveness of the life principle in the laboratory, the way in which life continues to defy mechanistic analysis; and he points to the rise of chaos theory, to a new appreciation of creativity and spontaneity in evolution, to the Gaian hypothesis of James Lovelock, and to the mystery of "dark matter" in contemporary physics, all of which ideas, he believes, are leading toward "a post-mechanistic world-view," in which nature once more becomes alive, spontaneous, creative, and unpredictable. "These developments," he writes, "have brought back many of the features of animate nature denied in the mechanistic revolution; in effect, they have begun to reanimate nature."[20]

We have heard the claim before that the newest theories in science will save us from the culture of materialism; Alfred North Whitehead, for example, made similar predictions back in the 1920s.[21] But even if we grant Mr. Sheldrake his argument that science is undergoing profound change, one that will have deep cultural effects, then we must still admit that a new science alone will not be enough to produce a new culture. We will also need a new post-materialist economics, if that is not a contradiction in terms, in which economic philosophers put back into the picture all that Adam Smith and his disciples have left out: the full economy of nature, the intrinsic worth of all beings, the beauty and wonder of the cosmos. The environmental crisis is making the modern mind obsolete. It demands a new economics, a new science, a new world-view to replace materialism. But where is the new Adam Smith who will help reveal the direction in which we ought to fly?

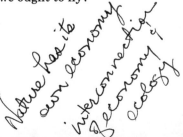

Notes

◆

Preface

1. Joseph Wood Krutch, *The Twelve Seasons: A Perpetual Calendar for the Country* (New York: William Sloane, 1949), 11.

Chapter 1

1. *The Travels of William Bartram,* ed. Mark Van Doren (New York: Dover, 1928; orig. pub. 1791), 107.

2. *The Journals of Lewis and Clark,* ed. Frank Bergeron (New York: Penguin, 1989), 36–37.

3. Frank Gilbert Roe, *The North American Buffalo: A Critical Study of the Species in Its Wild State* (Toronto: University of Toronto Press, 1951), 505. A higher estimate of 75 million came from Ernest Thompson Seton, in *Life Histories of Northern Animals* (New York: Charles Scribner's Sons, 1989), I, 292. See also Dan Flores, "Bison Ecology and Bison Diplomacy: The Southern Plains from 1800 to 1850," *Journal of American History,* 78 (September 1991), 465–85. According to Flores, "the Southern Plains might have supported an average of about 8.2 million bison, the entire Great Plains perhaps 28-30 million" (471).

4. "Letter of Coronado to the king, from the province of Tiguex, October 20, 1541," in *Narratives of the Coronado Expedition, 1540–1542,* ed. George P. Hammond and Agapito Ray (Albuquerque: University of New Mexico Press, 1940), 186.

5. A. W. Schorger, *The Passenger Pigeon: Its Natural History and Extinction* (Norman: University of Oklahoma Press, 1955), 204. Schorger estimates there were originally three, possibly five, billion of the birds. He also cites Roger Tory Peterson's estimate of 1941 that there were then six billion breeding birds of all species in the United States, or a density of about three birds per acre. See also Peter Matthiessen, *Wildlife in America,* revised ed. (New York: Viking, 1987).

6. See William M. Denevan, ed., *The Native Population of the Americas in 1492* (Madison: University of Wisconsin Press, 1976), esp. 2–4, 289–92. Denevan comes up with the figure of 4.4 million, slightly larger than Harold Driver's figure of 3.5 million, for Greenland, Canada, Alaska, and the rest of the United States; and for all of the Americas, he estimates

a native population of 57.3 million, a figure that might have varied 25 percent either way. For a much larger estimate, see Henry F. Dobyns, *Their Number Became Thinned: Native American Population Dynamics in Eastern North America* (Knoxville: University of Tennessee, 1983), 34–45. Dobyns arrives, by a series of extrapolations from estimated food supply, at the figure of eighteen million living north of civilized Mesoamerica in the early years of the sixteenth century, before introduced diseases struck them down. Most of his book deals with Florida, which he figures had nearly 800,000 aboriginal inhabitants—a number that is at least eight times larger than anyone else has found. Many demographers do not find Dobyns's methods or conclusions very reliable.

7. These calculations are based on data from *The Times Atlas of the World,* 7th ed. (London: Times Books Ltd., 1988).

8. See Lester R. Brown, "Reconsidering the Automobile's Future," *State of the World, 1984,* ed. Brown et al. (New York: Norton, 1984), 157–74.

9. Sam H. Schurr and Bruce C. Netschert, *Energy in the American Economy, 1850–1975* (Baltimore: Johns Hopkins University Press, 1960), 36. Having cut a lot of cordwood myself to burn through New England winters, I find their figures suspiciously high. They also calculate that the total U.S. consumption of energy in 1850 was 2,357 trillion BTUs, while in 1976 it was 80,681 trillion. See also Martin V. Melosi, *Coping with Abundance: Energy and Environment in Industrial America* (Philadelphia: Temple University Press, 1985).

10. World Resources Institute and the International Institute for Environment and Development, *World Resources 1988–89* (New York: Basic Books, 1988), 306.

11. Thomas Jefferson, *Notes on the State of Virginia* (New York: Harper Torchbooks, 1964; orig. pub. 1785), 48. A good discussion of this theme, and of eighteenth-century American ideas of nature generally, is Daniel Boorstin, *The Lost World of Thomas Jefferson* (Boston: Beacon Press, 1948), chaps. 1–3. I have discussed some of these ideas at more length in my book *Nature's Economy: A History of Ecological Ideas* (New York: Cambridge University Press, 1977), chap. 2.

12. *The Age of Reason,* Part I (orig. 1794), in *Thomas Paine: Representative Selections,* ed. by Harry Hayden Clark (New York: Hill & Wang, American Century Series, 1961), 278.

13. Garry Wills shrewdly analyzes its tenacity in *Reagan's America: Innocence at Home* (New York: Random House Vintage, 1987).

Chapter 2

1. *The Journal of Jacob Fowler,* ed. Elliott Coues (Lincoln: University of Nebraska Press, 1970), 30–31. Fowler was born in New York in 1765, later moved to Kentucky, where he married a widow and kept a farm near Covington.

2. "Translation of a Letter from Coronado to the King, October 20, 1541," in George Parker Winship, "The Coronado Expedition, 1540–1542," *14th Annual Report of the Bureau of American Ethnology, 1892–1893, Part I* (Washington: Government Printing Office, 1896), 582.

3. Sheridan Ploughe, *History of Reno County Kansas* (Indianapolis: B. F. Bowen, 1917), I, 327–29; Tim Stuckey, *Reno County: The Early Years* (Pretty Prairie, Kans.: Prairie Publications, 1985).

4. On this nature-vs.-culture split I have profited from reading Neil L. Jamieson and George W. Lovelace, "Cultural Values and Human Ecology: Some Initial Considerations," in *Cultural Values and Human Ecology in Southeast Asia,* ed. Karl L. Hutterer, A. Terry Rambo, and George Lovelace, Center for South and Southeast Asian Studies, University of Michigan, No. 27 (Ann Arbor: University of Michigan Press, 1985), 27–54; and Alice E. Ingerson, "Some Practical Effects and Radical Uses of the Nature/Culture Dichotomy" (unpublished essay).

5. A useful introduction to the field are the essays by William Cronon, Alfred Crosby,

Carolyn Merchant, Stephen Pyne, Richard White, and myself in "A Roundtable: Environmental History," *Journal of American History*, 76 (March 1990), 1087–1147; my own contribution to that discussion is reprinted in this book under the title, "Transformations of the Earth." Also see Donald Worster, ed., *The Ends of the Earth: Essays on Modern Environmental History* (New York: Cambridge University Press, 1988).

6. See Arthur F. McEvoy, *The Fisherman's Problem: Ecology and Law in the California Fisheries, 1850–1980* (New York: Cambridge University Press, 1986).

7. See, for example, F. E. Graedel and P. J. Crutzen, "Atmospheric Trace Constituents," in *The Earth As Transformed by Human Action*, ed. B. L. Turner II, et al. (Cambridge: Cambridge University Press, 1990), 300–301.

8. Lewis Mumford, *The Pentagon of Power* (New York: Harcourt Brace Jovanovich, 1970), 393.

9. Andrew B. Appleby, "Epidemics and Famine in the Little Ice Age," *Climate and History: Studies in Interdiscipinary History*, ed. Robert I. Rotberg and Theodore K. Rabb (Princeton: Princeton University Press, 1981), 63–84. The pioneering studies in this area were H. H. Lamb, *Climate: Present, Past and Future* (London: Methuen, 1972), and Emmanuel Le Roy Ladurie, *Times of Feast, Times of Famine: A History of Climate Since the Year 1000*, trans. Barbara Bray (London: Allen and Unwin, 1972).

10. See L. N. Gumilev, *Searches for an Imaginary Kingdom: The Legend of the Kingdom of Prester John*, trans. R. E. Smith (Cambridge: Cambridge University Press, 1988).

11. Joy McCorriston and Frank Hole, "The Ecology of Seasonal Stress and the Origins of Agriculture in the Near East," *American Anthropology*, 93 (March 1991), 46–69.

12. John U. Nef, "An Early Energy Crisis and Its Consequences," *Scientific American*, 237 (1977), 140–51; Richard Wilkinson, *Poverty and Progress: An Ecological Perspective on Economic Development* (New York: Praeger, 1973), chap. 4; I. G. Simmons, *Changing the Face of the Earth: Culture, Environment, History* (Oxford: Basil Blackwell, 1989), 296–306.

13. Vaclav Smil, *The Bad Earth: Environmental Degradation in China* (New York: Sharpe, 1984), section 2.1.

14. R. P. Sieferle, "The Energy System—a Basic Concept of Environmental History," in *The Silent Countdown: Essays in European Environmental History*, ed. P. Brimblecombe and C. Pfister (Berlin and Heidelberg: Springer-Verlag, 1990), 14–15.

15. E. Schramm, "Experts in the Smelter Smoke Debate," *ibid.*, and 197; P. Brimblecombe and C. Bowler, "Air Pollution in York, 1850–1900," *ibid.*, 183.

16. See, for instance, Stephen J. Pyne, *Burning Bush: A Fire History of Australia* (New York: Henry Holt, 1991). The quotation is from page 82.

17. Buffon, "Des époques de la nature" (1779), in *Oeuvres complètes de Buffon* (Paris: Pourrat Frères, 1838), I, 479–569.

18. James Hutton, *Theory of the Earth* (Edinburgh: Cadell, Davie, Creech, 1795), II, 562.

19. An ecologist who has begun to study the landscape as influenced by human history is Norman Christensen of Duke University. See his essay, "Landscape History and Ecological Change," *Journal of Forest History*, 33 (July 1989), 116–25.

20. C. P. Snow, *The Two Cultures and the Scientific Revolution* (New York: Cambridge University Press, 1963; orig. given as Rede Lectures in 1959), 4–5.

Chapter 3

1. A good example of this earlier fusion of interests is the English naturalist and historian, Gilbert White (1720–93). See Donald Worster, *Nature's Economy* (New York, 1977), 3–11.

2. There is another trend, other than the ecological, that comes out of Darwinism—the sociobiological. Because it seems less useful to the historian, I neglect it here. Interested readers, however, might consult the work of Edward O. Wilson in this area, along with that

of William Hamilton, R. L. Trivers, D. P. Barash, and Konrad Lorenz. A provocative essay (and more directly relevant to history) is Donald Campbell's "On the Conflicts between Biological and Social Evolution and between Psychology and Moral Tradition," *American Psychologist,* XXX (1975), 1103–26. See also Richard Alexander, *Darwinism and Human Affairs* (Seattle, 1979); and N. A. Chagnon and W. G. Irons, eds., *Evolutionary Biology and Human Social Behavior* (North Scituate, Mass., 1979).

3. *Pacific Historical Review,* XLI (1972), 271–372. The main themes addressed in this issue were conservation, water development, wilderness, national parks, and the Department of the Interior. For new directions in the field, see the most recent issues of *Environmental History Review,* published by the American Society for Environmental History. Topics now include energy, environmental policies in the Netherlands, drought and revolution, and landscape aesthetics.

4. On Webb's work there are two book-length studies: Necah Furman, *Walter Prescott Webb: His Life and Impact* (Albuquerque, 1976); and Gregory Tobin, *The Making of a History: Walter Prescott Webb and "The Great Plains"* (Austin, 1976). On Malin, consult Robert Bell, "James C. Malin and the Grasslands of North America," *Agricultural History,* XLVI (1972), 414–24; and Robert Johannsen, "James C. Malin: An Appreciation," *Kansas Historical Quarterly,* XXXVII (1972), 457–66.

5. Webb, "Geographical-Historical Concepts in American History," *Annals of the Association of American Geographers,* L (1960), 87.

6. Malin, *On the Nature of History: Essays about History and Dissidence* (Lawrence, Kans., 1954), 27.

7. The sharpest attack on Webb's approach was Fred Shannon's "An Appraisal of Walter Prescott Webb's 'The Great Plains: A Study in Institutions and Environment,'" *Critiques of Research in the Social Sciences* (New York, 1940).

8. I have made this point in greater detail in my *Dust Bowl: The Southern Plains in the 1930s* (New York, 1979), 205–6; see also my *Nature's Economy,* 242–48.

9. See the massive intellectual biography by G. L. Ulmen, *The Science of Society: Toward an Understanding of the Life and Work of Karl August Wittfogel* (The Hague, 1978), esp. 89–103; also, see Ulmen, "Wittfogel's Science of Society," *Telos,* XXIV (1975), 81–114. The 1929 essay appeared in the journal *Unter dem Banner des Marxismus.*

10. The sources of this idea are traced by Anne Bailey and Josep Llobera in their *The Asiatic Mode of Production* (London, 1981), 13–45.

11. Wittfogel's seminal statement of this theme was his "Die Theorie der orientalischen Gesellschaft" (1938), which has been translated as "The Theory of Oriental Society" in *Readings in Anthropology,* ed. Morton Fried (2nd ed., 2 vols., New York, 1968), II, 179–98.

12. Originally published by Yale University Press and reissued as a Vintage paperback by Random House in 1981, with a new introduction by the author.

13. Wissler, *Man and Culture* (New York, 1923), and *The Relation of Nature to Man in Aboriginal North America* (New York, 1926). See also Alfred Kroeber, *Cultural and Natural Areas of Native North America* (Berkeley, 1939). June Helm discusses this early work in "The Ecological Approach in Anthropology," *American Journal of Sociology,* LXVII (1962), 630–31.

14. Steward, *Theory of Culture Change: The Methodology of Multilinear Evolution* (Urbana, 1963), 31.

15. Robert Murphy, "Introduction: The Anthropological Theories of Julian H. Steward," in *Evolution and Ecology: Essays on Social Transformation by Julian H. Steward,* ed. Jane Steward and Robert Murphy (Urbana, 1977), 1.

16. Steward, *Theory of Culture Change,* 37.

17. *Ibid.,* 40–42.

18. This symposium was later published in Steward, *et al., Irrigation Civilizations: A Comparative Study* (Washington, D.C., 1955). No papers were included on modern irrigation

civilizations, but, despite this serious omission, the crossfertilization between history and anthropology was a significant achievement. See Steward's later essay of tribute, "Wittfogel's Irrigation Hypothesis," in Steward and Murphy, *Evolution and Ecology,* 87–99.

19. Netting, *Cultural Anthropology* (Menlo Park, Calif., 1977), 4. The parallel with history is obvious; however, unlike anthropology, history's first stage was "politics," and it still has not gotten very far from it.

20. Some of these are monographs, others are articles. A good sampler is Andrew Vayda, ed., *Environment and Cultural Behavior: Ecological Studies in Cultural Anthropology* (Garden City, N.Y., 1969). For overviews of the field, see Donald Hardesty, *Ecological Anthropology* (New York, 1977); John Bennett, *The Ecological Transition: Cultural Anthropology and Human Adaptation* (New York, 1976); Richard and Patty Watson, *Man and Nature: An Anthropological Essay in Human Ecology* (New York, 1969); and J. N. Anderson, "Ecological Anthropology and Anthropological Ecology," in *Handbook of Social and Cultural Anthropology,* ed. J. J. Honigman (Chicago, 1974), 477–97.

21. Vayda and Rappaport, "Ecology, Cultural and Non-Cultural," in *Introduction to Cultural Anthropology,* ed. James Clifton (Boston, 1968), 492.

22. Rappaport, "Nature, Culture, and Ecological Anthropology," in *Man, Culture, and Society,* ed. Harry Shapiro (London, 1971), 247, 261–64. Also see his *Pigs for the Ancestors* (New Haven, 1968).

23. Among Harris's brilliant and feisty works, the most useful here are *The Rise of Anthropological Theory: A History of Theories and Culture* (New York, 1968), chap. 23, where he discusses Steward's, Wittfogel's, and his own theories; and *Cannibals and Kings: The Origins of Cultures* (New York, 1977), which ranges widely over history.

24. I have discussed Odum's work in *Nature's Economy,* 311–13.

25. Vayda and Bonnie McCay, "New Directions in Ecology and Ecological Anthropology," *Annual Review of Anthropology,* IV (1975), 294–95. Among the leading new textbooks are Paul Colinvaux, *Introduction to Ecology* (New York, 1973); Eric Pianka, *Evolutionary Ecology* (3rd ed., New York, 1982); Robert Ricklefs, *The Economy of Nature* (New York, 1976); and *Ecology* (2nd ed., New York, 1979).

26. See, for example, Jonathan Friedman, "Marxism, Structuralism and Vulgar Materialism," *Man,* IX (1974), 444–69. Harris is the main vulgarian.

27. Harris takes up the theories of Marx in his *Cultural Materialism: The Struggle for a Science of Culture* (New York, 1979), x–xi, 216–57. Some of that discussion was provoked by Marshall Sahlins's attack on Harris's "business mentality," in "Culture as Protein and Profit," *New York Review of Books,* XXV (Nov. 13, 1978), 45–53.

28. I echo here some comments by Immanuel Wallerstein in *The Capitalist World-Economy* (Cambridge; 1979), ix–x.

29. Originally published in French in 1975. The American edition was brought out in 1978. See especially Part One, "The Ecology of the Montaillou: The House and the Shepherd." Another and even more extraordinary work out of France is Fernand Braudel's *The Mediterranean and the Mediterranean World in the Age of Philip II,* trans. Siân Reynolds (New York, 1973), esp. I, 25–275, on "The Role of the Environment."

30. McNeill, *Plagues and Peoples* (Garden City, N. Y., 1976). Chapter 5 is very suggestive for the ecological study of the roots of capitalism and industrialism, though McNeill does not himself make the connections. Someone who does is Richard Wilkinson in *Poverty and Progress: An Ecological Perspective on Economic Development* (New York, 1973), 212. See also Harris, *Cannibals and Kings,* chap. 14; and E. L. Jones, "Environment, Agriculture, and Industrialization in Europe," *Agricultural History,* LI (1977), 491–502; E. L. Jones, *The European Miracle: Environments, Economics, and Geopolitics in the History of Europe and Asia* (Cambridge, 1981).

31. Darling, "The Ecological Approach to the Social Sciences," *American Scientist,* XXXIX (1951), 248.

32. My own study of the Dust Bowl was such an attempt; see footnote 7 for citation. There is also John Bennett's *Northern Plainsman: Adaptive Strategy and Agrarian Life* (Chicago, 1969), but the ecological study of modern agricultural history has only just begun.

33. See Crosby, "Ecological Imperialism: The Overseas Migration of Western Europeans as a Biological Phenomenon," *Texas Quarterly,* XXI (1978), 10–22. Also, see Wilbur Jacobs, "The Fatal Confrontation: Early Native-White Relations on the Frontiers of Australia, New Guinea, and America—A Comparative Study," *Pacific Historical Review,* XL (1971), 283–309; and Calvin Martin, *Keepers of the Game: Indian-Animal Relationships and the Fur Trade* (Berkeley, 1978). One of the great classics in frontier ecology is Owen Lattimore's *Inner Asian Frontiers of China* (Boston, 1951).

34. Sahlins, "Culture and Environment: The Study of Cultural Ecology," in *Horizons of Anthropology,* ed. Sol Tax (Chicago, 1964), 145.

35. The work of conservation historians like Samuel Hays, Roderick Nash, and Donald Swain has been very illuminating on these questions, though not placed in this particular perspective. For excellent recent work on the link between changing ideas of nature and changing human ecologies, see Carolyn Merchant, *The Death of Nature: Women, Ecology, and the Scientific Revolution* (San Francisco, 1980); and Keith Thomas, *Man and the Supernatural World: A History of the Modern Sensibility* (New York, 1983).

Chapter 4

1. Aldo Leopold, *A Sand County Almanac, and Sketches Here and There* (1949; reprint, New York, 1987), 205.

2. *Ibid.* When the soil is destroyed by a volcanic eruption or some other catastrophe, another process called primary succession begins, in which species that can gain a foothold on bare rock or subsoil invade and proliferate. A clear discussion of both types of succession can be found in Paul R. Ehrlich, *The Machinery of Nature* (New York, 1986), 268–71.

3. Leopold was aware that the story had more complexity to it; "we do not even know," he admitted, "where the bluegrass came from—whether it is a native species, or a stowaway from Europe." Leopold, *Sand County Almanac,* 206.

4. I take the phrase from Alfred Crosby, Jr., *Ecological Imperialism: The Biological Expansion of Europe, 900–1900* (New York, 1986).

5. The best effort to trace the emergence of the field, at least in one influential part of the world, is Richard White, "American Environmental History: The Development of a New Historical Field," *Pacific Historical Review,* 54 (Aug. 1985), 297–335. White argues that the study of frontier and western history has been the formative influence on this field. Another important source of ideas, quite removed from the influence of Frederick Jackson Turner, has been French historians and geographers, particularly Fernand Braudel, Lucien Febvre, and Emmanuel Le Roy Ladurie, all associated with the journal *Annales.*

6. George Woodwell, "On the Limits of Nature," in *The Global Possible: Resources, Development, and the New Century,* ed. Robert Repetto (New Haven, 1985), 47.

7. A good guide to this field is J. Robert Dodd and Robert J. Stanton, *Paleoecology: Concepts and Applications* (New York, 1981).

8. The phrase "modes of production" originated with Karl Marx, who used it in more than one way. In some cases he was referring to "the material mode," defined by G. A. Cohen as "the way men work with their productive forces, the kinds of material process they set in train, the forms of specialization and division of labour among them." In other cases, Marx employed the phrase to denote "social properties of the production process," including the purpose controlling production (whether for use or exchange), the form of the producer's surplus labor, and the means of exploiting producers. Then, again, at times he seems to have meant both material and social aspects at once. See G. A. Cohen, *Karl Marx's Theory of History: A Defense* (Princeton, 1978), 79–84.

9. Useful theoretical background for this study are Julian H. Steward, *The Theory of Culture Change: The Methodology of Multilinear Evolution* (Urbana, 1955), 30–42; and Marvin Harris, *Cultural Materialism: The Struggle for a Science of Culture* (New York, 1979), 46–76.

10. The classic explication of the ecosystem concept is Eugene Odum, *Fundamentals of Ecology* (Philadelphia, 1971), 8–23.

11. The debate is summarized in Paul R. Ehrlich and Jonathan Roughgarden, *The Science of Ecology* (New York, 1987), 541–52. Detailed criticisms of the stable ecosystem idea include Robert May, *Stability and Complexity in Model Ecosystems* (Princeton, 1973); Paul Colinvaux, *Why Big Fierce Animals Are Rare* (Princeton, 1978), 199–211; Margaret B. Davis, "Climatic Instability, Time Lags, and Community Disequilibrium," in *Community Ecology,* ed. Jared Diamond and Ted J. Case (New York, 1986), 269–84; and S. J. McNaughton, "Diversity and Stability," *Nature,* May 19, 1988, pp. 204–5.

12. Eugene P. Odum, "Properties of Agroecosystems," in *Agricultural Ecosystems: Unifying Concepts,* ed. Richard Lowrance, Benjamin R. Stinner, and Garfield J. House (New York, 1986), 5–11. See also George Cox and Michael Atkins, *Agricultural Ecology* (San Francisco, 1979). The scientific pioneers in applying ecology to agriculture were Karl H. W. Klages, *Ecological Crop Geography* (New York, 1942); and Wolfgang Tischler, *Agrookologie* (Jena, 1965).

13. Omer C. Stewart, "Fire as the First Great Force Employed by Man," in *Man's Role in Changing the Face of the Earth,* ed. William L. Thomas, Jr. (2 vols., Chicago, 1956), I, 115–33; Stephen Pyne, *Fire in America: A Cultural History of Wildland and Rural Fire* (Princeton, 1982); and Emily W. B. Russell, "Indian-Set Fires in the Forests of the Northeastern United States," *Ecology,* 64 (Feb. 1983), 78–88.

14. Harold C. Conklin, "The Study of Shifting Cultivation," *Current Anthropology,* 2 (Feb, 1961), 27–61; John W. Bennett, "Ecosystemic Effects of Extensive Cultivation," *Annual Review of Anthropology,* 2 (1973), 36–45; Robert McC. Netting, "Agrarian Ecology," *ibid.,* 3 (1974), 24–28.

15. Mark Nathan Cohen, *The Food Crisis in Prehistory: Overpopulation and the Origins of Agriculture* (New Haven, 1977), 18–70; D. C. Darlington, "The Origins of Agriculture," *Natural History,* 79 (May 1970), 46–57; Stuart Struever, ed., *Prehistoric Agriculture* (Garden City, 1971); Kent V. Flannery, "The Origins of Agriculture," *Annual Review of Anthropology,* 2 (1973), 271–310; Ester Boserup, *The Conditions of Agricultural Growth: The Economics of Agrarian Change under Population Pressure* (Chicago, 1965); Ester Boserup, "The Impact of Scarcity and Plenty on Development," in *Hunger and History: The Impact of Changing Food Production and Consumption Patterns of Society,* ed. Robert I. Rotberg and Theodore K. Rabb (Cambridge, Eng., 1983), 185–209. Boserup denies that there are any ultimate environmental limits on population growth; scarcity, in her view, always generates greater innovation and abundance.

16. According to Norman Hudson, soil may be formed under natural conditions at the rate of one inch in three hundred to one thousand years; good farming techniques can speed up this process considerably. See Norman Hudson, *Soil Conservation* (Ithaca, 1971), 38. See also M. Witkamp, "Soils as Components of Ecosystems," *Annual Review of Ecology and Systematics,* 2 (1971), 85–110. On the role of climate in history see, for example, Reid Bryson and Thomas J. Murray, *Climates of Hunger: Mankind and the World's Changing Weather* (Madison, 1977); and Robert I. Rotberg and Theodore K. Rabb, eds., *Climate and History: Studies in Interdisciplinary History* (Princeton, 1981). On the major types of water control in history, see Donald Worster, *Rivers of Empire: Water, Aridity, and the American West* (New York, 1985), 17–60.

17. Miguel A. Altieri, *Agroecology: The Scientific Basis of Alternative Agriculture* (Boulder, 1987), 69–71; Harold C. Conklin, "An Ethnological Approach to Shifting Agriculture," in *Environment and Cultural Behavior,* ed. A. P. Vayda (New York, 1979), 228.

18. One of the best descriptions of the mosaic in traditional agriculture can be found in

Georges Bertrand, "Pour une histoire écologique de la France rurale," in *Histoire de la France rurale,* ed. Georges Duby (3 vols., Paris, 1975), I, 96–102. See also E. Estyn Evans, "The Ecology of Peasant Life in Western Europe," in *Man's Role in Changing the Face of the Earth,* ed. Thomas, 217–39. The incredibly long-lived agricultural systems of East Asia, as they existed before the twentieth century forced decisive changes on them, are described in Franklin H. King, *Farmers of Forty Centuries* (Madison, 1911).

19. Karl Polanyi, *The Great Transformation: The Political and Economic Origins of Our Time* (New York, 1944).

20. One of the few scholars to grapple with this transformation on the local level is Victor Skipp, *Crisis and Development: An Ecological Case Study of the Forest of Arden, 1570–1674* (Cambridge, Eng., 1978). For background to the period, see Phyllis Deane, *The First Industrial Revolution* (Cambridge, Eng., 1979), 20 52. On the transition to capitalism in the rural United States, see Steven Hahn and Jonathan Prude, eds., *The Countryside in the Age of Capitalist Transformation: Essays in the Social History of Rural America* (Chapel Hill, 1985). Unfortunately, this collection of essays includes no discussion of the ecological changes that accompanied, and may have contributed to, the social changes.

21. A good recent discussion is Eric Wolf, *Europe and the People without History* (Berkeley, 1982), 73–100.

22. Polanyi, *Great Transformation,* 30, 41.

23. For an insightful discussion of the new market in land, see William Cronon, *Changes in the Land: Indians, Colonists, and the Ecology of New England* (New York, 1983), 54–81.

24. On monocultures, see Lech Ryszkowski, ed., *Ecological Effects of Intensive Agriculture* (Warsaw, 1974). This authority observes that Soviet bloc nations have followed the West in adopting monocultural farming, with many of the same environmental ill effects. See also Tim P. Bayliss-Smith, *The Ecology of Agricultural Systems* (Cambridge, 1982), 83–97, which deals with a Russian collective farm. Since Marxists accede to the view that capitalism achieves the final technological domination of nature and argue that communism is simply a rearrangement of the ownership of the technology, it is hardly surprising that they have not represented any real alternative from an ecological standpoint. On specialization in the pinmaker's trade as a model of capitalist development, as perceived in 1776, see Adam Smith, *An Inquiry into the Nature and Causes of the Wealth of Nations* (New York, 1937), 4–5.

25. Alfred Crosby, Jr., "The British Empire as a Product of Continental Drift," in *Environmental History: Critical Issues in Comparative Perspective,* ed. Kendall E. Bailes (Lanham, 1985), 553–76.

26. Sources for this discussion include J. D. Chambers and G. E. Mingay, *The Agricultural Revolution, 1750–1880* (New York, 1966), 54–76; Eric Kerridge, *The Agricultural Revolution* (London, 1967), 181–348; G. E. Fussell, "Science and Practice in Eighteenth-Century British Agriculture," *Agricultural History,* 43 (Jan. 1969), 7–18; and D. B. Grigg, *The Agricultural Systems of the World: An Evolutionary Approach* (London, 1974), 152–86.

27. I do not deny that science has become, in many places and ways, a handmaiden of modern market agriculture; see, for example, the criticisms of two scientists: Richard Lewins and Richard Lewontin, *The Dialectical Biologist* (Cambridge, Mass., 1985).

28. Donald Worster, *Dust Bowl: The Southern Plains in the 1930s* (New York, 1979). The literature on the ecology and human settlement of the Great Plains is voluminous. Good introductions include Walter Prescott Webb, *The Great Plains* (Boston, 1931); James C. Malin, *The Grassland of North America: Prolegomena to Its History* (Lawrence, 1947); and Brian W. Blouet and Frederick C. Luebke, eds., *The Great Plains: Environment and Culture* (Lincoln, 1979). About the adjoining corn belt, which has much in common with the Plains, see Allan N. Auclair, "Ecological Factors in the Development of Intensive Management Ecosystems in the Midwestern United States," *Ecology,* 57 (Late Spring 1976), 431–44.

29. John S. Steinhart and Carol E. Steinhart, "Energy Use in the U.S. Food System," *Science,* April 19, 1974, pp. 307–16; William Lockeretz, ed., *Agriculture and Energy* (New

York, 1977); David Pimentel, "Energy Flow in Agroecosystems," in *Agricultural Ecosystems*, ed. Lowrance, Stinner, and House, 121–32.

30. David Pimentel et al., "Land Degradation: Effects on Food and Energy Resources," *Science*, Oct. 8, 1976, pp. 149–55. These authors argue that due to intensive, continuous cultivation, annual sediment loss via surface runoff increased from about 3 billion tons nationally in the 1930s to 4 billion tons in recent years. Other scientific critiques of modern agriculture appear in Miguel A. Altieri, Deborah K. Letourneau, and James R. Davis, "Developing Sustainable Agroecosystems," *Bioscience*, 33 (Jan. 1983), 45–49; and Stephen R. Gliessman, "An Agroecological Approach to Sustainable Agriculture," in *Meeting the Expectations of the Land: Essays in Sustainable Agriculture and Stewardship*, ed. Wes Jackson, Wendell Berry, and Bruce Colman (San Francisco, 1984), 160–71.

31. See Paul Sears, *Deserts on the March* (Norman, 1980), 170–86.

Chapter 6

1. Thomas Jefferson quoted in Edwin Morris Betts, *Thomas Jefferson's Farm Book* (Princeton: Princeton University Press, 1953), 42. On Ruffin, see Avery Craven, *Soil Exhaustion as a Factor in the Agricultural History of Virginia and Maryland, 1606–1860* (Gloucester, Mass.: Peter Smith, 1965), 134–42.

2. Russell Lord, *The Care of the Earth* (New York: Mentor, 1962), 190. Hugh Hammond Bennett's most important work was *Soil Conservation* (New York: McGraw-Hill, 1939). See also Wellington Brink, *Big Hugh, The Father of Soil Conservation* (New York: McMillan, 1951), and Stanley W. Trimble, "Perspectives on the History of Soil Erosion Control in the Eastern United States," *Agricultural History*, 59 (April 1985), 162–80.

3. Hugh Bennett and W. R. Chapline, "Soil Erosion as a National Menace," reprinted in *Agriculture in the United States: A Documentary History*, ed. Wayne D. Rasmussen (New York: Random House, 1975), III. 2043.

4. *Ibid.*, 2047–48.

5. Donald Worster, *Dust Bowl: The Southern Plains in the 1930s* (New York: Oxford University Press, 1979), 13–14.

6. *Ibid.*, 213.

7. *Ibid.*, 190–91.

8. Bennett, "Development of Natural Resources: The Coming Technological Revolution on the Land," *Science*, 3 (January 1947). 3.

9. Alistair Cooke, *A Generation on Trial* (New York: Knop, 1951), 28.

10. Bennett, "Development of Natural Resources," 4.

11. Charles Hardin, *The Politics of Agriculture: Soil Conservation and the Struggle for Power in Rural America* (Glencoe, Ill.: Free Press, 1952), 102.

12. *Ibid.*, 103.

13. United States Department of Agriculture, *Agricultural Statistics, 1984* (Washington: Government Printing Office, 1984), 482–86.

14. United States Department of Agriculture, *Basic Statistics, 1977 National Resources Inventory* (Washington: Soil Conservation Service, 1980). See also USDA, *Soil, Water and Related Resources in the United States: Status, Condition, and Trends: 1980 RCA Appraisal*, Part I (Washington: Government Printing Office, 1981), 96–99.

15. J. Douglas Helms, "Walter Lowdermilk's Journey: Forester to Land Conservationist," *Environmental Review*, 8 (Summer 1984), 138.

16. Office of Management and Budget, *Budget of the United States Government, Fiscal Year 1986* (Washington: Government Printing Office, 1985), 8–42 and 8–43.

17. Edward Hyams, *Soil and Civilization* (New York: Harper Colophon, 1976), 26–27.

18. Hans Jenny, unpublished interview with Kevin Stuart, 1983. The author wishes to thank Stuart for furnishing a copy of this interview. See also Jenny, "The Making and

Unmaking of a Fertile Soil," in *Meeting the Expectations of the Land: Essays in Sustainable Agriculture and Stewardship,* eds. Wes Jackson, Wendell Berry, and Bruce Colman (San Francisco: North Point, 1984), 42–55.

Chapter 7

1. U.S. Department of Agriculture, *A Time to Choose: Summary Report on the Structure of Agriculture* (Washington, D.C.: U.S. Department of Agriculture, January 1981), 23–27.

2. This public attitude, which has shown up in Gallup and Harris polls, is supported by social researchers studying the impact of large-scale farms on community development and democratic politics. See Isao Fujimoto, "Farming in the Rockies: A Humanistic Perspective," in *The Future of Agriculture in the Rocky Mountains,* ed. E. Richard Hart (Salt Lake City, Utah: Westwater Press, 1980), 74–75; and Walter Goldschmidt, *As You Sow: Three Studies in the Social Consequences of Agribusiness* (Montclair, N.J.: Allanheld, Osmun, 1978).

3. Kenneth L. Robinson, "The Impact of Government Price and Income Programs on Income Distribution in Agriculture," *Journal of Farm Economics,* 47, no. 5 (December 1965): 1225–34.

4. In 1979, there were 6.2 million persons living on farms, or 3 percent of the national population. That number is based on the current definition of a farm, which does not count places with less than $1,000 a year in farm sales. That is also a way of declaring, for the purposes of the government, that noncommercial agriculture does not exist. USDA, *A Time to Choose,* 34.

5. In 1900, there were 838,591,744 acres of American land in farms; by 1978, the total was 1,029,694,535 acres. Most of the increase in farmland occurred before World War II, but most of the decline in the number of farms took place, rather precipitously, after the war. See U.S. Bureau of the Census, *Thirteenth Census of the United States,* vol. 5, *Agriculture* (Washington, D.C.: U.S. Government Printing Office, 1913), 28; *1978 Census of Agriculture* (Washington, D.C.: U.S. Government Printing Office, 1981), vol. 51, pt. 51, p. 1.

6. See James Turner, *The Chemical Feast* (New York: Grossman, 1970), chap. 5; and Jim Hightower, *Eat Your Heart Out* (New York: Crown, 1975).

7. USDA, *A Time to Choose,* 75.

8. Peter Manniche, *Living Democracy in Denmark* (Toronto: Ryerson Press, 1952), 236.

9. James Risser, "A Renewed Threat of Soil Erosion: It's Worse Than the Dust Bowl," *Smithsonian,* II, no. 12 (March 1981): 127.

10. The ecological approach to farming appears to have more serious support in some European countries than in the United States. See, for instance, the officially sponsored Dutch report, R. Boerringa, ed., *Alternative Methods of Agriculture* (Amsterdam: Elsevier, 1980); and Gil Friend, "Biological Agriculture in Europe," *CoEvolution Quarterly,* Spring 1978, pp. 60–64. In the United States, research and support have so far come from outside government and established agricultural schools. See, for example, Wes Jackson's *New Roots for Agriculture* (San Francisco: Friends of the Earth, 1980); and Richard Merrill, ed., *Radical Agriculture* (New York: New York University Press, 1976), especially pt. 5.

11. The book was first published in 1927 by Harper & Brothers. Rölvaag was a professor of Norwegian literature in Minnesota and wrote in his native Norse. Two editions are available at this writing: the 1927 edition is still published by Harper & Row, in hardback, and there is a 1965 edition, also from Harper & Row, in paperback.

Chapter 8

1. Robert Frost, "The Gift Outright," first read before the Phi Beta Kappa Society, the College of William and Mary (1941) and read again at the presidential inauguration of John

F. Kennedy (1961). Reprinted in *The Poetry of Robert Frost* (New York: Holt, Rinehart and Winston, 1969), 348.

2. J. Hector St. Jean de Crèvecoeur, "On the Situation, Feelings, and Pleasures of an American Farmer," *Letters from an American Farmer* (New York: Signet Classic, 1963; orig. pub. 1782), 48. Crèvecoeur was a loyalist and, during the Revolutionary War, was forced to leave the country.

3. Thomas Jefferson, *Notes on the State of Virginia* (New York: Harper Torchbooks, 1964; orig. pub. 1784–85), 157.

4. The original public domain came together in less than a century of war, negotiation, and purchase. If one leaves aside the vital but overlapping cessions from the first inhabitants, the Indians, the major acquisitions went thus:

Cessions by original states (1781–1802)	237 million acres
Louisiana Purchase (1803)	560 "
Florida Purchase (1819)	46 "
Oregon Compromise (1846)	183 "
Mexican Treaty (1848)	339 "
Purchase from Texas (1850)	79 "
Gadsden Purchase (1853)	19 "
Alaska (1867)	375 "
	1,828

To these figures must be added, to get the whole territory of the United States, the lands of the original states (305 million acres) and Texas (170 million acres), which were never part of the public domain, and lands of the island possessions, Hawaii, Puerto Rico, Guam, and American Samoa. See Marion Clawson and Burnell Held, *The Federal Lands: Their Use and Management* (Lincoln: University of Nebraska Press, 1957), 21. Also, Frederick Merk, *History of Westward Movement* (New York: Knopf, 1978), chap. 28; and Paul W. Gates, *A History of Public Land Law Development* (Washington: Public Land Law Review Commission, 1968).

5. The 60 percent that remains in private hands is highly concentrated; 3 percent of the population owns almost all of it—that is, owns 55 percent of all American land. Fewer than six hundred companies and corporations own about 11 percent of the nation's total area and 23 percent of all private land in America. See Peter Wolf, *Land in America: Its Value, Use, and Control* (New York: Pantheon Books, 1981), xiii. In general, this book provides an excellent survey of the ways in which land uses and values are changing in the country.

6. Two of the leading spokesmen for this point of view are John Baden and Richard Stroup. See their article, "Private Rights, Public Choices, and the Management of National Forests," *Western Wildlands*, 2 (Autumn 1975), 5–13.

7. Leopold, "The Land Ethic," *Sand County Almanac* (New York: Oxford University Press, 1987; orig. pub. 1947), 224. Two essential books for understanding the evolution of Leopold's thinking are Curt Meine, *Aldo Leopold: His Life and Work* (Madison: University of Wisconsin Press, 1988); and J. Baird Callicott, ed. *Companion to A Sand County Almanac: Interpretive and Critical Essays* (Madison: University of Wisconsin Press, 1987).

8. *Ibid.*, 213.

Chapter 9

1. Henry Nash Smith, *Virgin Land: The American West as Symbol and Myth* (Cambridge: Harvard University Press, 1950); Bernard DeVoto, *The Course of Empire* (Boston: Houghton Mifflin, 1952); Paul Horgan, *Great River: The Rio Grande in North American History* (New York: Holt, Rinehart and Winston, 1954); Wallace Stegner, *Beyond the Hun-*

dredth Meridian: John Wesley Powell and the Second Opening of the West (Boston: Houghton Mifflin, 1953); Walter Prescott Webb, *The Great Frontier* (Boston: Houghton Mifflin,
1952).

2. Vernon Parrington, *The Beginnings of Critical Realism in America, 1860–1920,* vol. 3
of *Main Currents in American Thought* (Norman: University of Oklahoma Press, 1987). 23–
26.

3. Leonard J. Arrington, *Great Basin Kingdom: An Economic History of the Latter-Day
Saints, 1830–1900* (Cambridge: Harvard University Press, 1958), 35.

4. Leonard J. Arrington and Davis Bitton, *The Mormon Experience* (New York: Vintage
Books, 1979), 115.

5. Charles Hillman Brough, *Irrigation in Utah* (Baltimore: Johns Hopkins Press, 1898),
28, 75. For an overview, see George D. Clyde, "History of Irrigation in Utah," *Utah Historical
Quarterly,* 27 (January 1959), 27–36.

6. Brough, *Irrigation in Utah,* 33. A recent, comprehensive survey of early economic
development may be found in Charles S. Peterson's *Utah: A History* (New York: W. W. Norton, 1977), chap. 3.

7. Cit. B. H. Roberts, *A Comprehensive History of the Church of Jesus Christ of Latter-
Day Saints: Century I* (Salt Lake City: Deseret News Press, 1930), III, 269.

8. Arrington, *Great Basin Kingdom,* 34.

9. *Ibid.,* 35.

10. *Ibid.,* 386.

11. *Ibid.,* 409.

12. *Ibid.,* 410–11. Arrington writes: "As the waste involved in the short-sighted,
unplanned, and ruthless exploitation of other Western frontiers became more apparent, the
Mormon pattern became increasingly appreciated—became recognized as prophetic of the
pattern which the entire West would ultimately have to adopt. . . . The design of the Kingdom, once despised as backward, is now part of the heritage which Americans are passing
on to governments and peoples in many parts of the world."

13. Nel Anderson, *Desert Saints: The Mormon Frontier in Utah* (Chicago: University of
Chicago Press, 1966), 383.

14. Thomas O'Dea, *The Mormons* (Chicago: University of Chicago Press, 1957), 198.

15. George Thomas, *The Development of Institutions Under Irrigation, with Special Reference to Early Utah Conditions* (New York: Macmillan, 1920), 18.

16. Richard T. Ely, "Economic Aspects of Mormonism," *Harper's Magazine,* 106 (April
1903), 669.

17. Richard Slotkin, *Regeneration Through Violence: The Mythology of the American
Frontier, 1600–1860* (Middletown, Conn.: Wesleyan University Press, 1973).

18. I have drawn this argument from Richard Slotkin's *The Fatal Environment: The
Myth of the Frontier in the Age of Industrialization, 1800–1890* (New York: Atheneum,
1986), esp. chap. 3.

19. Arrington, *Great Basin Kingdom,* 25–26.

20. William E. Smythe, *The Conquest of Arid America* (Seattle: University of Washington, 1969; orig. pub. 1889, rev. ed., 1905), 56, 327, 330–31.

21. John A. Widtsoe, *Success on Irrigation Projects* (New York: John Wiley & Sons,
1928), 138.

22. Illustrative is the declaration by Brigham Young's chief counsellor Heber C. Kimball:
"Those that will live the religion of Christ will have orchards." Cited by Jeanne Kay and
Craig J. Brown, "Mormon Beliefs about Land and Natural Resources, 1847–1877," *Journal
of Historical Geography,* 11 (1985), 261.

23. For a fine example of this mythologizing of landscape see Clifton Johnson, *Highways
and Byways of the Rocky Mountains* (New York: Macmillian, 1910), 158, which speaks
enthusiastically of "tall Lombardy poplars" lining the streets of the ideal Mormon village,

of "life-giving water" flowing in ditches, and of "lucious pastures" in the surrounding country.

24. George H. Williams, *Wilderness and Paradise in Christian Thought* (New York: Harper & Bros., 1962), 12–15.

25. I have discussed this massive expansion of the reclamation program in my book, *Rivers of Empire: Water, Aridity, and the Growth of the American West* (New York: Pantheon, 1985), Part VI. See also Marc Reisner, *Cadillac Desert: The American West and Its Disappearing Water* (New York: Viking, 1986), chaps. 5–12.

Chapter 10

1. Actually, Taoist writers dealt with flood control more than irrigation, but their water philosophy of noninterference has many modern applications. For a useful discussion of their ideas, see Joseph Needham, *Science and Civilization in China* (Cambridge: Cambridge University Press, 1971), vol. 4, pt. 3, pp. 235–51.

2. Aldo Leopold, *Round River* (New York: Oxford University Press, 1953).

3. Robert Curry, "Watershed Form and Process: The Elegant Balance," *Co-Evolution Quarterly*, Winter 1976–77,pp. 14–21.

4. Much of what follows is based on these sources: Gamal Hamdan, "Evolution of Irrigation Agriculture in Egypt," in *A History of Land Use in Arid Regions*, ed. L. Dudley Stamp (Paris: UNESCO, 1961), 119–42; Karl Butzer, *Early Hydraulic Civilization in Egypt* (Chicago: University of Chicago Press, 1976); Desmond Hammerton, "The Nile River—A Case History," in *River Ecology and Man*, eds. Ray Oglesby, Clarence Carlson, and James McCann (New York: Academic Press, 1972), 171–214; John Waterbury, *Hydropolitics of the Nile Valley* (Syracuse, N.Y.: Syracuse University Press, 1979); and Robert Tignor, "British Agricultural and Hydraulic Policy in Egypt, 1882–1892," *Agricultural History*, 37, no. 2 (April 1963): 63–74.

5. Karl Wittfogel, *Oriental Despotism: A Comparative Study of Total Power* (New Haven, Conn.: Yale University Press, 1957). This is a controversial effort to link water technology to centralized authority in Asian history. Consult also, among the large number of titles on this theme, Marvin Harris, *Cannibals and Kings: The Origins of Cultures* (New York: Random House, 1977), chap. 13; and William Mitchell, "The Hydraulic Hypothesis: A Reappraisal," *Current Anthropology*, 14 (December 1973), 532–534.

6. I have discussed this process in my "Hydraulic Society in California: An Ecological Interpretation," *Agricultural History*, 56, no. 3 (July 1982): 503–12.

7. U.S. Water Resources Council, *The Nation's Water Resources, 1975–2000* (Washington, D.C.: U.S. Government Printing Office, 1978), vol. I, pp. 28–29. The 1975 coterminous U.S. rate was estimated at 159 million gallons a day withdrawn for agriculture out of a total of 339 million gallons a day.

8. C. Richard Murray and E. Bodette Reeves, *Estimated Use of Water in the United States in 1970*, U.S. Geological Survey Circular 676 (Washington, D.C.: U.S. Government Printing Office, 1972), 22–23. Of the 140 million acre-feet of water withdrawn nationally for irrigation in that year, 82 million acre-feet were considered "consumed"—that is, no longer available for stream flow or other uses.

9. "The Browning of America," *Newsweek*, 97 (23 February 1981), 29–30. For a comparable decline, see David Todd, "Groundwater Utilization," in *California Water: A Study in Resource Management*, ed. David Seckler (Berkeley: University of California Press, 1971), 174–189.

10. Curry, "Watershed Form and Process," 17–18.

11. The state-financed California State Water Project, which takes the Sierra snowmelt from the north to agribusiness operations in Kern County and to the Los Angeles area, has

a huge energy deficit. Pumping alone requires thirteen billion kilowatt hours a year, while the project generates only five billion. These figures are taken from Jeffrey Lee, "The Energy Costs of the California Water Project" (Pamphlet, Water Resources Center Archives, University of California at Berkeley, 1973).

12. Marty Bender and Wes Jackson, "American Food: S/Oil and Water," *The Land Report,* Winter 1981, p. 13. See also Margaret Lounsbury, Sandra Hebenstreit, and R. Stephen Berry, *Resource Analysis: Water and Energy as Linked Resources,* Water Resources Center, Research Report 134 (Urbana: University of Illinois, July 1978), 118–75.

13. The salinity problem is discussed in the following: Myron Holburt and Vernon Valantine, "Present and Future Salinity of Colorado River," *Journal of the Hydraulic Division, Proceedings of American Society of Civil Engineers* 98 (March 1972), 503–20; Gaylord Skogerboe, "Agricultural Impact on Water Quality in Western Environment," in *Environmental Impact on Rivers,* ed. Hsieh Wen Shen (Fort Collins, Colo.: Privately published, 1973), 12–1 to 12–25; George Cox and Michael Atkins, *Agricultural Ecology* (New York: W. H. Freeman, 1979), 300–308.

14. J. F. Poland and G. H. Davis report that at least 30 percent of California's pumped land has subsided; in some places the drop is nearly thirty feet. "Land Subsidence Due to Withdrawal of Fluids," *Reviews in Engineering Geology,* 2 (1969), 187–269.

15. Charles Goldman, "Biological Implications of Reduced Freshwater Flows on the San Francisco-Delta System," in Seckler, *California Water,* 109–124; Robert Hagan and Edwin Roberts, "Ecological Impacts of Water Projects in California," *Journal of the Irrigation and Drainage Division: Proceedings of American Society of Civil Engineers,* 91 (March 1972), 25–48. The latter is a most comprehensive account and a model of wishy-washy conclusions.

16. The danger posed by deteriorating dams is far more serious than the public realizes. One study indicates that dams are 10,000 times more likely to cause a major disaster than are nuclear power plants. Gaylord Shaw, "The Nationwide Search for Dams in Danger," *Smithsonian,* 9 (April 1978), 36.

17. See, for example, the remarks by Joseph Sibley, Congressman from Pennsylvania, in *Congressional Record,* 21 January 1902, p. 836; and of Gilbert Tucker, editor of *Country Gentleman,* in *Congressional Record,* 13 June 1902, pp. 6723–24.

18. Charles Howe and William Easter, *Interbasin Transfer of Water: Economic Issues and Impacts* (Baltimore: Johns Hopkins University Press, 1971), 138–40, 144–45, 167. See also Richard Berkman and W. Kip Vicusi, *Damming the West* (New York: Grossman, 1973), 17–23.

19. James Risser, "A Renewed Threat of Soil Erosion: It's Worse Than the Dust Bowl," *Smithsonian,* II, no. 12 (March 1981): 127. Other areas with serious erosion are Iowa, which has lost half of its splendid topsoil in a century, and the Palouse country of eastern Washington, losing seventeen million tons from a million acres of cropland—as much as 200 tons per acre.

20. Some engineers are beginning to question the old hubris. Elmo Huffman of California's Department of Water Resources writes: "We must learn that meddling is not synonymous with management. . . . In many cases, the wisest management is simply to preserve things as they now are, or, at the most, only attempt to heal the wounds so carelessly inflicted by man in the past." "Role of the Civil Engineer in Total Watershed Development and Management," in *Development of the Total Watershed,* Irrigation and Drainage Conference, American Society of Civil Engineers (1966), 43–44. See also Gilbert White, "A Perspective of River Basin Development," *Law and Contemporary Problems,* 22 (Spring 1977), 157–187, which suggests some changing attitudes.

21. A similar recommendation comes from the study team headed by the impeccably conservative agricultural economist Earl Heady. See National Water Commission, *Water Policies for the Future* (Washington, D.C.: U.S. Government Printing Office, 1973), 141. The Heady group, however, simply wanted no new projects authorized.

22. Bureau of Reclamation, *Water and Land Resource Accomplishments: 1977,* p. 8.

23. The Third World, facing far more intense population pressures, may be forced into more and more environmental violence to survive. Simply to keep pace with their food needs, they will require by the year 2000 some twenty-two million hectares of new irrigation land, according to the prognosis of the Food and Agriculture Organization in *Water for Agriculture,* E/Conference, 70/II, 29 January 1977, p. 4.

24. Leopold's "The Land Ethic" essay appears in his *Sand County Almanac* (New York: Oxford University Press, 1949). His son Luna Leopold is one of the foremost hydrological experts in the United States and author of such technically sophisticated works as *Water in Environmental Planning.* See his own trenchant critique of American resource policy, "Ethos, Equity, and the Water Resource," *Environment,* 32 (March 1990): 16–20, 37–42.

Chapter 11

1. "Endless Frontier," *Time Magazine,* 58 (July 30, 1951), 48–51.

2. Arthur E. Morgan, *Dams and Other Disasters: A Century of the Army Corps of Engineers in Civil Works* (Boston: Porter Sargent, 1971).

Chapter 12

1. Quoted in World Commission on Environment and Development, *Our Common Future* (Oxford and New York: Oxford University Press, 1987), 64. See also Sandbrook, *The Conservation and Development Programme for the UK: A Response to the World Conservation Strategy* (1982); *Our Common Future: A Canadian Response to the Challenge of Sustainable Development* (Ottawa: Harmony Foundation of Canada, 1989); and Raymond F. Dasmann, "Toward a Biosphere Consciousness," in *The Ends of the Earth: Perspectives on Modern Environmental History,* ed. Donald Worster (New York: Cambridge University Press, 1988), 281–85.

2. Robert G. Lee, "Sustained-Yield and Social Order," in *History of Sustained-Yield Forestry: A Symposium,* ed. Harold K. Steen (n.p.: Forest History Society, 1984), 94–95. See also Heinrich Rübner, "Sustained-Yield Forestry in Europe and Its Crisis During the Era of Nazi Dictatorship," *ibid.,* 170–75; and Claus Wiebecke and W. Peters, "Aspects of Sustained-Yield History: Forest Sustention as the Principle of Forestry—Idea and Reality," *ibid.,* 176–83.

3. Bernhard E. Fernow, *Economics of Forestry* (New York: T. Y. Crowell, 1902), 20.

4. I have found two books by Michael Redclift useful here: *Development and the Environment Crisis: Red or Green Alternatives?* (London: Methuen, 1984); and *Sustainable Development: Exploring the Contradictions* (London: Methuen, 1987). See too Sharachchandram M. L'el'e, "Sustainable Development: A Critical Review," *World Development,* 19 (June 1991), 607–21.

5. Clem Tisdell, "Sustainable Development: Differing Perspectives of Ecologists and Economists, and Relevance to LDCs," *World Development,* 16 (March 1988), 373–84.

6. Arthur A. Goldsmith and Derick W. Brinkerhoff define sustainability as a condition in which an institution's "outputs are valued highly enough that inputs continue." See their book, *Institutional Sustainability in Agriculture and Rural Development: A Global Perspective* (New York: Praeger, 1990), 13–14.

7. Wes Jackson, Wendell Berry, and Bruce Colman, eds., *Meeting the Expectations of the Land: Essays in Sustainable Agriculture and Stewardship* (San Francisco: North Point Press, 1984), x.

8. An example of how these older ecological theories still influence the advocates of sus-

tainable development is P. Bartelmus, *Environment and Development* (London: Allen and Unwin, 1986), 44.

9. Daniel B. Botkin, *Discordant Harmonies: A New Ecology for the Twenty-first Century* (New York: Oxford University Press, 1990), 10, 62.

10. *Ibid.,* 62

11. *Ibid.,* 6, 183, 189, 193.

12. See also Arthur McEvoy, *The Fisherman's Problem: Ecology and Law in California Fisheries, 1850–1980* (New York: Cambridge University Press, 1986), 6–7, 10, 150–51.

13. Botkin, *Discordant Harmonies,* 190.

Chapter 13

1. Paul Sears, *Deserts on the March,* 3rd ed. (Norman: University of Oklahoma Press, 1959), 162.

2. *Ibid.,* 177.

3. Donald Worster, *Nature's Economy: A History of Ecological Ideas* (New York: Cambridge University Press, 1977).

4. This is the theme in particular of Clement's book *Plant Succession* (Washington: Carnegie Institution, 1916).

5. Worster, *Nature's Economy,* 210.

6. Clement's major rival for influence in the United States was Henry Chandler Cowles of the University of Chicago, whose first paper on ecological succession appeared in 1899. The best study of Cowles's ideas is J. Ronald Engel, *Sacred Sands: The Struggle for Community in the Indiana Dunes* (Middletown, Conn.: Wesleyan University Press, 1983), 137–59. Engel describes him as having a less deterministic, more pluralistic notion of succession, one that "opened the way to a more creative role for human beings in nature's evolutionary adventure" (150). See also Ronald C. Tobey, *Saving the Prairies: The Life Cycle of the Founding School of American Plant Ecology, 1895–1955* (Berkeley: University of California, 1981).

7. Sears, *Deserts on the March,* 142.

8. This book was co-authored with his brother Howard T. Odum, and it went through two more editions, the last appearing in 1971.

9. Eugene P. Odum, *Fundamentals of Ecology* (Philadelphia: W. B. Saunders, 1971), 8.

10. Odum, "The Strategy of Ecosystem Development," *Science,* 164 (18 April 1969), 266.

11. The terms "K-selection" and "r-selection" came from Robert MacArthur and Edward O. Wilson, *Theory of Island Biogeography* (Princeton: Princeton University Press, 1967). Along with Odum, MacArthur was the leading spokesman for the view of nature as a series of thermodynamically balanced ecosystems during the 1950s and 60s.

12. Odum, "Strategy of Ecosystem Development," 266. See also Odum, "Trends Expected in Stressed Ecosystems," *BioScience,* 35 (July/August 1985), 419–22.

13. A book of that title was published by Earl F. Murphy: *Governing Nature* (Chicago: Quadrangle Books, 1967). From time to time, Eugene Odum himself seems to have caught that ambition or lent his support to it, and it was certainly central to the work of his brother, Howard T. Odum. On this theme see Peter J. Taylor, "Technocratic Optimism, H. T. Odum, and the Partial Transformation of Ecological Metaphor after World War II," *Journal of the History of Biology,* 21 (Summer 1988), 213–44.

14. A very influential popularization of Odum's view of nature (though he is never actually referred to in it) is Barry Commoner's *The Closing Circle: Nature, Man, and Technology* (New York: Knopf, 1971). See in particular the discussion of the four "laws" of ecology (33–46).

15. Communication from Malcolm Cherrett, *Ecology,* 70 (March 1989), 41–42.

16. See Michael Begon, John L. Harper, and Colin R. Townsend, *Ecology: Individuals,*

Populations, and Communities (Sunderland, Mass.: Sinauer, 1986). In another textbook, Odum's views are presented critically as the traditional approach: R. J. Putnam and S. D. Wratten, *Principles of Ecology* (Berkeley: University of California Press, 1984). More loyal to the ecosystem model are Paul Ehrlich and Jonathan Roughgarden, *The Science of Ecology* (New York: Macmillan, 1987); and Robert Leo Smith, *Elements of Ecology,* 2nd ed. (New York: Harper & Row, 1986), though the latter admits that he has shifted from an "ecosystem approach" to more of an "evolutionary approach" (xiii).

17. William H. Drury and Ian C. T. Nisbet, "Succession," *Journal of the Arnold Arboretum,* 54 (July 1973), 360.

18. H. A. Gleason, "The Individualistic Concept of the Plant Association," *Bulletin of the Torrey Botanical Club,* 53 (1926), 25. A later version of the same article appeared in *American Midland Naturalist,* 21 (1939), 92–110.

19. Joseph H. Connell and Ralph O. Slayter, "Mechanisms of Succession in Natural Communities and Their Role in Community Stability and Organization," *The American Naturalist,* 111 (Nov.–Dec. 1977), 1119–44.

20. Margaret Bryan Davis, "Climatic Instability, Time Lags, and Community Disequilibrium," in *Community Ecology,* ed. Jared Diamond and Ted J. Case (New York: Harper & Row, 1986), 269.

21. James R. Karr and Kathryn E. Freemark, "Disturbance and Vertebrates: An Integrative Perspective," *The Ecology of Natural Disturbance and Patch Dynamics,* ed. S.T.A. Pickett and P. S. White (Orlando, Fla.: Academic Press, 1985), 154–55. The Odum school of thought is, however, by no means silent. Another recent compilation has been put together in his honor, and many of its authors express a continuing support for his ideas: L. R. Pomeroy and J. J. Alberts, eds., *Concepts of Ecosystem Ecology: A Comparative View* (New York: Springer-Verlag, 1988).

22. Orie L. Loucks, Mary L. Plumb-Mentjes, and Deborah Rogers, "Gap Processes and Large-Scale Disturbances in Sand Prairies," in Pomeroy and Alberts, *ibid.,* 72–85.

23. For the rise of population biology see Sharon E. Kingsland, *Modeling Nature: Episodes in the History of Population Biology* (Chicago: University of Chicago Press, 1985).

24. An influential exception to this tendency is F. H. Bormann and G. E. Likens, *Pattern and Process in a Forested Ecosystem* (New York: Springer-Verlag, 1979), which proposes (in chap. 6) the model of a "shifting mosaic steady-state." See also P. Yodzis, "The Stability of Real Ecosystems," *Nature,* 289 (19 February 1981), 674–76.

25. Paul Colinvaux, *Why Big Fierce Animals Are Rare: An Ecologist's Perspective* (Princeton: Princeton University Press, 1978), 117, 135.

26. Thomas Söderqvist, *The Ecologists: From Merry Naturalists to Saviours of the Nation. A Sociologically Informed Narrative Survey of the Ecologization of Sweden, 1895–1975.* (Stockholm: Almqvist & Wiksell International, 1986), 281.

27. This argument is made with great intellectual force by Ilya Prigogine and Isabelle Stengers, *Order Out of Chaos: Man's New Dialogue with Nature* (Boulder: Shambala/ New Science Library, 1984). Prigogine won the Nobel Prize in 1977 for his work on the thermodynamics of nonequilibrium systems.

28. An excellent account of the change in thinking is James Gleick, *Chaos: The Making of a New Science* (New York: Viking, 1987). I have drawn on his explanation extensively here. What Gleick does not explore are the striking intellectual parallels between chaotic theory in science and post-modern discourse in literature and philosophy. Post-Modernism is a sensibility that has abandoned the historic search for unity and order in nature, taking an ironic view of existence and debunking all established faiths. According to Todd Gitlin, "Post-Modernism reflects the fact that a new moral structure has not yet been built and our culture has not yet found a language for articulating the new understandings we are trying, haltingly, to live with. It objects to all principles, all commitments, all crusades—in the name of an unconscientious evasion." On the other hand, and put more positively, the new sensibility leads to a new emphasis on democratic coexistence: "a new 'moral ecology'—that

in the preservation of the other is a condition for the preservation of the self." Gitlin, "Post-Modernism: The Stenography of Surfaces," *New Perspectives Quarterly,* 6 (Spring 1989), 57, 59. See also N. Catherine Hayles, *Chaos Bound: Orderly Disorder in Contemporary Literature and Science* (Ithaca: Cornell University Press, 1990), esp. chap. 7.

29. The paper was published in *Science,* 186 (1974), 645–47. See also Robert M. May, "Simple Mathematical Models with Very Complicated Dynamics," *Nature,* 261 (1976), 459–67. Gleick discusses May's work on pages 69–80 of *Chaos.*

30. W. M. Schaeffer, "Chaos in Ecology and Epidemiology," in *Chaos in Biological Systems,* ed., H. Degan, A. V. Holden, and L. F. Olsen (New York: Plenum Press, 1987), 233. See also Schaeffer, "Order and Chaos in Ecological Systems," *Ecology,* 66 (Feb. 1985), 93–106.

31. John Muir, *My First Summer in the Sierra* (1911; Boston: Houghton Mifflin, 1944), 157.

32. Prigogine and Stengers, *Order Out of Chaos,* 312–13.

33. Much of the alarm that Sears and Odum, among others, expressed has shifted to a global perspective, and the older equilibrium thinking has been taken up by scientists concerned about the geo- and biochemical condition of the planet as a whole and about human threats, particularly from the burning of fossil fuels, to its stability. One of the most influential texts in this new development is James Lovelock's *Gaia: A New Look at Life on Earth* (Oxford: Oxford University Press, 1979). See also Edward Goldsmith, "Gaia: Some Implications for Theoretical Ecology," *The Ecologist,* 18, nos. 2/3 (1988): 64–74.

Chapter 15

1. These events occurred in 1980 and were extensively covered in the Honolulu *Advertiser,* though little noticed on the mainland. My information also comes from a discussion with the American protester Dexter Cate in his home in Hilo, Hawaii, in July 1980.

2. This statement has appeared frequently in the organization's brochures and its now defunct newspaper, *Greenpeace Chronicles.*

3. Masao Watanabe, "The Conception of Nature in Japanese Culture," *Science,* 183 (25 Jan. 1974), 279. The literature on this subject seems all to be written in the past tense, as though whatever was true of Japanese culture in the past has remained true today.

4. Quoted in Charles Cleaver, *Japanese and Americans: Culture Parallels and Paradoxes* (Minneapolis: University of Minnesota Press, 1976), 66.

5. Japan has a very active environmental movement of its own, but reformers there are so far almost wholly preoccupied with the problem of *kogai,* or harm to people caused by industrial pollution, and with seeking compensation. See Julian Gresser, *Ecology Law Quarterly,* 3 (Fall 1973), 765–6. "Somewhat curiously," he adds, "no thought has been given in Japan, with the Buddhist-Shinto tradition, to the proposition that the environment itself has rights to its own integrity, a concept proposed in the West."

6. Robert Bellah, *Tokugawa Religion: The Values of Pre-Industrial Japan* (Glencoe, Ill.: Free Press, 1957), chap. V.

7. Lynn White Jr., "The Historical Roots of Our Ecologic Crisis," *Science,* 155 (10 March 1967), 1203–7. See also his reply to critics, "Continuing the Conversation," in Ian Barbour, ed., *Western Man and Environmental Ethics* (Reading, Mass.: Addison-Wesley, 1973), 55–64. White's original essay was reprinted, with several interesting other perspectives on the nature-religion debate, in *Ecology and Religion in History,* ed. David and Eileen Spring (New York: Harper & Row, 1974).

8. Edward A. Armstrong, *Saint Francis: Nature Mystic* (Berkeley: University of California Press, 1973). Armstrong writes: "[St. Francis] is the patron saint, not of those who view the enjoyment of nature as an end in itself nor in pantheistic appreciation, but of those who, taking pleasure—sometimes rising to ecstatic delight—in the exuberance and diversity of Creation, thankfully regard them as expressions of divine splendor, sacramental intima-

tions of glories beyond human apprehension. (17). Also see René Dubos, *A God Within* (New York: Scribners, 1972), chap. 8.

9. A number of books expressing this revival of the stewardship idea have appeared in print, including: Ian G. Barbour, ed., *Earth Might Be Fair: Reflections of Ethics, Religion, and Ecology* (Englewood Cliffs: Prentice-Hall, 1972); John Carmody, *Ecology and Religion: Toward a New Christian Theology of Nature* (New York: Paulist Press, 1983); Albert J. Fritsch, *A Theology of the Earth* (Washington: CLB Publishers, 1972); and Bernard Evans and Gregory D. Cusack, eds., *Theology of the Land* (Collegeville, Minn.: Liturgical Press, 1987). Some of those authors are Catholics, but Protestants have seemed to play the leading role in the discussion to date. For that perspective see John Cobb, Jr., *Is It Too Late? A Theology of Ecology* (Beverly Hills: Bruce, 1972); Richard Cartwright Austin, *Beauty of the Lord: Awakening the Senses* (Atlanta: John Knox Press, 1988); Richard Baer, Jr., "Land Misuse: A Theological Concern," *Christian Century* (12 Oct. 1966): 1239–41; Richard L. Means, "Ecology and the Contemporary Religious Conscience," *ibid.* (3 Dec. 1969): 1546–49; Joseph Sittler, Jr., "A Theology for Earth," *The Christian Scholar* (June 1954): 367–74; Paul H. Santmire, *Brother Earth: Nature, God, and Ecology in a Time of Crisis* (New York: T. Nelson, 1970).

10. Lawrence D. Geller, *Pilgrims in Eden: Conservation Policies at New Plymouth* (Wakefield, Mass.: Pride Publications, 1974). For a contrasting view of early New England Protestants as nature-haters see Roderick Nash, *Wilderness and the American Mind,* 3rd ed. (New Haven: Yale University Press, 1982), chap. 2.

11. I take the phrase from Harold L. Lunger, *The Political Ethics of Alexander Campbell* (St. Louis: Bethany Press, 1954), chap. I.

12. These biographical details come from William Culp Darrah, *Powell of the Colorado* (Princeton: Princeton University Press, 1951), 3–29.

13. Robert Shankland, *Steve Mather of the National Parks,* 3rd ed. (New York: Knopf, 1970), 12. Also see Peter Wild, *Pioneer Conservationists of Western America* (Missoula: Mountain Press Publishing, 1979), chap. 5.

14. Esther Lanigan Stineman, *Mary Austin: Song of a Maverick* (New Haven: Yale University Press, 1989), 17–18; and Kevin Starr, "Mary Austin: Mystic, Writer, Conservationist," *Sierra Club Bulletin,* 61 (Nov.–Dec. 1976), 34. In her excellent study, Stineman presents Austin as simply a rebel from a Methodist upbringing, while I suspect that there was a more complex emotional legacy.

15. William O. Douglas, *The Three Hundred Year War: A Chronicle of Ecological Disaster* (New York: Random House, 1972), 198. Douglas discusses his childhood influences in his autobiography, *Go East, Young Man: The Early Years* (New York: Random House, 1974), chaps. I–II.

16. Stephen Fox, *John Muir and His Legacy: The American Conservation Movement* (Boston: Little, Brown, 1981).

17. Two recent books deal cogently with the founding and early intellectual milieu of the Sierra Club: Michael P. Cohen, *The History of the Sierra Club, 1892–1970* (San Francisco: Sierra Club Books, 1988), 8–15; and Michael L. Smith, *Pacific Visions: California Scientists and the Environment, 1850–1915* (New Haven: Yale University Press, 1987), 143–65.

18. For background on the Campbellite movement see: Walter Wilson Jennings, "Origin and Early History of the Disciples of Christ" (Ph.D. dissertation, University of Illinois, 1918), chaps. III–VI; David E. Harrell, Jr., *Quest for a Christian America: The Disciples of Christ and American Society to 1866* (Nashville: Disciples of Christ Historical Society, 1966); S. Morris Eames, *The Philosophy of Alexander Campbell* (Bethany, West Va.: Bethany College, 1966); and Sidney Ahlstrom, *A Religious History of the American People* (New Haven: Yale University Press, 1972), 445–52. For general background, see T. Scott Miyakawa, *Protestants and Pioneers: Individualism and Conformity on the American Frontier* (Chicago: University of Chicago Press, 1964), though the author does not give much attention to the Campbellite group.

19. Robert Frederick West, *Alexander Campbell and Natural Religion* (New Haven: Yale University Press, 1948), 53.

20. Fox, *John Muir and His Legacy;* Michael Cohen, *The Pathless Way: John Muir and American Wilderness* (Madison: University of Wisconsin Press, 1984). Fox does describe Muir's position as "the religion of conservation," but disassociates it entirely from Protestantism. Cohen, who has written the single best study of Muir's intellectual development, cites my argument (282). Frederick Turner mentions the Campbells briefly in his *Rediscovering America: John Muir in His Time and Ours* (New York: Viking, 1985), 29. Whatever Daniel Muir's influence on John, it is important to note that Daniel was not, as many writers persist in maintaining, a strict Calvinist; in his view the Calvinist doctrine of predestination was an unacceptable form of elitism.

21. John Muir, *The Story of My Boyhood and Youth* (1916; Madison: University of Wisconsin Press, 1965), 41.

22. Cited in William Badé, *The Life and Letters of John Muir* (Boston: Houghton Mifflin, 1924), I, 20–22.

23. Quoted by Linnie Marsh Wolfe, *Son of the Wilderness: The Life of John Muir* (Madison: University of Wisconsin Press, 1973), 21–22.

24. John Muir, *A Thousand Mile Walk to the Gulf* (Boston: Houghton Mifflin, 1916), 136–40; Badé, *Life and Letters of John Muir,* I, 43.

25. I have been influenced in my argument and whole treatment of Muir by Philip Greven, *The Protestant Temperament: Patterns of Child-rearing, Religious Experience, and the Self in Early America* (New York: Knopf, 1977). Greven's discussion of the "evangelical" type (in Part Two) is especially provocative for the study of environmentalism.

26. Badé, *Life and Letters of John Muir,* I, 23–25.

27. John Muir, "The American Forests," *Atlantic Monthly,* 80 (August 1987), 145–57. Also Muir, *The Yosemite* (New York: Century Co., 1912), 262, on the Hetch Hetchy controversy; and Nash, *Wilderness and the American Mind,* chap. 10.

28. A suggestive book that brings out Muir's religious disposition is Richard Cartwright Austin, *Baptized into Wilderness: A Christian Perspective on John Muir* (Atlanta: John Knox Press, 1987).

29. Roderick Frazier Nash, *The Rights of Nature: A History of Environmental Ethics* (Madison: University of Wisconsin, 1989), 41.

30. Linnie Marsh Wolfe, ed., *John of the Mountains: The Unpublished Journals of John Muir* (Madison: University of Wisconsin Press, 1966), 137–38.

31. Ernst Troeltsch, *The Social Teachings of the Christian Churches,* trans. Olive Wyon (New York: Harper & Row), II, 617–30, 632–33. Also see Michael Walzer, *The Revolution of the Saints* (Cambridge: Harvard University Press, 1965).

32. Martin Marty, *Righteous Empire: The Protestant Experience in America* (New York: Dial Press, 1970), esp. Parts I–II.

33. *The Autobiography of Benjamin Franklin,* ed. Leonard Labaree et al. (New Haven: Yale University Press, 1964), 172, 204–5. The urban environment was, in Franklin's phrase, one of the important things "that I conceiv'd to want Regulation."

34. Gifford Pinchot, *The Fight for Conservation* (Seattle: University of Washington Press, 1967), 88.

35. *Not Man Apart: The Magazine of the Friends of the Earth,* 19 (Dec. 1989–Jan. 1990), 15. John McPhee calls David Brower a pagan [*Encounters with the Archdruid* (New York: Farrar, Straus, and Giroux, 1971)], but he seems to me to be decidedly more a classic American Protestant in temperament than paganistic or druidical.

36. Quoted in Max Weber, *The Protestant Ethic and the Spirit of Capitalism,* trans. Talcott Parsons (New York: Charles Scribner's Sons, 1958), 121.

37. Ralph Barton Perry described Puritanism as a "cult of misanthropy," which is of course a description many observers attach to environmentalism. See Perry, *Puritanism and Democracy* (New York: Vanguard Press, 1944), 190.

38. This is the view of Lewis Lapham, editor of *Harper's Magazine,* cited by Deborah Baldwin in "Harper's War on Environmentalism," *Ecology Action,* 10 (21 Oct. 1978), 4–8. One of Lapham's favorite writers, William Tucker, similarly accuses environmentalists of being fanatical puritans, in "Of Mites and Men," *Harper's,* 257 (Aug. 1978), 58.

39. Quoted in Sacvan Bercovitch, *The American Jeremiad* (Madison: University of Wisconsin Press, 1978), 6.

40. "Civil Disobedience," *Walden and Other Writings of Henry David Thoreau* (New York: Modern Library, 1950), 645.

41. Perry, *Puritanism and Democracy,* chap. 16.

42. Alexis de Tocqueville, *Democracy in America,* translated by George Lawrence and edited by J. P. Mayer (New York: Anchor Books, 1969), 451–52.

43. Richard Cartwright Austin, "Three Axioms for Land Use," *Christian Century,* 94 (12 Oct. 1977), 910–11.

44. William Clebsch, *American Religious Thought: A History* (Chicago: University of Chicago Press, 1973), xvi.

45. Clarence Faust and Thomas Johnson, eds., *Jonathan Edwards: Representative Selections* (New York: American Book Company, 1935), 60–61. See also Douglas Elwood, *The Philosophical Theology of Jonathan Edwards* (New York: Columbia University Press, 1960), 28–30.

46. Jonathan Edwards, *Images or Shadows of Divine Things,* ed. Perry Miller (New Haven: Yale University Press, 1948), 94.

47. I am referring to Perry Miller's essay, "From Edwards to Emerson," in *Errand into the Wilderness* (Cambridge: Harvard University Press, 1956), chap. VIII. See also Catherine L. Albanese, *Nature Religion in America from the Algonkian Indians to the New Age* (Chicago: University of Chicago Press, 1990), chap. 3.

48. Donald Fleming has maintained that the "conservation movement has been the main institutional legacy" of the nineteenth-century Transcendentalists. See his "Roots of the New Conservation Movement," *Perspectives in American History,* VI (1972), 8.

49. Barry Commoner, *The Closing Circle: Nature, Man, and Technology* (New York: Knopf, 1971). Essentially Commoner defines the environmental crisis as a problem in industrial pollution and, therefore, human health. His ecological conscience, though undeniably real, is very different from Muir's embrace of the wilderness and its "people."

50. The influence may, of course, also go the other way. See for instance Maymie and William Kimes, "Ryozo Azuma: The John Muir of Japan," *Sierra Club Bulletin,* 64 (July-Aug. 1979), 42–4.

Chapter 16

1. Peter M. Vitousek, Paul R. Ehrlich, Anne E. Ehrlich, and Pamela A. Matson, "Human Appropriation of the Products of Photosynthesis," *BioScience,* 36 (June 1986), 368–73. People use directly, as food, fuel, fiber, or timber, only about 3 percent of the net primary production of the earth; but nearly 40 percent when one adds in all the productivity of lands devoted entirely to human activities (e.g., croplands) and the productive capacity lost as a result of converting land to cities and forests to pastures or because of desertification, erosion, or other overuse.

2. World Resources Institute and the International Institute for Environment and Development, *World Resources, 1988–89* (New York: Basic Books, 1988), 17, 71, 89–95.

3. For recent appraisals of the human health effects of ozone depletion see the statements of Margaret L. Kripke and Thomas B. Fitzpatrick, in *Stratospheric Ozone Depletion,* Hearing before the Subcommittee on Health and Environment of the House Committee on Energy and Commerce, 25 January 1990 (Washington: Government Printing Office, 1990), 238–41 and 248–62.

4. Lynn White, Jr., "The Historical Roots of Our Ecologic Crisis," *Science,* 155 (10 March 1967), 1206.

5. *Ibid.,* 1205.

6. The leading historian of population is E. A. Wrigley, who has tried to discover the grassroots causes of the English demographic explosion, using parish registers going back to the sixteenth century to understand the changing relations of fertility to nuptiality, real wages, and food prices. See E. A. Wrigley and R. S. Schofield, *The Population History of England, 1541-1872: A Reconstruction* (Cambridge: Harvard University Press, 1981).

7. Karl Jaspers, *The Origin and Goal of History* (New Haven: Yale University Press, 1959), 1–21. According to Jaspers, the Axial Period was a nearly simultaneous spiritual flowering occurring in three widely separated places—China, India, and the Middle East—in which rationality replaced primitive mythology, speculative philosophy appeared for the first time, and religion took on an ethical content.

8. J. B. Bury, *The Idea of Progress: An Inquiry into Its Origin and Growth* (New York: Macmillan, 1932), 5.

9. Descartes, *Discourse on the Method,* in *The Philosophical Writings of René Descartes,* trans. John Cottingham, Robert Stoothoff, and Dugald Murdoch (Cambridge: Cambridge University Press, 1985; orig. pub. 1637), I, 142–43. For a useful discussion of Descartes's view of animals see Keith Thomas, *Man and the Natural World: A History of the Modern Sensibility* (New York: Pantheon, 1983), 33–35.

10. *The Works of Francis Bacon,* ed. James Spedding (New York, 1872–78), I, 47–48, 398. See also William Leiss, *The Domination of Nature* (Boston: Beacon Press, 1972); Carolyn Merchant, *The Death of Nature: Women, Ecology, and the Scientific Revolution* (San Francisco: Harper & Row, 1980), 164–90: Lewis Mumford, *The Power of the Pentagon* (New York: Harcourt Brace Jovanovich, 1970), 105–29.

11. Quoted by William Cronon, *Changes in the Land: Indians, Colonists, and the Ecology of New England* (New York: Hill and Wang, 1983), 40–41.

12. Robert L. Heilbroner, *The Worldly Philosophers: The Lives, Times, and Ideas of the Great Economic Thinkers,* 6th ed. (New York: Simon & Schuster, 1986), 42–74. For a discussion of the connections between the rise of economics and the Scientific Revolution see William Letwin, *The Origins of Scientific Economics* (Garden City, N.Y.: Anchor Books, Doubleday & Co., 1965).

13. John Rae, *Life of Adam Smith* (New York: A. M. Kelley, 1965; orig. pub. 1895), esp. chap. XVI. See also John Cunningham Wood, ed., *Adam Smith: Critical Assessments* (London: Croom Helm, 1983), in four volumes. The first two volumes deal with *The Wealth of Nations* and with Smith's place in the general currents of eighteenth-century intellectual history; but nowhere do they discuss his view of nature.

14. Adam Smith, *An Inquiry into the Nature and Causes of the Wealth of Nations,* ed. Edwin Cannan (New York: Modern Library, 1937; orig. pub. 1776).

15. This passage is from Locke's *Some Considerations of the Consequences of the Lowering of Interest and Raising the Value of Money* (published in 1696). Smith quotes it in the introduction to his work (lvii).

16. Smith, *An Inquiry . . .,* 344, 527–28.

17. For the ecological legacy of Marxism (albeit filtered through the Stalinist military-imperial mentality of the twentieth-century U.S.S.R.), see Marshall Goldman, *The Spoils of Progress: Environmental Pollution in the Soviet Union* (Cambridge: Massachusetts Institute of Technology Press, 1972); and Douglas R. Weiner, *Models of Nature: Ecology, Conservation, and Cultural Revolution in Soviet Russia* (Bloomington: Indiana University Press, 1988). For recent reports of Soviet bloc pollution and environmentalism see "Environmental Awakening in the Soviet Union," *Science,* 241 (26 Aug. 1988): 1033–35; and Dick Thompson, "The Greening of the U.S.S.R.," *Time,* 133 (2 Jan. 1989): 68–69.

18. For a history of this phrase and its evolution into the science of ecology, see my book, *Nature's Economy: A History of Ecological Ideas* (New York: Cambridge University Press,

1977). The phrase has had a double life, serving at once to reinforce the economistic, materialistic bias of modern thought and to critique that bias as flawed and destructive.

19. I discovered long after writing this essay some similar views expressed by Wendell Berry in more eloquent and profound words than any I have written here. Berry distinguishes between the "Great Economy" and the "little economy" created by humans. "A little economy," he writes, "may be said to be good insofar as it perceives the excellence of [the Great Economy's] benefits and husbands and preserves them. It is by holding up this standard of goodness that we can best see what is wrong with the industrial economy. For the industrial economy does not see itself as a little economy; it sees itself as the only economy." Berry, "Two Economies," *Home Economics* (San Francisco: North Point Press, 1987), 64.

20. Rupert Sheldrake, *The Rebirth of Nature: The Greening of Science and God* (London: Century, 1990), 75. The leading scientific critique of Cartesianism is *The Dialectical Biologist* (Cambridge: Harvard University Press, 1985), by Richard Lewins and Richard Lewontin; however, they base their critique on the outworn dialectical materialism of Karl Marx, not on some altogether new paradigm. For the Gaian hypothesis, see James Lovelock, *Gaia: A New Look at Life on Earth* (Oxford: Oxford University Press, 1979); and *The Ages of Gaia: A Biography of Our Living Earth* (Oxford: Oxford University Press, 1988). The essential idea in the thesis is that the collective action of all living organisms keeps the earth fit for life and stable over long periods of time.

21. Alfred North Whitehead, *Science and the Modern World* (New York: Macmillan, 1925), chaps. 7–8.

Index

◆

Aborigines, 23
Adaptation, 32, 38, 54
Aesthetics, 144, 181–83, 196, 199–200
Agribusiness, 77, 86–87, 140
Agriculture: and agricultural revolutions, 42, 60; and capitalism, 42; and characteristics of good farming, 91–93; complexity of, 64–65; and ecology, 42, 64–70; as an ecosystem, 50–51, 52–53; and the engineering ecstasy, 140; and equilibrium, 66–67; and the government, 65, 66, 87; and healthier people, 91; history of, 65–66; and the individual, 66–67; and a just society, 91–92; and the market economy, 60, 67, 69, 70, 88, 90; and modes of production, 50, 52–63; need for reform of, 65; need for restraints on, 66–67; and need for vision, 70; and number of farms, 89–90; origins of, 22; and politics, 86; pressures/constraints on, 68–69; and productivity, 85; and the public good, 84–94; public opinion about, 87–88; and questions about agricultural policy, 86; and science, 60, 69–70; and soil issues, 77–78, 92–93; subsidization of, 66, 87; success/failure in, 68; and surpluses, 85–86; and sustainable development, 147–48; and technology, 77; uniqueness of American, 66–67; and water issues, 126–27, 131–34, 140; and wealth/profit, 70, 85, 86–87, 88–89, 90; and yeoman farmers, 100–101. *See also* Agroecosystem; Irrigation; Rural communities

Agriculture, U.S. Department of, 85
Agroecosystem: and capitalism, 56–63; characteristics of an, 52–53, 55–56; and chemicals, 61–62; definition of an, 52; as destructive/constructive, 55–56; and expertise, 62; and fossil fuels, 61, 62; instability in the, 61–62; and management, 54–55; and modes of production, 56–63; as a monoculture, 58–63; simplification of the, 58–63; and soil issues, 61; species in an, 58–59; and subsistence, 56, 57–58; and technology, 61
Alaska, 102, 162
Altieri, Miguel A., 55
American commons, 104–5, 107
American Society for Environmental History, 31
Anderson, Nels, 116
Andrus, Cecil, 139
Anthropocentrism, 187–88
Anthropology, 34, 37–39, 40–41. *See also* Ecological anthropology
Army Corps of Engineers, 18, 138–39
Arrington, Leonard J., 112–17, 118–19, 122
Ascetic discipline, 196, 197–98
Asian societies, 33. *See also* Japan
Aswan Dam, 126
Atmosphere, 204
Audubon Society, 111
Austin, Mary, 190
Automobiles, 7, 11–12

Bacon, Francis, 212
Balance. *See* Equilibrium
Bartram, William, 3
Beauty, 174, 182–83, 199–200, 213
Behavior, laws of, 43–44
Bellah, Robert, 186
Bennett, Hugh Hammond, 72–73, 74, 77, 79
Bennett, John, 36
Berry, Wendell, 148
Bethal, James, 128
"Biological Populations with Nonoverlapping Generations" (May), 168
Biology: and culture, 37; and land-management professionals, 107; and a post-materialist world-view, 219
Bluegrass, 46
Boserup, Ester, 54
Botkin, Daniel, 150, 151, 152, 153
Brower, David, 197, 200
Brown, Lester R., 143
Brundtland Report, 143, 146, 153
Buddhism/Zen Buddhism, 186–87, 188, 198
Buffalo/bison, 4, 104
Buffon, Georges-Louis Leclerc de, 24
Building a Sustainable Society (Brown), 143
Bureau of Agricultural Economics, U.S., 76
Bureau of Land Management, U.S., 137
Bureau of Reclamation, U.S., 116, 121, 130, 135, 136, 137–38, 139
Bureau of Soils, U.S., 73
Bureaucracies, 106–8, 126, 139
Burnet, Gilbert, 198
Bury, J. B., 211
"Butterfly effect," 168–69

California, 127
Campbellism, 191–94, 195
Cancer, 205
Capitalism: and agriculture/agroecosystem, 42, 56–63; and America as a model society, 14–15; and ascetic discipline, 197; and environmental destruction, 185, 187; and equilibrium, 180; and industrialism, 178–80; and land issues, 58, 105; and Marxism, 56–57; and modes of production, 56–63; and the Mormons, 113–17; and the myth of the frontiersman, 117–18; questions about the emergence of, 56; and religion, 187, 197; and a reorganization of nature, 57–58; and science, 60; social effects of, 62; as a success/failure, 62–63; and sustainable development, 145, 154; and

water issues, 113–17; and wealth/profit, 58. *See also* Market economy
Carson, Rachel, 21, 23, 170, 182, 200
Carter, Jimmy, 139
Causality, and history, 49–50
Change, explanations for, 39–40. *See also* Chaos theory; Succession
Chaos theory, 162–70, 219
Chapline, W. R., 73
Chemicals, 61–62, 75, 133, 140, 148, 204
Chlorinated hydrocarbons, 23
Chlorofluorocarbons, 204–5
Christianity. *See* Religion
Clements, Frederic L., 158–59, 160, 162, 163, 164, 165, 168, 175
Climate, 21–22, 54–55, 129, 164, 168–69, 204
Climax theory (Clements), 158–59, 160, 163, 164–65, 170, 175
Coachella Valley, 129
Coal, 7–8, 22
Cody, Buffalo Bill, 17
Cognized model of nature (Rappaport), 38
Cohen, Michael, 192–93
Colinvaux, Paul, 166
Collectivism. *See* Public good
Colorado River, 127, 129, 131
Commoner, Barry, 21, 201
Commons, American, 104–5, 107
"Commonwealth" concept, 113
Communal ownership, 93–94, 110–11
Conklin, Harold, 36
Connell, Joseph, 163
Conquest of Arid America, The (Smythe), 120
Conservation: and the American commons, 104–5, 107; characteristics of, 156–57; criticisms of, 108–9; and economics, 107, 108; emergence of movement for, 103; and the engineering ecstasy, 140; and equilibrium, 157, 158; and land issues, 103, 104–5, 107–9; legacy of movement for, 105; and morality, 156–57, 158, 196–97; and Progressivism, 73; purpose of movement for, 103; as a religion, 190; and technology, 131, 157; and the voluntary practice of conservation, 109; and water issues, 131. *See also* Soil issues
Constitution, U.S., 95–101, 104, 111
Cooke, Alistair, 77
Corruption, and land issues, 99–100, 101
Cotton kingdom, 65–66
Cow Creek, 16–18
Crèvecoeur, J. Hector St. John de, 98–99
Crosby, Alfred, Jr., 43, 46, 59
Cultural anthropology, 36
Cultural core, 35, 36

Cultural diversity, 38
Cultural ecology, 34–44
Cultural evolution, 34–35, 37, 38
Culture: and the agroecosystem, 58–63; and biology, 37; and change, 178; of cooperation, 116; and ecology, 34–44, 68; and the eighteenth-century myth, 8–9; and the engineering ecstasy, 137; and environmental crisis, 207, 209–19; and environmental destruction, 8–9; and environmental history, 48; and the Garden of Eden myth, 9–12; genetic basis of, 40; and "the habit of aesthetic apprehension," 181–82; and history (discipline), 24, 27, 41–42; in Japan, 186–87; and language, 26; and materialism, 28, 34–44, 210–19; and nature, 20, 27–28, 37; nutrition as basis of, 38–39; and a post-materialist world-view, 218–19; and the public good, 85; and science, 24, 25, 26, 28–29, 219; of scientists, 177; and soil issues, 76, 78; source of change in, 181–82; and the "two cultures," 28–29; and wealth/profit, 85, 88–89; and "why" questions, 27; and work behavior patterns, 35–36
Culture-area concept (Wissler), 34–35
Curry, Robert, 124, 128

Dams, building of, 136–41
Dams and Other Disasters (Morgan), 138–39
Dark matter, 219
Darling, Frank Fraser, 42
Darwin, Charles, 12, 25, 30, 31, 32, 149, 168, 174
Darwinism, 38, 114, 166, 167–68
Dating of nature, 25–26
Davis, Margaret, 164
Democracy: and environmental destruction, 187; and environmentalism, 195–96; and land issues, 104–5, 109; and religion, 187, 195–96; and technology, 136; and water issues, 122; and wealth/profit, 103
Democritus, 20
Demography. *See* Population
Depression, 73–74, 86
Descartes, René, 20, 211–12
Deserts on the March (Sears), 157, 158
DeVoto, Bernard, 112, 113, 118
Discordant Harmonies (Botkin), 150, 151, 152, 153
Disturbances, 164–65, 166, 176
Douglas, William O., 190, 200
Drought, 59–62, 164–65
Drury, William, 162–63

Dust Bowl, 74–75, 76
"Dynamic ecology," 158–59

Ecological anthropology, 32–34, 35–37, 42–44
Ecological history. *See* Environmental history
Ecological imperialism, 46
Ecology: and agriculture, 42, 64–70; and the "Butterfly effect," 168–69; and change, 40; and the chaos theory, 162–70, 175–76; and the climax theory, 158–59, 160, 163, 164–65, 170, 175; and the conservation movement, 107–9; and culture, 34–44, 68; and "dynamic ecology," 158–59; and ecologists' view of nature, 52; and the ecosystem concept, 159–62, 164–65, 166, 170, 175; emergence of, 45; and the engineering ecstasy, 136; and environmentalism, 185–86; evolutionary, 166; expectations for, 156–57, 170; and experts, 158; goals of, 107–8; as a guide to understanding nature, 157–58; and history, 42–44; lack of certainty in, 68–69; and language, 162, 170; laws of, 53; and leadership in the future, 181; and Marxist anthropologists, 40–41; and materialism, 40–41; models of nature of, 68; and morality, 69–70, 156–57, 158; new permissiveness in, 152; popular impact of, 156–57; and population, 165, 166–67; and prediction, 41; and public policy, 107–9; and relativism, 151–52, 176–77; revisionism in, 151–52; and the strategy of development, 159–61; and sustainable development, 148–53, 157; topics of, 175–76; and water issues, 132–33
Ecology of Natural Disturbance and Patch Dynamics (White and Pickett), 164–65
Economics: and the conservation movement, 107, 108; and the engineering ecstasy, 136–37; and the environmental crisis, 210–19; and environmentalism, 144; and industrialism, 179; and land policies, 106–7, 108; and materialism, 210–19; and nature, 52; and order/change, 178, 179; and a post-materialist world-view, 218–19; and progress, 211; and sustainable development, 144, 145, 147, 151–52, 153; and water issues, 113, 124–25, 130. *See also* Market economy
Economy of nature, 217–18, 219
Ecosystem: and agriculture, 50–51; assumptions about, 175; and the chaos theory, 164–65, 166, 170; characteristics of an, 52–53, 165; and the climax theory, 175; conventional model of a, 50–51;

Ecosystem (*continued*)
definition of an, 50, 159; diminished use of term, 162, 164–65, 170; and ecology, 68, 159–62, 164–65, 166, 170, 175; and equilibrium, 51, 159–62; and fire, 23; as an important concept, 162; management of the, 54–55, 161; and native/new species and fauna, 53–54, 59; and nature as a series of ecosystems, 149, 159–62; number of species in an, 51, 52; questions about an, 51; rate of change in an, 153; and restoration, 175; and revisionism, 51; size of an, 50–51; and a strategy of development, 159–61; and subsistence, 56, 57–58; and succession, 161; and sustainable development, 149, 153–54; and technology, 161; textbooks' discussions about an, 25, 68, 162; theory of the, 159–61; and transformations, 50–63. *See also* Agroecosystem

Edwards, Jonathan, 199–200

Egalitarianism, and environmentalism, 196, 198–99

Egypt, 125–26, 128

Ehrlich, Paul, 21

Ely, Richard, 117

Emerson, Ralph Waldo, 200

Endangered habitats/species, 4, 154

Energy, 7–8, 22–23, 127–28, 159, 204

Engineering ecstasy, 135–41

England. *See* Great Britain

Enlightenment, 145–56, 192, 195

Environmental balance. *See* Equilibrium

Environmental crisis: and culture, 207, 209–19; and economics, 210–19; and ethics, 27; and industrialism, 218; long chain of, 206; and management, 207; and a market economy, 218; and materialism, 209–19; and a monoculture, 62; and population, 208–9; reasons for the, 26–27; and religion, 207–8, 209, 218; and science, 21, 207, 210–19; solution to the, 218–19; and technology, 207; and the "two cultures," 29; and wealth/profit, 209–19

Environmental destruction: amount of, 204; and capitalism, 185, 187; and costs of taking care of nature, 203–4; and democracy, 187; and ethics/values, 189; and inadequacy of knowledge, 206; and industrialism, 185; and irrigation, 129–31, 206; in Japan, 185–87; and land issues, 103; and management, 204, 206; and order/change, 180; and population, 204; and progress, 188; and religion, 185–202; remedies for, 184–202; and science, 185, 187, 206; and surprises, 205, 206; and technology, 185, 187; and water issues, 133–34, 204; and wealth/profit, 203–4

Environmental determinism, 46

Environmental history: assumptions of, 46–47; and climate changes, 21–22; contributions of, 21; and culture, 48; emergence of, 20–29, 31, 45, 47; and food, 42; goals of, 47, 63; and history, 31–32; and the history of nature, 48; levels for pursuing, 48–50; material/topics for, 47–48; mission of, 31; and the parson-naturalist synthesis, 31; purpose/function of, 48; research topics in, 24; and science, 63; and technology, 48–49

Environmental movements. *See* Conservation movement; Environmentalism; Sustainable development

Environmental transformations. *See* Transformations

Environmentalism: and aesthetics, 144, 196, 199–200; and ascetic discipline, 196, 197–98; and beauty, 199–200; and costs of taking care of nature, 203–4; and democracy, 195–96; and economics, 144; and egalitarianism, 196, 198–99; and the eighteenth-century myth, 12; emergence of, 142; and the engineering ecstasy, 137, 140; and environmental history, 47; and ethics/values, 144; goals of, 142–43; and guilt/atonement for destruction of the wilderness, 9; and the human impact on nature, 166; and individualism, 196, 198–99; and morality, 189, 195, 196–97, 201; as negative, 152; and a pluralistic society, 201–2; and politics, 142, 154; and popular concern, 47; and questions confronting environmentalists, 201–2; and rationalism, 192, 195; and redemption, 188, 195; and religion, 185–202. *See also* Sustainable development

Equilibrium: and agriculture, 66–67; and capitalism, 180; and the chaos theory, 162–70; and conservation, 157, 158; and Darwinism, 167–68; and ecosystems, 51, 159–62; as functional, 173; and the individual, 66–67; and industrialism, 180; and the public good, 84–85; and rural societies, 66–67; in society, 180; and soil issues, 79; and succession, 162; and sustainable development, 149–53; and wealth, 67. *See also* Homeostasis

Ethics/values: and conservation as an ethic, 156–57; and the environmental crisis, 27; and environmental destruction, 189; and environmentalism, 144; and the "land ethic," 108–10; and materialism, 210; and modern views of

nature, 13; and nature, 52; and religion, 189; of rural societies, 67; and soil issues, 83; and sustainable development, 155; and transformations, 49; and water issues, 134. *See also* Morality
Europe, pollution in, 22–23
Evolution, 30–44, 149, 154, 155, 166, 167, 174, 217, 219. *See also* Cultural evolution; Darwin, Charles; Darwinism
Experts, 62, 149, 154, 158. *See also* Professional managers
Extinction of species, 4, 10–11, 12, 27, 43, 97, 154, 204, 206

Farming: characteristics of good, 91–93; and farm surpluses, 85–86. *See also* Agriculture; Agroecosystem
Fernow, Bernhard, 145
Feudalism, 42, 97–98
Fifth Amendment, 98
Fire, 23, 46, 150, 164–65
Fish and Wildlife Service, U.S., 107
Flaming Gorge Dam, 136
Florida, 127
Food/nutrition, 38–39, 42, 147. *See also* Agriculture; Agroecosystem
Forest Service, U.S., 137, 138
Forests: and the conservation movement, 104; depletion of, 22, 27, 103; and disturbances, 176; and environmental destruction, 204; Japanese assault on, 187; legislation about, 188; management of, 144–45; and moral activism, 196; regeneration of, 138; and stewardship, 188; and succession, 162–63; and sustainable development, 144–45, 150–51
Fossil fuels, 7–8, 22, 61, 62, 128, 133, 204
Fowler, Jacob, 16–17
Fox, Stephen, 190, 192–93
Franck, Sebastian, 197
Franklin, Benjamin, 196, 197
Freiberg, Germany, 22–23
Freud, Sigmund, 30
Friends of the Earth, 197
Frontier, 42–43, 45–46, 117–18, 191–94, 195
Frost, Robert, 96
Functionalism, 40, 173
Fundamentals of Ecology, The (Odum), 159

Gaia: An Atlas of Planet Management (Meyers), 143
Gaian hypothesis (Lovelock), 219
Garden of Eden, 9–15, 172
Garrison Diversion Unit (North Dakota), 137
Geertz, Clifford, 36–37
Geological Survey, U.S., 127

Geology, historical, 24
"Geopolitics, Geographical Materialism, and Marxism" (Wittfogel), 32
Germany, 144–45
Giants in the Earth (Rölvaag), 93–94
Gleason, Henry A., 163
Glen Canyon Dam, 136, 137
Government: and agriculture, 65, 66, 87; and land issues, 95–111; and materialism, 211; and water issues, 125–26
Grand Coulee Dam, 136, 137
Grasslands of North America, 32, 164
Great Basin Kingdom (Arrington), 112–17
Great Britain, 23, 60, 157, 162
Great Plains, 60–61, 62, 63, 66, 74–75, 77, 127. *See also* Dust Bowl
Greed, 13–15, 143, 216, 218–19
Greenhouse effect, 26–27
Greenpeace, 185–86, 201
Groundwater, 129, 133

Hardin, Charles, 77–78
Harris, Marvin, 37, 38–39, 40, 41, 42, 43–44
Health, 91, 147
Historical geology, 24
Historiography, 31
History: of agriculture, 65–66; and causality, 49–50; of nature, 18–19, 48, 53–54, 63; political uses of, 39; and population as a historical force, 48; standard accounts of American, 19; of transformations, 18–19, 48, 53–54. *See also* Environmental history; History (discipline); Natural history
History (discipline): as a clustering of interests, 41–42; and cultural ecology, 34–44; and culture, 24, 27, 41–42; and dates, 25–26; and ecological anthropology, 32–34, 42–44; and ecology, 42–44; and environmental history, 31–32; and evolution, 30–44; language of, 26; as natural history, 30–44; and revisionism, 51; and the sciences, 20–24; and scientists as historians, 24–25; and specialization, 19–20; and textbooks, 19, 24; and "why" questions, 27. *See also* Environmental history
Homeostasis, 37–39, 160–61. *See also* Equilibrium
Hoover, Herbert, 105
Hoover Dam, 128, 136
Hopkins, Gerard Manley, 18
Horgan, Paul, 112, 113, 118–19
Human nature, 13–15, 27, 215
Humans: as animals with ideas, 37–38; and assumptions in environmental history, 46–47; and the environmental crisis, 207;

Humans (*continued*)
  impact on nature of, 203–19; and modes
  of production, 56–57; right of, to give
  order to nature, 151–52; superiority of,
  188, 207. *See also* Population
Huntington, Ellsworth, 34
Hurricanes, 46
Hutchinson, G. Evelyn, 159
Hutchinson, Kansas, 17–18
Hutton, James, 24
Hyams, Edward, 82
Hydraulic society, 33, 126

Idaho, 127
Iki island (Japan), 185–86
Immigration, 6–7, 8, 46
Imperial Irrigation District, 129
Individualism: and agriculture, 66–67; and
  the chaos theory, 165–66; and
  environmentalism, 196, 198–99; and
  equilibrium, 66–67; and land issues,
  109–10; and the market economy, 67; and
  the Mormons, 113, 117; and myths, 117–
  18, 121; and soil issues, 83; and water
  issues, 117
"Individualistic Concept of the Plant
  Association, The" (Gleason), 163
Industrialism, 7, 23, 42, 148, 154, 178–80,
  181, 185, 218
Interdependency, and the chaos theory, 169
International Union for the Conservation
  of Nature, 143
Irrigation, 36, 113, 114–22, 125–31, 132,
  136, 137–38, 206

Jantzen, Daniel, 21
Japan, 185–87, 201, 217
Jaspers, Karl, 210
Jefferson, Thomas, 3, 10–11, 59, 72, 100–
  102, 109, 148
Jeffries, Richard, 182
Jenny, Hans, 82
Journal of the Arnold Arboretum, 162–63
Juday, C., 159
Judeo-Christianity. *See* Protestantism;
  Religion
Just society, and characteristics of good
  farming, 91–92

Kentucky, 45–46
Kroeber, Alfred, 34

Ladurie, LeRoy, 42
"Land ethic," 108–10, 134, 183
Land issues: and an American commons,
  104–5, 107; and amount of public land,

104; and bureaucracies, 106–8; and
capitalism, 58, 105; and communal
ownership, 110–11; and the conservation
movement, 103; and the Constitution,
95–101, 104, 111; and corruption, 99–100,
101; and democracy, 104–5, 109; and
economics, 106–7, 108; and
environmental destruction, 103; and
feudalism, 97–98; and the government,
76, 95–111; government purchase/sales
of, 76, 101–2; and individualism, 109–10;
and land as a commodity, 58; and land
controls, 110–11; and the "land ethic,"
108–10, 134, 183; and management of
land, 105–8, 109; and the market
economy, 99; and materialism, 216–17;
and the Mormons, 115; and nature as
land, 58; and private/public land, 95–
111; and the public good, 103; and soil
issues, 110; and virtue, 100–101; and
wealth/profit, 100–101, 102, 103, 108
Land professionals, 106–7
Land Utilization Project, 76
Language: and anthropology, 37; and
  cultural evolution, 37; and culture, 26;
  and ecology, 162, 170; of history
  (discipline), 26; of the sciences, 26; and
  sustainable development, 144
Lao-tzu, 201
Laws: of behavior, 43–44; of ecology, 53;
  of human nature, 215; of nature, 25,
  211
LeClercq, Chrétien, 213
Lee, Richard, 36–37
Lee, Robert, 145
Leopold, Aldo, 45–46, 108–10, 111, 124,
  125, 134, 170, 171–75, 180–83
Letters from an American Farmer
  (Crèvecoeur), 98–99
Lewis and Clark expedition, 3–4
Lindeman, Raymond, 159
Locke, John, 215
Lorenz, Edward, 168–69
Loucks, Orie, 176
Louisiana Purchase, 101–2
Lovelock, James, 219
Lowdermilk, Walter, 79
Lucretius, 20

MacArthur, Robert, 168
McNeill, William, 42
Malin, James, 19, 31, 32, 33–34, 36
Management: and the agroecosystem, 54–
  55; of ecosystems, 54–55, 161; and the
  environmental crisis/destruction, 204,
  206, 207; of forests, 144–45; and land
  issues, 105–8, 109; by professionals, 145,
  146, 161; and sustainable development,

144–45, 146; and technology, 161; and
water issues, 54–55, 125–26, 133

Market economy: and agriculture, 60, 67,
69, 70, 88, 90; and America as a model
society, 14–15; definition of, 57–58; and
the environmental crisis, 218; impact on
environment of a, 63; and individualism,
67; and land issues, 99; and modes of
production, 56–58; and morality, 57–58;
as part of capitalism, 56–58; and people's
wants, 87; and the public good, 88–89, 90;
and science, 60; and soil issues, 72, 73–
74, 75, 76, 78, 83; and sustainable
development, 147; and water issues, 113,
133, 140; and wealth/profit, 70

Marx, Karl, 30, 32–34, 41, 179–80, 201, 217

Marxism, 32–34, 40–41, 56–57, 154, 179–80,
217

Massachusetts, 65, 113, 188

Massengale, Martin, 128

Materialism: and beauty, 213; and culture,
28, 34–44, 210–19; and ecological
anthropology, 32–34; and ecology, 40–41;
and economics, 210–19; and the
environmental crisis, 209–19; and ethics/
values, 210; and land issues, 216–17; and
Marxism, 217; and progress, 211, 212–13;
and rationality, 211, 212–13; and
religion, 210; and science, 210–19; and
secularism, 212–13; and sustainable
development, 143, 144, 153, 154, 155; and
technology, 211; and value (of things),
215–16. *See also* Wealth/profit

Mathematical models, and the chaos
theory, 168

Mather, Stephen, 190

May, Robert, 168

Meadows, Dennis and Donella, 21

Mechanical determinism, 40

Mesopotamia, 54, 129

Meyers, Norman, 143

Miller, Perry, 200

Modes of production, 49, 50, 52–63

Monocultures, 59–62, 161

Montaillou: The Promised Land of Error
(Ladurie), 42

Morality: and beauty, 183; and
conservation, 156–57, 158, 196–97; and
ecology, 69–70, 156–57, 158; and
environmentalism, 189, 195, 196–97, 201;
and irrigation, 117–22; and the market
economy, 57–58; and the marriage of
agriculture and ecology, 69–70; and
myths, 117–22; and water issues, 117–22,
124–25, 134; and wealth/profit, 122. *See
also* Ethics/values

Morgan, Arthur, 138–39

Mormons, 112–17, 119–20, 121, 122

Morris, William, 182

Muir, John, 169, 170, 182, 189, 190–96, 200,
202

Multinational corporations, 146, 211

Mumford, Lewis, 21

Myth: definition of, 117; of the
frontiersman, 117–18; irrigation, 117–22;
of the lone individual, 117–18, 121; and
morality, 117–22; and redemption, 117–
18, 121; of rugged individualism, 118;
and rural communities, 148; of the West,
117–22

Nash, Roderick, 195

National Cancer Institute, 205

National Park Service, 107, 137, 190

National Reclamation Act (1902), 129–30

National Resource Inventory, 79

Natural gas, 7–8

Natural history, 30–44

Nature: America as a destroyer of, 15;
characteristics of, 10–11, 52; cognized
model of, 38; as a commodity, 145; and
common ground between history and
science, 28–29; complexity of, 69–70; in
constant flux, 150–52; control/
understanding of, 69–70; as a creative
work, 183; and culture, 20, 27–28, 37;
ecologists' view of, 52; ecology's models
of, 68; and economics, 52; economy of,
217–18, 219; and the eighteenth-century
myth, 9–12, 13; as a flow of energy, 159;
and history (discipline), 30–44; history
of, 18–19, 48, 53–54, 63; and the history/
science split, 20–22; human impact on,
203–19; as land, 58, 188; laws of, 25, 211;
modern views of, 12–13; as a norm/
standard for civilization, 151–52; as
orderly/chaotic, 70, 151–52, 162–70, 176–
83; as physical matter, 211–12; respect
for, 170, 173, 174; rights of, 195; as a
round river, 124–27; as a series of
ecosystems, 149, 159–62. *See also* Garden
of Eden; Wilderness

Nature Conservancy, 111

Navajo Dam, 136

Nebraska, 128

Negative feedback mechanisms, 38, 43

Neolithic revolution, 54, 56

Netting, Robert, 36

New Deal, 116

New England, 65

"New Light on the Changing Forest"
(Loucks), 176

Newton, Isaac, 25, 168

Nile River, 125–26

Nisbet, Ian, 162–63

North Dakota, 137

Nutrition. *See* Food/nutrition

O'Dea, Thomas, 116
Odum, Eugene P., 39, 159–61, 162–63, 165, 166, 168, 170
Oil, 7–8, 22, 162
Olney, Warren, 190–91
On the Origin of Species (Darwin), 12, 25
Order: origins of, 173–74; and religion, 173–74; and restoration, 171–83; scientific doubt about, 175–76. *See also* Chaos theory; *specific ecologist or concept*
Oriental Despotism (Wittfogel), 33–34
Our Common Future (Brundtland), 143, 146, 153
Ozone, 205

Pacific Historical Review, 31
Paine, Thomas, 11
Pantheism, 198
Parkman, Francis, 19
Parrington, Vernon, 113
Parson-naturalist synthesis, 31
Patch dynamics, 164–65, 166
Pests/pesticides, 23, 61, 110, 133, 164
Physics, 175, 219
Pickett, S. T. A., 164–65
Pinchot, Gifford, 106, 108, 145, 190, 196–97
Pioneering process, 42–43
Plato, 20
Pluralism, and environmentalism, 201–2
Polanyi, Karl, 56, 57–58
Political institutions, and sustainable development, 147
Politics: and agriculture, 86; and the chaos theory, 166; and environmentalism, 142, 154; and soil conservation, 77–78; and sustainable development, 143, 154, 155
Politics of Agriculture, The (Hardin), 77–78
Pollution, 22–23, 147, 187
Population: and the chaos theory, 165, 166–67; and disturbances, 165; and ecology, 165, 166–67; and the environmental crisis, 208–9; and environmental destruction, 6–7, 8, 204; as a historical force, 42, 48; and religion, 208–9; and sustainable development, 143, 147; and transformations, 54; and water issues, 132; and wealth/profit, 209; in the wilderness, 5–6
Powell, John Wesley, 112, 118, 189–90
Prigogine, Ilya, 169
Prince William Sound oil spill, 162
Productivity, 85, 161. *See also* Modes of production
Professional managers, 145, 146, 161
Progress: and Darwinism, 38, 167–68; and economics, 211; and environmental destruction, 188; and materialism, 211, 212–13; and succession, 162; and

sustainable development, 143, 144, 145, 152, 154; and technology, 211
Progressivism, 73
Protestantism, and environmentalism, 185–202. *See also* Religion
Public good: and agriculture, 84–94; and culture, 85; and environmental balance, 84–85; examples of, 91–93; and land issues, 103; and the market economy, 88–89, 90; and the Mormons, 113–17, 119–20, 122; and rural communities, 87–89, 93–94; and soil issues, 75; and wealth/profit, 88–89, 90
Public land, 98–111
Public opinion: about agriculture, 87–88; and costs of taking care of nature, 203–4
Public policy: and ecology, 107–9; and science, 68. *See also* Public good
Puritans, 113, 188

Racial minorities, 91–92
Rain forests. *See* Forests
Rappaport, Roy, 37–38, 39, 40–41, 43
Rationalism, 192, 195, 211, 212–13
Ratzel, Friedrich, 34
Reclamation, 121, 130, 132, 138
Reclus, J. J. E., 34
Redemption, 117–22, 188, 195
Regeneration-through-violence myth, 117–18, 121
Relativism, and ecology, 151–52, 176–77
Religion: and capitalism, 187, 197; conservation as a, 190; and democracy, 187, 195–96; diversity in, 201; and the environmental crisis/destruction, 185–202, 207–8, 209, 218; and environmentalism, 188; and ethics/values, 189; and the frontier, 191–94, 195; and materialism, 210; and order, 173–74; and population, 208–9; and science, 174, 187, 207; and stewardship, 187–88; and technology, 121, 187, 207. *See also* Mormons; Protestantism
Restoration: and aesthetics, 181–83; and beauty, 182–83; and the ecosystem concept, 175; and the engineering ecstasy, 140; and evolution, 174; and industrialism, 181; mission of, 175; and order/change, 171–83
Risser, James, 130–31
Rivers: and the engineering ecstasy, 135–41; thinking like, 123–34
Roe, Frank Gilbert, 4
Rölvaag, O. E., 93–94
Roosevelt, Franklin D., 74
Roosevelt, Theodore, 196
Ruffin, Edmund, 72

Rural communities: commonalities in, 93–
94; and equilibrium, 66–67; and myths,
148; and the public good, 87–89, 93–94;
and soil issues, 80–81; and sustainable
development, 148; as utopias, 100–101;
values of, 67

Safe optimum notion, 152–53
Sahlins, Marshall, 36, 43
St. Francis of Assisi, 218
Salt poisoning, 128–29, 137–38, 140
Sand County Almanac, A (Leopold), 172
Sandbrook, Richard, 143
Santa Fe Trail, 17
Schaefer, William, 168
Science: and aesthetics, 181; and
agriculture, 60, 69–70; aim of modern,
212; and capitalism, 60; criticisms of, 25;
and culture, 24, 25, 26, 28–29, 219;
culture of, 26, 177; and dates, 25–26; and
the environmental crisis, 21, 207, 210–19;
and environmental destruction, 185, 187,
206; and environmental history, 63; and
history (discipline), 20–22, 27; language
of, 26; and leadership in the future, 181;
and the market economy, 60; and
materialism, 210–19; and models of
nature, 177–78; need for challenging the
authority of, 157–58; and need for vision,
70; and order/change, 181; and a post-
materialist world-view, 218–19; and
public policy, 68; and religion, 174, 187,
207; and surprises, 206; and sustainable
development, 144–45; and the "two
cultures," 28–29; and water issues, 124.
See also specific science
Scientific textbooks, 24, 25
Scientists, as historians, 24–25
Sears, Paul, 157, 158, 159, 161, 170
Secondary ecological succession, 46
Secularism: and materialism, 212–13; and
sustainable development, 143, 154
Semple, Ellen, 34
"Sensitive dependence on initial
conditions," 168–69
Seton, Ernest Thompson, 4
Shasta Dam, 136
Sheldrake, Rupert, 219
Sieferle, R. P., 22
Sierra Club, 12, 166, 190–91
Silent Spring (Carson), 21
Slatyer, Ralph, 163
Slotkin, Richard, 118, 121
Smith, Adam, 14, 30, 58, 214–16, 217, 219
Smith, Henry Nash, 112, 118
Smythe, William, 120
Snow, C. P., 28–29
Social change, 177–78

Social Darwinism, 114, 166–67
Social equilibrium, 180
Social institutions, and sustainable
development, 147
Social sciences, 40
Socialism. *See* Marxism
Socialization of investment, 115
Söderqvist, Thomas, 166
Soil Conservation Service (SCS), 71–79, 80
Soil Erosion Act (1935), 71–78
"Soil Erosion as a National Menace"
(Chapline), 73
Soil issues: and agriculture/agroecosystem,
61, 77–78; and the amount of soil
erosion, 79; and characteristics of good
farming, 92–93; and chemicals, 75; and
the collective good, 75; consequences of
erosion of, 79–80; and the conservation of
soil, 72; and the creation of soil, 82–83;
and culture, 76, 78; and equilibrium, 79;
and ethics/values, 83; and fossil fuels,
61; importance of, 81–83; and
individualism, 83; and land issues, 76,
110; legislation about, 71–78; and the
management of soil, 71–79; and the
market economy, 72, 73–74, 75, 76, 78, 83;
and politics, 77–78; and rural societies,
80–81; and the soil community, 82; and
sustainable development, 148; and
technology, 75–76, 77, 80, 82; and
transformations, 54; and water issues,
123–24, 128–29, 130–31, 133; and wealth/
profit, 72, 75, 76
South, 65–66
Specialization: and the agroecosystem, 58–
63; and history (discipline), 19–20
Stegner, Wallace, 112, 118
Stenger, Isabelle, 169
Steward, Julian, 35–37
Stewardship, 122, 137, 138, 174, 187–88,
189
Strategy of development, 159–61
Stratosphere, 205
Subsidization: of agriculture, 66, 87; for
irrigation, 132
Subsistence agriculture, 56, 57–58
Succession, 46, 158–66
"Succession" (Drury and Nisbet), 162–63
Surpluses, farm, 85–86
Surprises, and environmental destruction,
205, 206
Survival techniques, 36
Sustainable development: and agriculture,
147–48; and capitalism, 154; criteria for,
146–47, 149, 152–53; and ecology, 148–53,
157; and economics, 144, 145, 147, 151–
52, 153; and ecosystems, 149, 153–54;
and the Enlightenment, 145–56; and

Sustainable development (*continued*)
  equilibrium, 149–53; and ethics/values,
  155; and experts/managers, 144–45, 146,
  154; flaws in concept of, 153–55; and
  food, 147; and greed, 143; and health,
  147; and industrialism, 148, 154; and
  language, 144; and management, 144–45,
  146; and the market economy, 147; and
  materialism, 143, 144, 153, 154, 155; and
  normal "yield"/"output," 152–53; and
  political institutions, 147; and politics,
  143, 154, 155; and pollution, 147; and
  population, 143, 147; and prediction, 153;
  and progress, 143, 144, 145, 152, 154; and
  rural communities, 148; and the safe
  optimum notion, 152–53; and science,
  144–45; and secularism, 143, 154; and
  social institutions, 147; and socialism,
  154; and soil issues, 148; and technology,
  143, 152; and time frames, 146–47; and
  water issues, 147
Symbiotic relationships, 160

Tage, Kenzo, 186
Tansley, A. G., 175
Technology: and adaptation, 32; and the
  agroecosystem/agriculture, 61, 77; and
  change, 178; and the chaos theory, 170;
  and conservation, 131, 157; and cultural
  ecology, 35; and democracy, 136; and
  ecosystems, 161; and the engineering
  ecstasy, 136, 138, 140, 141; and
  environmental crisis, 207; and
  environmental destruction, 7, 8, 185, 187;
  environmental history's study of impact
  of, 48–49; and forest depletions, 22;
  impact of, 23, 48–49; in Japan, 187; and
  management, 161; and materialism, 211;
  as means of altering nature, 23; and
  progress, 211; and redemption, 121; and
  religion, 121, 187, 207; and soil issues,
  75–76, 77, 80, 82; and sustainable
  development, 143, 152; and
  transformations, 48–49; and water
  issues, 121, 131, 136, 138, 140, 141
Tennessee, 78, 130–31
Tennessee Valley Authority, 126
Teton Dam, 136
Texas, 127
Textbooks, 19, 24, 25, 68, 159, 162
Theory of Cultural Change (Steward), 35
Third World, 56
Thomas, George, 116–17
Thoreau, Henry David, 27, 182, 198, 200,
  201
Three Hundred Years War, The (Douglas),
  190
Tocqueville, Alexis de, 198

Tomlinson, H. M., 182
Transcendentalism, 200
Transformations: and adaptation, 54; and
  climate, 54–55; and ecology's models of
  nature, 68; and ecosystems, 50–63; and
  ethics/values, 49; and the "great
  transformation," 56, 57–58; history of,
  18–19, 48, 53–54; and modes of
  production, 48–49, 50, 52–63; and
  perceptions/ideology, 49; and population,
  54; and soil issues, 54; and technology,
  48–49; and water issues, 54–55, 126
Turner, Frederick, 19, 31, 193
"Two cultures," 28–29

Underground water, 66
United Nations, 204
United States: as a Garden of Eden, 9–15;
  as a model society, 13–15
Urbanization, 19
Utah. *See* Mormons

Value (of things), and materialism, 215–16
Values. *See* Ethics/values
Vásquez de Coronado, Francisco, 4, 16–17
Vayda, Andrew, 37, 39
Virtue: and irrigation, 116–17; and land
  issues, 100–101
Vogt, William, 180

Watanabe, Masao, 186
Water issues: and agriculture, 126–27, 131–
  34, 140; and bureaucracy, 126; and
  capitalism, 113–17; and conservation,
  131; and democracy, 122; and
  disturbances, 164–65; and ecology, 132–
  33; and economics, 113, 124–25, 130; and
  the engineering ecstasy, 135–41; and
  environmental destruction, 133–34, 204;
  and fossil fuels, 133; and funding of
  water projects, 137; in the future, 132–34;
  and the government, 125–26; and the
  importance of water cycles, 18; and
  individualism, 117; legislation about,
  110; management of, 54–55, 125–26, 133;
  and the market economy, 113, 133, 140;
  and morality, 117–22, 124–25, 134; and
  the Mormons, 112–17, 119–20, 121, 122;
  and a new "homestead program," 132;
  and population, 132; questions about,
  18–19; and reclamation, 121, 130, 132,
  138; religious metaphor about, 124; and
  the round-river concept, 124–25, 133; and
  salt poisoning, 128–29, 137–38, 140; and
  science, 124; as an SCS priority, 77; and
  soil issues, 77, 79, 123–24, 128–29, 130–
  31, 133; and stewardship, 122; and
  sustainable development, 147; and

technology, 121, 131, 136, 138, 140, 141; and thinking like a river, 123–34; and transformations, 54–55, 126; and the water cycle as a model of the natural world, 124; and a water ethic, 134; and a watershed, 124–25, 134; and wealth/ profit, 113, 114, 122. *See also* Cow Creek; Dust Bowl; Great Plains; Irrigation
Watt, James, 139, 200
Wealth of Nations, The (Adam Smith), 214–16
Wealth/profit: Adam Smith's views of, 214–16; and agriculture, 70, 85, 86–87, 88–89, 90; and capitalism, 58; costs of, 103; and costs of taking care of nature, 203–4; and culture, 85, 88–89; and democracy, 103; and the engineering ecstasy, 136; and environmental crisis/ destruction, 203–4, 209–19; and equilibrium, 67; and land issues, 100– 101, 102, 103, 108; and the market economy, 70; and materialism, 214–16; and morality, 122; and population, 209; and the public good, 88–89, 90; restraints on, 67; and soil issues, 72, 75, 76; and water issues, 113, 114, 122
Webb, Walter Prescott, 31–32, 33–34, 36, 112, 118
Whale/dolphin issue, 185–86, 201

Wheat, 60–61
White, Lynn, Jr., 187–89, 207–9, 218
White, P. S., 164–65
Whitehead, Alfred North, 181, 219
Why Big Fierce Animals Are Rare (Colinvaux), 165–66
Widstoe, John A., 119–20
Wilderness, 4–9
Wilderness Society, 12
Wildlife, 103–4, 188
Wilson, Edward O., 21
Wind, 62, 79, 164–65. *See also* Dust Bowl
Wissler, Clark, 34
Wittfogel, Karl, 32–34, 36, 126
Woodruff, Wilford, 114
Woodwell, George, 47–48
Work behavior patterns, 35–36
World Conservation Strategy (International Union for the Conservation of Nature), 143

Yellowstone National Park, 104
Yeoman farmers, 100–101, 148
York, Alvin, 80–81
York, England, 23
Young, Brigham, 114–15

Zoning, 110–11